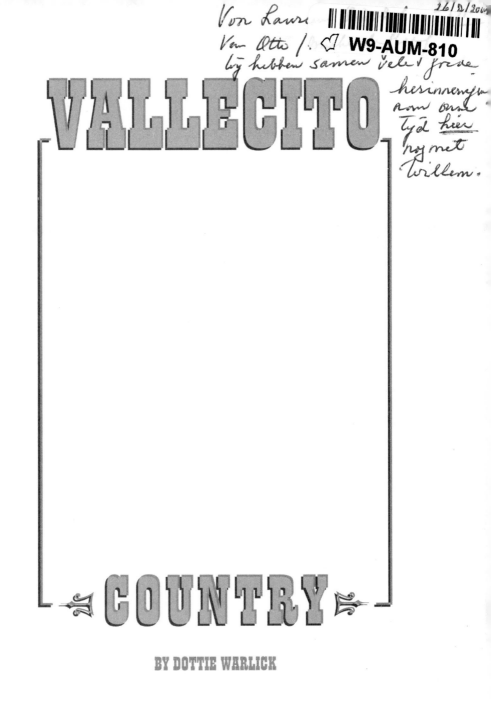

VALLECITO COUNTRY

BY DOTTIE WARLICK

WESTERN REFLECTIONS PUBLISHING COMPANY®

Montrose, Colorado

2003
First Edition
Printed in the United States of America

ISBN 1-890437-76-X

Library of Congress Control Number: 2003102019

Cover and Book Design by Laurie Goralka Design
Cover photo: Rock Lake — A high altitude lake above Vallecito. (Warlick
Collection)

Western Reflections Publishing Co.®
219 Main Street
Montrose, Colorado 81427

westref@montrose.net
www.westernreflectionspub.com

TABLE OF CONTENTS

ACKNOWLEDGEMENTS

I am deeply indebted to the many people that helped me find my way through the many trails I had to follow to be able to write this narrative. When I started, I didn't quite realize how involved this project would be, and how much help I would need to finally reach the end of this journey from the past. I extend my heartfelt thanks to everyone that helped me along the way.

A number of the Southern Ute people helped me locate some of their tribal members that I needed to contact, or they gave me additional information themselves. Among them were: Eugene and Dixie Naranjo, Everett Burch, Neil Cloud, Shirley Goodtracks, Lorraine Baker, Archie Baker, Sylvian Valdez, Robert Baker, Debby Cuthair Lucero, Sherri Salazar, Southern Ute Museum Director Lynn Brittner, and John Baker, Museum Curator.

Also, I am forever indebted to the individual Ute people that I interviewed for this book. Most are gone from this earth now, but I feel extremely grateful that I had the opportunity to talk with them and listen to their life stories. It was a wonderfully enlightening experience to hear the memories of the Ute people first hand. I will always treasure these memories and remember the graciousness of the Southern Ute people.

I also want to thank everyone else that took the time from their busy lives to dig back into their memories to tell me their almost forgotten family stories. These interviews were the highlights of this whole project for me.

I especially thank the ones who rummaged through their family relics and trusted me enough to lend me their old, treasured pictures that I could reproduce and share with my readers. Donna Becker and Ed Wommer were especially helpful in that respect, but there were many others.

Everyone at Fort Lewis College Southwest Studies Center in Durango, including former Director Dr. Richard Ellis, was very helpful, as was Robert McDaniel from the La Plata Historical Society. Special thanks go to Dr. Duane Smith, a noted author and well-known and respected history professor at Fort Lewis College. He has helped guide me through the book writing process, as well as giving me inspiration that was sorely needed at times. I will always remain grateful for his time and help.

My most valuable help came from my very good friend, Rosie Geier. Without her help and support I could never have waded through the myriad of old records and information that I needed for the actual writing of this book. Her help in making charts on land ownership was invaluable. Two other special friends, Wayne Myers and Jan Pierce, gave additional help. To these great friends, who gave so willingly of their time and my son Glenn, who gave me technical support, I give my special thanks.

And to my husband, Dave, I owe an extra special "thank you" for his help on the maps included in the book, for all the years he has put up with my comings and goings as I searched for the needed information, and the many hours at my computer. He went to great lengths to help me find the time I needed to wrap up this project before I, too, go to the great beyond and all these great old memories are lost forever.

INTRODUCTION

How is it possible to put together many separate colorful scraps of memories and facts and blend them into a cohesive quilt of early times and people? Some scraps of information came from written records, and many of the scraps came directly from peoples' memories. The prospect of doing this task overwhelmed me as I was getting near the end of my long hours of research. A book, I finally decided, can only be attempted by starting with the first stitch in time and adding scrap upon scrap of information as time advanced until I finally had my quilt.

After living in Vallecito for a number of years and hearing the almost forgotten stories of the Valley's early days from my husband's family and other old-timers, I felt compelled to try to preserve the treasure of information that is being forever lost with the passage of time.

In the pursuit of this goal, I have also spent countless hours searching old records and newspaper files. My research has taken me to Fort Lewis College, Durango Public Library, National Archives in Denver, Spanish Archives in Santa Fe, and Southern Ute Headquarters in Ignacio.

However, my most interesting research came from numerous pleasurable hours spent in personal interviews with old-timers and their relatives, who were, without exception, more than willing to help me recapture some of the memories and happenings of the almost forgotten "good old days." In reality, these were usually anything but easy times; but one does tend to remember the good times, and there were an abundance of stories to be recorded.

At times I found discrepancies between different folks' viewpoints or memories of long ago events. One can expect this after such a long time. When possible, I used written records to help clarify dates, spelling of names, or other differences of opinion; but in the long run, I don't believe a few differences in viewpoints is of earth shaking importance.

I apologize in advance for any misspelling of names or other misinformation. It isn't always easy to find the correct spellings. There are many variations even in written records. I also do apologize if I have unintentionally left anyone out that should have been included.

I am deeply indebted to all of the generous souls who tried so willingly to help me in this search for the preservation of old memories. Too many of these people have already said their last farewells.

"A NATION THAT FORGETS ITS PAST HAS NO FUTURE"
Quote from unknown author

VALLECITO AREA MAP

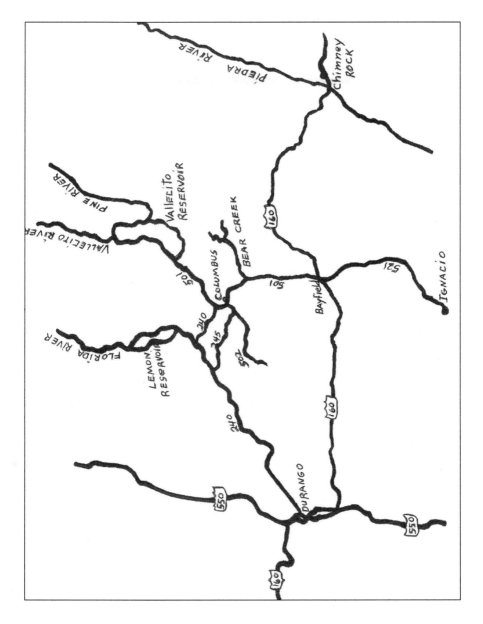

PART ONE

❧ *Blending of Cultures* ❧

Caption for picture on reverse page: View of Emerald Lake and Wilderness area from top of Middle Mountain. (Warlick Collection)

CHAPTER 1

The Old Ones

I t seems impossible to try to write of Vallecito without including at least a bit of information on the earlier inhabitants who also enjoyed this entrancing valley and mountain hideaway. They were living here long before the white man knew of the valley's existence; and even though the present-day occupants and visitors feel such a deep sense of love and possession of this place, one has to be saddened at the way its former inhabitants were forced from the spot that they also claimed and loved.

There are many theories as to where the earliest inhabitants came from, but the most accepted theory seems to be that they were nomadic hunters from Asia who crossed the Bering Strait when the Ice Age had created a land bridge and eventually migrated down into what now is Colorado.

The Folsom People, who were named for an archaeological find near Folsom, New Mexico, were nomadic hunters who traveled throughout most of the western part of our continent, including present-day Colorado. Little record exists of their habitation except for their beautiful stone tools. The Desert People foraged and farmed on the Western Slope of the Rockies. They were ancestors of the Basketmakers and Anasazi Indians, who later would abandon Mesa Verde for more favorable locations.

The oldest "Desert People" were of small stature and were referred to as the "The Ancient Ones" by the later Indians. Traces of these ancient people are plentiful in Vallecito, southwestern Colorado, as well as the rest of the Four Corners Region. The Chimney Rock Spiritual Center is the closest Anasazi ruin site to Vallecito. Going east from Bayfield on Highway 160 for approximately twenty-six miles to the intersection of Highway 151 and then turning south for approximately eight miles, you will find the entrance to the site. Tours can be taken which explore the many kivas and ceremonial pits and it is fascinating to hike up to the old ranger station that gives a wonderful view of the mesa's towering chimneys and the Piedra River and the valley that lie far below.

Historians believe that the Chimney Rock location is an outpost of the larger, more popular culture at Chaco Canyon, which is located in the northwest corner of New Mexico. While Chimney Rock isn't as large or quite as spectacular as Chaco Canyon or Mesa Verde, it is impressive in its own way. It is believed to have been a spiritual center that housed a number of "priests." There is evidence that for some unknown reason scores of turkeys were raised on this high outcropping. The Piedra River would have been the only source of water with the exception of infrequent rains. It was a splendid place to see the first signs of enemy marauders, which must have influenced the choice of location.

The Mesa Verde ruins to the west of Durango and the Chaco Canyon ruins in New Mexico are quite extensive and tell a remarkable story of the lives of the ancient people who constantly had to be on the lookout for enemy invaders. The Mesa Verde ruins show that their occupation started around two thousand years ago and thrived until around

The Chimney Rock archeological site was once occupied by the Anasasis and is believed to have been a spiritual center that housed a number of priests.

Cliff Palace at Mesa Verde archeological site near Cortez, Colorado, west of Durango. (Warlick Collection)

1200 A.D.; but then suddenly and rather mysteriously, Mesa Verde was vacated. It is not known for certain just why these peoples abandoned their homes in this fashion, but they seemed to have migrated down to the south where the climate was more favorable.

In about 1300 the Utes forced the Anasazi out of present-day Colorado and made the mountains and surrounding lands their home. At one time, the Utes ranged over a vast section of present-day Colorado, northern New Mexico and eastern Utah. They migrated from the lower elevations to the higher mountainous areas as the warmer weather came, and then descended back to the lower country with the coming of fall. In the lower elevations they could hunt the antelope and other small game that would be used to help them get through the long, cold winters.

The Utes had seven distinct bands. The Uinta, Tabeguache, Yampa, and Parianucs made up the bands known as the "Northern Utes;" while the Muache, Capote, and Weminuche were known as the "Southern Utes." These bands, which called themselves "Yuutaas," roamed freely across the central Rocky Mountains and were sometimes called the "Blue Sky People." They were both respected and feared by the neighboring Indian tribes. The "Yuutaas" were among the first of the tribes to acquire the "magic dogs" [horses] from the Spanish invaders. Soon they were accomplished horsemen; and due to their mobility and shrewdness, they created increasing waves of fear among other Indian tribes.

By the early 1800s American fur trappers were in the area of Vallecito. Kit Carson was later influential in the United States choosing Ouray to represent the Utes in treaty discussions with the United States in 1859. This was probably due to Ouray's ability to speak Ute, Apache, English, and Spanish as well as his exceptional negotiating skills, dignity, and charm. He acquired these skills while being raised in a Spanish home near Taos. Many of the Utes didn't approve of Ouray being chosen as overall chief since he had not come up through the ranks as most chiefs had done. Therefore many Utes never really accepted Ouray as their chief. Nevertheless, he was an eloquent speaker and managed to charm the government representatives from Washington, D.C., thereby keeping his people from being moved to the reservation for far longer than any other Indian tribe.

With the influx of whites in the 1859 gold rush, the coming of settlers, and the ever-growing involvement of the military, the lives of all the Colorado Indians grew increasingly harried as they were pushed farther from their original territories. After numerous treaties with the United States, the Utes were in 1868 left with just the western quarter of the Territory of Colorado.

The Southern Utes, whose territory included Vallecito, resisted reservation life longer than most other tribes, but with the mining boom that hit the San Juan Mountains in 1874, the influx of settlers swarming into Colorado as the result of the enactment of the Homestead Act in 1862, and Colorado attaining statehood in 1876, they were forced to settle on the present-day Southern Ute Reservation. This is a fifteen-mile by seventy-three mile strip of land along the southern border of Archuleta, La Plata, and Montezuma counties.

When the Meeker Massacre occurred in 1879 it really put the white community in an uproar. Something had to be done to tame these wild heathens! The Northern Utes had attacked the Indian agent, Nathan Meeker, and other white men who happened to be at the agency. When Meeker's body was found lying among the dead men, a stake was driven through his mouth. The attackers considered him to be a liar and felt this was a just end to the man. This tragic incident created such an outcry that the news spread clear to Europe. The Utes were confined to reservations in southern Colorado and eastern Utah in 1881.

The Dawes Act of 1887 established the right of Indians to become citizens of the United States. It also established the concept of individual land allotments (or homesteads) for Indians, as well as the right for tribal lands to continue to be held in common by the whole tribe.

The Hunter Act of 1895 permanently settled the Ute's reservation disputes and offered private farms for individual tribal members. The bill allowed the Indians who did not want to live on their individual land, to sell it to other settlers. This resulted in a checkerboard pattern of land ownership within some of the reservation land. The act provided that 160 acres of land would be allotted to each adult male Indian who petitioned for such. Those Utes not willing to accept a land allotment were permitted to live communally on the western part of the Southern Ute Reservation. The members of the Ute tribe were split on this decision. Most of the Muache and Capote Utes accepted individual allotments in the eastern part of the reservation. They became known as the "Southern Utes." Their headquarters was established in Ignacio, a small settlement of a few ranching families. It is located approximately twenty-six miles to the south of Vallecito, with the town of Bayfield being midway between the two.

Chief Ignacio and the majority of his Weminuche band moved to the western portion of the reservation to continue their communal way of living. They later became known as the "Ute Mountain" Utes. They originally had their headquarters at Navajo Springs but later moved to Towaoc, which is near the present-day town of Cortez.

Buckskin Charlie (also known as Sapiah) and Severo served as leaders after this split; and after Severo's death in 1913, Buckskin Charlie served as chief for both the Capotes and the Muaches. He was quite popular with his own people as well as the whites, and was involved in several negotiating sessions in Washington. He was once presented with a Peace Medal, which he wears in most of his photographs. Buckskin Charlie's son, Antonio Buck, followed him as the Capote and Muache chief for a short time until the Untied States put the Indian Reorganization Act in place. The law stated that the Indians could no longer have a chief, but had to form a tribal council. Antonio Buck was then elected the first Tribal Chairman of the Southern Ute Tribe. This coincidently happened at the same time as Buckskin Charlie's death in 1936. Buckskin Charlie was ninety-six years old at the time.

An interesting aside to Buckskin's death was that he chose to be buried in traditional Ute style, and a thin strip of ochre was painted from his hairline down over one eye to his chin. This was precisely the way many pre-Columbian figures excavated from burial sites in Mexico and Central America (some dating from before the time of Christ) were painted. It is a Native American symbol of sickness or death.

From the earliest times, the Vallecito country was particularly dear to the hearts of the Utes. It contained many high mountain lakes, raging streams, foliage-covered valleys, stately forests, and the land was rich in medicinal herbs, game, and fish. During the cold months the Utes lived to the south in more permanent quarters and more temperate conditions, but when warm weather came they would head for the mountains to reap their welcome bounty.

The upper valley of the Vallecito River is mostly rugged and narrow, but in some areas it widens out with grassy banks and deep pools of clear, cold water. These pools were the favorite bathing places of the Utes. It was quite convenient for them to build sweathouses on the nearby riverbanks. After plunging naked into the icy, cold water of the pool, they would quickly go into the small sweathouses, and by throwing cold water onto hot rocks, they could get an excellent sweat bath. Then a second plunge into the icy pool made them feel clean, refreshed, and invigorated. The sweat bath was a regular practice among the Utes in the summer season, and the remains of some of the old sweathouses are still in evidence after all these years.

Because of the many loops and turns of the lower Vallecito River, the Indians gave the river the name of "Shu-ah-gauche," which means "crooked water." When the lake is at its lowest, one can still see the many tortuous turns and twists of the old riverbed as it winds down the mountain valley to join with the Los Pinos River, now commonly referred to as the "Pine River." Vallecito Reservoir covers the spot where these two rivers join and then continue their journey to the south where they empty into Navajo Lake near the New Mexico border.

When the northern boundary of the Ute reservation was laid out, it didn't come quite as far north as the present town of Bayfield, which is some twelve or so miles to the south of Vallecito. The Utes treasured the Vallecito country, but it was never to be considered Ute land again.

CHAPTER 2

The Explorers

T he Indians who were spread throughout the southwestern portion of what is now the United States were accustomed to being in conflict with neighboring tribes, but when the Spanish explorers discovered this vastly rich, mostly uninhabited country, major changes were soon taking place. The Europeans would soon initiate changes to the life style of these "savages," as the Spanish tended to think of them.

There are records of many different adventurers who came to make their fortune in the Southwest. The first of them was probably the Spaniard Alvar Munez Cabeza de Vaca, who with three companions, was shipwrecked near the Florida coast in 1528. After making their way to land, the group became totally lost and spent eight miserable years wandering through the harsh, unknown land while trying to make their way west to some sort of civilization. At times they were held captive by different tribes of Indians, but they were always able to either escape or make friends with these people.

De Vaca heard many intriguing stories of abundant gold and silver that could be found in the western mountains. The legend of the Seven Cities of Cibola, which were supposedly made of gold, was incredibly fascinating to de Vaca. Once back with their own people, they proceeded to relate and embellish upon the wondrous stories of treasures to be found in the land to the north of inhabited Mexico, which succeeded in increasing the desire of their audience for additional explorations to search for treasure. It is improbable that de Vaca's group made it any farther north than present-day New Mexico and Arizona, but they did precede Coronado into the southwest country and de Vaca's notes were of great value to Coronado when he planned his expedition.

In 1540 Francisco Coronado and his contingent left Mexico on their quest to discover if there was any truth to the persistent rumors of gold in the country to the north of Mexico. Two hundred and fifty men in heavy armor accompanied him on his northward route, pillaging Indian pueblos as they traveled. When they reached the site of the present-day Bernalillo, New Mexico, they set up their base camp. Coronado and his men then made their way into the southeast corner of present-day Colorado in 1541.

Various Spanish artifacts have been found in the San Juan Mountains, including a six-foot skeleton with armor, a dagger, and spurs nearby. These armaments were of the type the Spanish soldiers used around 1540, possibly indicating that the area was also visited by a detachment of Coronado's soldiers to explore the mountainous country in their search for the fabled treasure. Coronado's records didn't mention any problems with the Ute Indians, but later stories of attacks by Utes were widely circulated among the Spaniards.

The nomadic Utes could have come into contact with Coronado's group during their trading with the Plains Indians. The first mention of Utes is in the Spanish territorial records kept in the archives in Santa Fe, New Mexico in 1637. A meticulous scribe for Governor Luis de Rosas noted that a mountain tribe of dark-skinned Indians known as "Uticahs" (as the Utes called themselves) had come to own quite a number of Spanish horses. He told the story of a terrible battle between these Uticahs and the governor's troops. Approximately eighty Uticahs (probably Muaches) were captured and punished, then driven to Santa Fe in chains to start their lives as Spanish slaves. There they were forced into a life of hard labor in the dank, dark depths of gold and silver mines.

The Spaniards became well known for their ruthless treatment of captives. Since the Spaniards were ruled by the strict and severe demands that the Roman Catholic Church had placed upon its people in Europe, they therefore had no sympathy for people who were not Christian. In their estimation, these Indians were without souls, and thus were shown absolutely no mercy by their brutal captors. The Ute slaves soon started dying in ever-increasing numbers as the brutal treatment and extremely difficult working conditions wore them down. The Utes' lack of immunity to the white man's diseases added greatly to the number of deaths, so the Spaniards were constantly trying to round up more slaves to do their mining.

The Spanish slave-hunters were soon hampered drastically in their attempts to capture the Utes, as these wily adversaries became very skilled riders on their stolen Spanish ponies. In fact, the Utes soon started making sneak attacks on outlying Spanish ranches to obtain more "magic dogs." In just one sneak attack in 1659, more than three hundred horses were stolen and driven to Ute mountain hideouts. The Utes were such nomadic and cunning people that the Spaniards began to focus on the more docile Plains and Navajo Indians for their slave trade. Eventually the Spaniards even started trading horses to former Ute adversaries in return for slaves from other tribes. The Utes in turn used the little Spanish horses for trade with other tribes, and soon these ponies were distributed and put to use throughout the Southwest.

In 1765, Captain Juan Maria de Riviera led the first recorded official expedition into present-day Colorado to investigate the persistent rumors of rich gold and silver mines. However Spanish adventurers had been mining in the area for at least fifty years. Tree rings from timbers found in old mines in the San Juans date from 1712 to 1726. Many of the old Spanish markings can still be found in the mountains in the Weminuche Wilderness to the north of Vallecito and Pagosa Springs, according to Temple Cornelius' book, *Sheepherders Gold.* Present-day Vallecito occupants, fascinated by his story and using Cornelius' instructions, have searched and found some of the markings.

Cornelius chronicles a story about the most famous Spanish mining operation that was started around 1750 and terminated about 1770. This mine was named *"La Mina de la Ventana,"* meaning "Mine of the Window." It was located near a window-like opening in rocky outcroppings in the highest reaches of the Continental Divide northeast of Vallecito and northwest of the present-day town of Pagosa Springs.

The Spanish miners followed the Little Chama River north from Santa Fe and crossed the divide through a low pass at the head of the stream. From this location one could see the "window" and the 13,821-foot pyramid-shaped peak nearby, known as the "Rio Grande Pyramid," which guided them to the mine. The landmarks were over one hundred miles away but showed clearly in the high, rugged outline of the San Juan Mountains to the northwest.

The mine was located near the headwaters of the Rio Grande and was in close proximity to the head of the Los Pinos River (Pine River) and Ute Creek. The mine was located in such ruggedly treacherous, high altitude country that it could only be reached after a long and grueling trek of several days.

Trail to the "Rio Grande Pyramid" and "The Window," a break in the Continental Divide. These landmarks guided the Spanish to the famed "Mine of the Window" located nearby. (Warlick Collection)

Just ten days after the Declaration of Independence was signed, another expedition started west out of Santa Fe. Father Francisco Dominguez had orders from Mexico City to inspect the Catholic Indian missions of the Southwest and attempt to find a shorter route between settlements in New Mexico and the chain of missions that had been established in California. They were also ordered to look for evidence of gold along the way. The Spanish thought that some of the Indian tribes might have stashes of the coveted metal.

Father Dominguez had chosen a young priest by the name of Silvestre Velez de Escalante to accompany him on the journey. Escalante was a mission priest who was known to be a keen reporter and would be valuable in documenting the trip. Their planned route would head north, thereby avoiding the dangerous Grand Canyon area, and covering a portion of the Ute territory that was yet to be charted. The small group (comprised of several Indian guides, a couple of Spanish soldiers, and a few civilians) was quite optimistic as it left on its quest. The journey took them through the area of present-day Durango, then west to the Cherry Creek area and on northward through Montrose. As they crossed the wide Colorado River, their guide refused to continue into the territory that was ruled by tribes hostile to the Utes. A Lakota Indian assumed the guiding duties from this point and managed to lead the group to the shores of the Great Salt Lake. It was already September.

After talking with Indian traders, Captain Mura y Pacheco convinced Dominguez that the settlement of Monterey, in California, was too distant to be reached before winter, so they decided to head back to Santa Fe. The return trip was a harrowing experience as they made their way through the rugged terrain of desert and mountains. At one point, their supplies were so meager they killed and ate some of their horses. The weary, scruffy-looking group finally arrived back in Santa Fe on Jan. 2, 1777. The fifteen hundred mile trip was declared a failure and Dominguez was demoted. In reality, it proved to be very beneficial to the later mapmakers in helping to find a shorter route to California.

In those times the southwestern area of present-day Colorado was called "Provincia de Nabajoo" and was part of the Spanish land grants. Reasoning tells us that this name no doubt means "Land of the Navajos." The mountain ranges were known as "Sierra del Almagne," "Sierra de LaPlata," and "Sierra Grullso."

Many years before settlers arrived, a Spanish individual bequeathed the name "Vallecito," meaning "Little Valley," upon the lush land where the Vallecito and Pine Rivers flow. The name was more melodious and pleasing to the ear of the white settlers than the name the Indians used, "Shu-ah-gauche." Spanish influence can be found in the names of many places in southwest Colorado, including the Los Pinos, Piedra, Vallecito, Animas, and San Juan rivers as well as the towns of Durango, Cortez, Mancos, Hesperus, Hermosa, and the old mining town of La Plata. The Spaniards didn't conquer the rich land of Southwestern Colorado; however, they certainly did leave ample evidence of their presence.

The French also traveled through this new country. When the French explorer, LaSalle, arrived on the Texas coast of the vast Louisiana Territory known as New France, he established Fort St. Louis in 1685. It was quite a challenge in this formidable, unfriendly country. The uncharted territory had no marked boundaries, which made its exploration difficult. Even the most daring individuals gave pause to traversing this hostile terrain.

The many different Indian tribes that inhabited the area were not pleased to see the white invaders, but the French managed to have a much better relationship with the Indians than the Spaniards had. They showered the Indians with trinkets and other gifts to win their valuable friendship, which allowed the French to expand trade in their territory to outposts west of the Mississippi River. It was at these outposts that the stories of the Spanish mines in New Mexico filtered through to the French, stories that whetted their appetite for a taste of the riches that the Spanish were supposed to have found. They sent out an expedition, led by Commander Chevalier de Bourgmont, to travel into this unknown land to the west to gather information and chart the country. Bourgmont traveled as far as the Missouri River in 1724 before becoming too ill to travel far-

Two Summitville cabins shown here in 1999. The French were the first to mine this area around 1800 after a band of Indians they befriended told them there was much gold there. In the 1900s there was a large mining operation here. Summitville is reached from the east side of Wolf Creek Pass. (Photo D. Warlick)

ther. However he was able to meet the different Indian tribes and solidify their relations.

It was during one of these meetings that a tribe of Indians told Bourgmont that the Spaniards were capturing their people and forcing them to work in the silver mines near their villages. Some of these Indians wore beautifully crafted silver jewelry, which substantiated their stories. In 1739 an expedition led by Pierre and Paul Mallet left for the Rocky Mountains to try to establish trade with the Spanish. On this journey they found evidence of actual mining activities.

Around the same time, the Spanish were becoming quite annoyed with the Frenchmen who were trading and trapping in Spanish territory. They could see that the French were having increasing influence on the Indian population, and it made them quite uneasy. Because of the Seven Year War between France and Great Britain, the French were left without any territory on the American continent after 1762. When the Spanish took command of the Louisiana Territory, they were diplomatic in their approach and hired many of the French to help with the transition. One of the French employees was Louis Villamont, a captain in the Spanish Regiment. He was influential in sending a large French and French Canadian mining expedition, led by Pierre Lebreau, into the mountains of Colorado in 1799. The three hundred man expedition was officially launched to map the area from New Orleans to Colorado and New Mexico; however, their main purpose, unbeknownst to the Spanish, was to prospect for gold and silver.

After a long journey, the group reached the San Luis Valley in southern present-day Colorado where they came upon a band of Capote Utes who were engaged in a battle with a large force of Comanche Indians. The French joined the fight with the Utes, saving them from slaughter. In return for their help, the Utes led the French through South Fork and up Park Creek to the summit of the Continental Divide near Wolf Creek Pass. Here, they were told there was much gold. The Utes left them there, telling them to stay up on the mountain and to stay out of their sacred areas in the valley below. The Utes especially didn't want the French around Pagosa Springs where the treasured healing waters of the hot mineral springs were located.

The French did find a large strike of gold in the area of Summitville and also on the East Fork of the San Juan River. During the first winter, sixty-five miners died from mercury poisoning before they realized that mercury vapor was poisonous. The problem was that the weather was so miserably cold and there was so much snow on top of the tents, that the ventilation was poor. They had to store the frozen corpses until spring when the heavy frost left the ground and they could bury them. They wanted to make sure the Spanish couldn't find the bodies, as they didn't want them to know just how many Frenchmen were in the San Juans.

During the last part of the eighteenth century there happened to be a severe drought, meaning that the men on hunting details had to travel farther and farther in search of game. They stayed out of the valleys to avoid conflict with the Indians. This limited their territory so much that they moved westward, over to the heights above Pagosa and Vallecito in their search for meat for the hungry miners. The French continued to operate their mines at Summitville for about four years until the Utes warned them that the Spanish had asked them to help get rid of the French. They hurriedly covered up all signs of mining activity and buried the gold.

By this time, the Spanish had recruited a large number of Comanches and Apaches who swarmed down upon the French camp and drove them out. In the running battle that ensued, the French fled north along the Continental Divide. After days of travel and hardship, they finally reached the distant Arkansas River, but by now there were only a few Frenchmen left. Although some of the hidden gold was later dug up by another French expedition, much of the results of four years of the Frenchmen's gold still lies hidden on Treasure Mountain near Wolf Creek Pass.

The Spanish and French may have been the first to explore this country, but when they returned to Europe with tales of a wild, new land and the treasures it held, it created widespread interest throughout the European population. At the same time the infamous Inquisition was at its strongest, and the Roman Catholic Church had set up a tribunal to investigate loyalty of its followers. Suspected enemies of the church were imprisoned and tortured in ever-growing numbers. Some were even burned at the stake. The potato famine in Ireland also contributed to a mass exodus.

The religious and political upheaval, along with a chance to try for a better life in a wondrously rich, new country, sent people from all over Europe scurrying across the sea to America. Many of the immigrants settled on the east coast, but soon there were more and more venturing to the west, where farmland was plentiful and the search for gold caused great excitement and expectations. Railroads were built across the continent to haul people, supplies, and equipment to new locations.

There were a number of explorers together with French, Spanish, and American trappers who made their way across the uncharted land. The trappers traveled through new territory in search of furs to satisfy the European demands. They all contributed to the taming of the wild country of the West.

Adventurous men, including Lewis and Clark and Jedediah Smith, stayed more to the north in their explorations. Jim Bridger, Uncle Dick

Wooton, Bill Williams, Kit Carson, and Captain John Fremont were famous explorers who used Ute guides to help find their way through the wild and challenging Rocky Mountains of present-day Colorado, but most of these well known trappers and explorers, with the exception of Kit Carson, were not known to venture into the southern region of the San Juans. Carson was very involved in the San Juans and was instrumental in the negotiations between the Utes and the U. S. government.

Temple Cornelius noted in his book, *Sheepherders Gold,* that in the summer of 1935 or 1936, a sheepherder found some human bones in a small ravine on what was known as "Starvation Slope" near the crest of Ute Ridge, which is above Ute Creek in the central San Juans. The sheepherder thought the bones surely belonged to a Spanish mining party that had been mining in these parts in the late 1700s and figured he must be close to the Old Ute Mine that he had long been searching for.

He immediately went down to Durango and stirred up the interest of some locals with this exciting story. A group followed him to the location of his gruesome find, but upon closer inspection by the Durango citizens, they found the skeletons were only a short distance from the campsite of the ill-fated Fremont expedition of 1845. Much to the sheepherder's dismay, it was decided that the skeletons belonged to that party.

The exciting news of the seemingly endless discoveries of veins of gold and silver worth immeasurable wealth in the 1870s started the rush of greedy prospectors and various mining companies into the San Juans. The gold rush had been going on in California since 1849, when the Ralston brothers and several Cherokee Indians struck gold in Clear Creek near the present city of Denver. Since there was not enough gold for all the prospective gold seekers, the rush spread all the way down to the present-day Durango area.

While there were both Anglo trappers and miners who drifted through the San Juan Mountains in the early days, their stories and names are mostly unknown until Colonel Baker, and the prospecting party that he headed, arrived at the Animas River in 1861. They settled in what was called Baker's Park near the present-day town of Silverton. These prospectors were proficient at placer gold digging, but had no experience with gold found in veins or lodes. Therefore, they were not very successful in their search at this location. The winter of 1861-62 also took a huge toll in lives.

When the Civil War ended, many of the released soldiers, along with other wandering souls from the East, started the long, arduous trek toward the fabled riches in the West. The Homestead Act of 1862 caused many more courageous fellows to head west. In spite of some unrest between the Utes and the whites, there were initially only a few problems during the time when settlers started drifting into the Pine River Valley and the Vallecito area. However the territory was part of the Ute Indian Reservation, and as miners swarmed into it, there were more and more confrontations with the Utes. As the U. S. government negotiated a new treaty with the Utes, the white men broke more and more of the already existing treaties. At one point, the U. S. government gave orders for the military troops to keep the miners out of the Indian land; but it was an order that did not work as the gold-crazed miners were not about to be stopped in their mad search for treasure.

The citizens of Colorado were crying to the government to keep the Utes out of the state or at least out of the rich mining areas. The *Boulder News* stated: "An Indian has no more right to stand in the way of civilization and progress than a wolf or bear."

Finally, the Brunot Agreement was adopted in 1873. It cut the Ute's territory even further, and since they didn't fully understand the new agreement, they thought the miners would do their mining and exploring in the summer and then leave in the winter. Of course this wasn't the way it turned out. It was just another bitter pill for the Utes to swallow. If it hadn't been for Chief Ouray's skill at negotiating, the Southern Utes probably would have been driven from their last remaining piece of land in Colorado. The Northern Utes were driven into Utah.

There is little known about the earliest prospectors who wandered through the Vallecito country, but certainly some of the miners who had gone to the big rushes in Silverton and LaPlata Canyon soon became discouraged and drifted into the adjacent areas of Chicago Basin and Vallecito in their search for precious metals.

Most of the early arrivals started looking for a piece of land they could call their own. The start of agriculture soon became a way of life to many who settled in these parts. The communities of Silverton, La Plata, and Animas City, which were developing to support the mining efforts, all needed agriculture to keep pace with the need for food, hay and other agricultural products, so farmers and ranchers were a welcome addition to the growing population.

CHAPTER 3:

Indian Settlers

he diplomatic skills the Utes used in their dealings with the Spanish, the French, the Mexicans, and other explorers served them well in their relations with the trappers who took their game and the greedy swarms of men that had invaded their land in search of gold. Now the white settlers moved onto Ute land. Unlike the explorers, these people didn't just come for a while and then move on— they stayed and started farming, ranching, and even setting up retail stores to furnish supplies to the other settlers. The Indians were gradually being crowded out.

As bad as things were, the Utes fared better with the federal government than any other Indian tribe because of their cooperative attitude and their skill in negotiations. They weren't completely forced out of Colorado, and the Southern Utes around Ignacio even received some fairly decent farmland. They got to keep at least a part of the land they had always known and considered theirs, and ended up with ample water rights from the Pine and Piedra Rivers that flowed through the reservation.

After the passing of the Hunter Act in 1895, which gave every adult male Ute, who wanted it, their own parcel of land, the U. S. govern-

Upper Vallecito Valley before the lake was filled. Note crooked Vallecito Creek and see why the Utes named it "Shu-ah-gauche" meaning "Crooked Water." Pine River comes into left side of picture to join it. Circa mid 1930s. (Photo courtesy Kennon Decker)

ment decided to try to make the Utes into farmers so they could eventually become self-supporting. They sent farm equipment to the reservation to help put this plan in action.

Farming was a totally new concept to the nomadic Utes. It went completely against their nature to be tied to one spot, to settle down to the tedious job of plowing, and to plant fields instead of wandering wherever and whenever they chose. Is it any wonder that the Indian agent in Ignacio would come across some of the young braves merrily racing around the fields on their stripped-down farming machines? Many of them didn't take to farming at all and sold their land to white people, but some Utes eventually did try their hand at agricultural pursuits.

☞   ☞

Jim Weaselskin and his extended family were Northern Utes. Jim was born around 1850 and acquired his name from the numerous weasel skins he always wore. After the death of Chief Ouray in 1880, the Weaselskin family made the decision to come down to Southern Ute land to settle. If they had not done so at this time, they would have been forced to go to the reservation in Utah like the other Northern Utes. They settled on a fairly level piece of land along the Florida River that Jim found appealing.

For a while the family lived in a dugout with a wooden front. Dugouts were simply caves that were dug back into the side of a hill. They were not uncommon in early times when money and tools were scarce. Even some of the white settlers lived in dugouts for brief periods until they could build better quarters.

Yet life was good. Summers would find the Weaselskin family (including uncles, aunts, brothers, sisters, and children) packing up and beginning the long hike up the steep trail to Endlich Mesa, a spectacular high mountain mesa which sits above and to the west of the Vallecito River Valley. Endlich Mesa is dotted with tiny lakes, numerous rock formations, and a few random patches of trees. Because the mesa is located above tree line, the surrounding land below can be viewed for many miles in all directions. From this vantage point, one could go west and head down toward Durango, or go east by making a steep, treacherous descent down a narrow canyon created by one of the tributaries of the Vallecito River that winds its way into the valley below.

The white men who settled the Vallecito River Valley named one of Endlich Mesa's swift running streams "Weaselskin Creek," in honor of the old Indian who used this location as a summer pasture for his horses for many years. Weaselskin Creek empties into the Vallecito River just north of the present Vallecito Campground, to the north of the lake.

The Weaselskins had eighty to ninety head of horses that they drove up to the high summer range every summer. Here on the high mesa was an abundance of rich grasses to fatten the herd, compensating for the skimpy rations at their winter home below. The men made rope corrals to contain the horses while the Weaselskins roamed the mountains, hunting, trapping, and fishing. Sometimes the excursions took them many miles away, and sometimes they would go down from the mountains to the lower country to the east to hunt the antelope that grazed there.

The women and children spent much of the summer picking berries and gathering herbs in the surrounding country. These essentials could only be found in the warm months, and some grew only at these higher elevations. Hides had to be tanned, and the meat from the animals was either cooked for meals at this location or dried for future use. The animal skins would be used for the family's clothing or saved to sell or trade.

Sometimes members of the family ventured down one of the steep canyons to the Vallecito River that ran far below and took a refreshing sweat bath and swam in the cold, deep pools. It was a busy but enjoyable life that they led in this summer home.

After the first snowfall, they would start the long trek down from the mountains to their home. The horses didn't have to be driven this time. They could sense the change of seasons and once turned loose, they started racing for home.

When she was a child, Jim Weaselskin's granddaughter, Belle Cuthair, had the job of feeding the baby goats that the family raised. She thought that baby goats were some of the cutest animals alive, so she didn't mind this chore at all. The family also raised some of the goats for the white neighbors. "People were widely scattered in those days, and everyone had plenty of space," Belle remembered.

> *The whites we knew were real good people. They gave us some of their apples, potatoes, squash, beans, and corn. We dried the hominy to preserve it for later use.*
>
> *Our family lived on dried meat, mostly antelope, sheep, and rabbit. Antelope were plentiful around here then. We also dried soap weed, which we would peel and then cut the ribs to prepare it for eating in the winter. It was sweet tasting, like bananas.*
>
> *We also picked chokecherries, gooseberries, and raspberries and dried them for later use. For Christmas, we would butcher a hog. What a treat that was! This gave us a good supply of lard, headcheese, bacon, and ham hocks.*

Jim frequently stayed up at Vallecito, running trap lines and tanning hides for white people. There were bear, lions, beaver, wolves, and other smaller animals to trap. When he had a good supply, he would take the animal hides to the Indian Market in Denver where he sold them for a good price. Seldom would you see a deer in those days. They were so scarce that it was against the law to kill them.

Belle recounted:

> The whites even gave us lumber to build a wooden house so that we wouldn't have to live in the dugout, but after we built it, we didn't get to enjoy it for very long. Buckskin Charlie, who was Chief at the time, ran us off of that place because we came from the north and weren't Southern Utes.
>
> He was a half Apache from down around Tierra Amarilla. The Utes often frequented the northern part of New Mexico where the Apaches ranged, which accounts for some of the inter-mixing with the nearby Apache tribe. The Weaselskins had settled on reservation land that apparently was not assigned to them. Buckskin Charlie perhaps didn't feel these Northern Utes deserved such choice Southern Ute land and a nice, new wooden house.
>
> After that, the government gave us some land on the Animas River. It was rocky, no good land. You couldn't grow anything on it.

Their land is near the present Weaselskin Bridge that crosses the Animas River approximately ten miles south of Durango. Instead of rounding up horses to sell or trade, which had been their way of life, the Weaselskins were given some sheep to raise. It was a far cry from their earlier, happier days.

Weaselskin had a special group of companions that would often join him in his summer domain overlooking Vallecito. Among them were Old Washington, Old Tallian, Old Pelon, and Old Page Wright. The "Old" used before their names did not refer to their ages. It was used because they were the male heads of a family and accustomed to the old way of life. This group of Utes knew every nook and cranny in this mountain country.

Besides having Weaselskin Creek and Weaselskin Bridge named after him, Old Weaselskin had another claim to fame. He was well remembered for the legendary Weaselskin gold mine. The fabulously rich vein of gold was said to have nuggets by the handfuls. It is purportedly located somewhere up the Vallecito River, above the mouth of Weaselskin Creek.

Temple Cornelius, author of *Sheepherder's Gold* heard many stories from Old Washington when Washington lived on the Charlie Pargin place east of Chimney Rock. One of the stories was about Weaselskin's gold stash. The Pargin family heard many of the same tales during their close association with the Utes, and many stories were passed on to the present generation. Some, including the Weaselskin gold story, seem to have some substance to them. Many have searched for the treasure stash over the years with little success, or if some lucky person was successful, he is keeping it secret. If it was hidden as well as Old Weaselskin said it was, it may never be found, although some believers occasionally search the hills for it.

The story goes like this: On their trip to and from the mountains, the Ute Indians became well acquainted with the few settlers who lived along the way. They got to know the Charlie Waldner family who owned a ranch far up the Florida River above the present Lemon Reservoir just over the mountain to the west of Vallecito. Weaselskin often stopped there on his journeys to Durango, and the Waldners fed him a meal in order to cultivate his friendship. At this time the Indians still instilled a certain amount of fear in the settlers, and they figured it was safer to be on good terms with them.

The visits became a routine. As Weaselskin made his way from his mountain camp to Durango, he would stop by the Waldner ranch and have a meal. As he prepared to leave, he would give them a gold nugget to repay them for their kindness.

After a time, Mr. Waldner started thinking that he wasn't being fair, taking all these nuggets for just a few meals. He might cause Weaselskin to run out of his best trading commodity. On the next visit, when Weaselskin tried to pay, Waldner offered to give some of the gold back, but Weaselskin refused. He was happy with the arrangement. The white man's food was worth every nugget.

Weaselskin and some of his companions ventured into a store in Durango one day and found that the owner of the store had just boiled up a pan of wieners. The proprietor generously handed out a number of them to the eager group, and then was quite surprised when they gave him gold nuggets to repay him for the kindness he had shown them.

For many years the Utes continued to come up to their favorite hunting and herb-gathering spot, but after the white settlers started to settle on the Los Pinos and Vallecito Rivers, things started changing. It became increasingly difficult to get onto their choicest grounds and the Utes gradually lost their freedom to roam at will. However, in the very early 1900s, they did occasionally go up the Pine River to the large ranches located near the Weminuche Wilderness boundary. Belle remembered, "The people up at Granite Peaks used to want us to come up there and kill the bighorn sheep when there got to be too many. They thought that the sheep scared their horses. We got to keep the meat and hides. But that was a long time ago and that time is gone forever."

Jim died during the influenza epidemic in 1918 while living on his land allotment near the Sunnyside Bridge on the Animas River. This was the bridge that was later re-named "Weaselskin Bridge" in his honor.

"The government agent changed the Weaselskin name to Williams," Belle said. "This was what the Indian agents would do sometimes rather than deal with the hard to pronounce Indian names." As the Ute people were increasingly integrated into the now predominately white community, more emphasis was placed on education. Consequently Belle's father, Price Williams (whose Indian name was Onmacich) was one of the many young Indians who were sent to school at Old Fort Lewis in the early 1900s. The spot had been a military fort south of the town of Hesperus before it was changed into an Indian school. Since the Indians had been put on reservations, there was no need for the military personnel that were stationed here; so they started making preparations to permanently leave the site. The soldiers enjoyed getting to know the strange, young students who were no longer their enemies, and were especially fond of Price Williams. Belle remembered how proud Price was when he talked about the soldiers giving him a three-mule team, harness and wagon, along with some straw mattresses before they left their Ft. Lewis post.

Edna Baker, another of Weaselskin's granddaughters, was the daughter of John Russell and a cousin of Belle Cuthair. This branch of the family spent summers with the extended family in the early 1900s but settled on reservation land in Echo Canyon, to the south of Pagosa Springs.

⮜ ⮞

Weaselskin's good friend, Old Washington, had his allotted parcel of land just to the east of Chimney Rock in what became known as Washington Flats. Washington was not content to sit around twiddling his thumbs on his own land when there was more interesting country to explore. Accustomed to being on the move in his earlier days, a change in his life-long habits didn't come easily.

Around 1874 a party of prospectors told of rounding a bend along the Roaring Fork River and seeing a small hunting camp of Ute teepees. The Utes' leader walked toward them making a peace sign. He showed them a card that had been given to him in Denver that said, "This Indian's name is Washington and he is a good Indian."

Washington was an occasional visitor at the ranch Daniel Pargin homesteaded on Beaver Creek in 1877. Even after Daniel died, in 1882, his wife, Serelda, and her boys would sometimes see him coming by their ranch. When Ed, the youngest of the Pargin boys, left home and home-steaded in Fossett Gulch near the Piedra River in 1898, it didn't take long for Old Washington to develop the habit of also stopping by there.

Many times while she was busy in her kitchen, Ed's wife, Maggie, would get a strange feeling. Turning, she would find Old Washington standing stoically near the door, waiting until his presence was acknowl-edged, and then saying, "Me want bees-keet." Whereupon Maggie, quaking in her boots, would quickly hand him a bunch of biscuits and he would take his leave.

Washington was so used to the old ways that he didn't adjust well to farming life. He would much rather spend his time with Weaselskin and his group of friends as they wandered about hunting and trapping. He ended up selling his land to the Pargin boy, Daniel D. (who was called "Doll"). The land later went to Doll's son, Charles. The Pargins permitted Washington to stay on his old land holdings for as long as he lived.

In the late 1980s, a Pargin heir that wasn't familiar with the old family history was looking through the county land records in Pagosa Springs. To his great surprise, he thought that one of the Pargins had pur-chased the Washington Flats land from George Washington's heirs. This first appeared to be very exciting news, but it didn't take long to realize that the government agent had shown a sense of humor when he gave Old Washington a white man's name to replace his Indian name. With the excep-tion of the agent, no one had ever used the old Indian's first name before.

⊣ ⊢

Annetta Frost was the granddaughter of Antonio Buck, the son of the well-known Ute chief, Buckskin Charlie. Annetta was raised by her grandparents, and the family land allotment was passed down to her. Annetta always heeded her grandfather's advice to never sell the land and be forced to live on just a tiny scrap of land like so many of the Utes. Annetta married another tribal member, Jack Frost, and raised a family. They spent their entire lives on their land allotment, which lies a few miles south of Bayfield.

The Utes ran their cattle on range permits above Vallecito in the 1920s and 1930s. One of the highlights of Jack Frost's boyhood was when he turned eleven and he was finally allowed to help drive the cattle up to the summer range in Chicago Basin in the high country, northwest of Vallecito. He would ride with his father, Andrew Frost, his uncles, John Carl and Sam, and Rob Richards — all tribal members. What a thrill it was to actually be considered old enough to do a man's job!

Southern Ute Tribal Members. Standing: Susan Williams, John Russell's wife; John Russell, Marie Frost, Scott Hay's wife; Emma Buck (Towee), Buckskin Charlie's wife; Buckskin Charlie; Victor Frost. Seated: Marie Tobias; Scott Hayes; Theodosia Frost; White Frost. (Courtesy Southern Ute Archives, Denver Public Library, Western History Department, 04302)

The first day they drove the cattle up to Red Creek where they stopped for the night. The next day they made the steep climb up to Carbonate Basin, their next stopping place. On the third day they would go up to their final destination in Chicago Basin where the cattle would feed on their summer range. In the fall the cattle would be moved back down to lower country as they couldn't survive the treacherous winter snows in the high country.

At the same time Buckskin Charlie and Rob Richards ran their cattle up East Creek to the east of the Vallecito Valley. When Buckskin Charlie dropped out of the cattle business, Frost's family took over his range. The Forest Service regulated these ranges then as they do now. Later on, the Indian cattle were put into an association, because they had to combine the herds to have enough cattle to get a coveted range permit.

In the 1930s when Jack was older, Bruce Sullivan was putting on rodeos on his ranch at Vallecito. The Utes would ride horseback all the way to the ranch, arriving about noon. There was a five-dollar charge to ride in such events as calf roping, bronco riding, and wild-cow milking. The

Left to right: Antonio Buck, Francis Buck and Chief Buckskin Charlie who was wearing his prized Benjamin Harrison 1890 Peace Medal. His son, Antonio Buck followed him as Chief of the Southern Utes for a short time until the Utes went to the Tribal Counsel form of government. He then was in the position of Tribal Chairman. (Animas Museum Photo Archives)

rodeos were the highlights of the summers for both Indians and whites. It was perhaps gratifying to the Indians to be able to out do or at least keep pace with the white cowboys at the rodeo events.

Jack was a member of the "Pine River Valley Polo Club," a talented team that played in a World Champion Polo Match in Albuquerque, New Mexico. Two Texas teams, a team from Cortez, and the Pine River team made it to the play-offs. The team from San Angelo, Texas beat the Pine River team in the championship game; however, the Pine River team did get to play in the "Big One."

As the older Utes and the white settlers continued to be in contact with one another, a certain amount of trust and friendship eventually developed among them and grew stronger as time progressed. At this point, the Utes really didn't have much choice, but each race realized the good side of their former enemies.

⊰ *Early White Settlers* ⊱

VALLECITO TRAILS & WATERWAYS

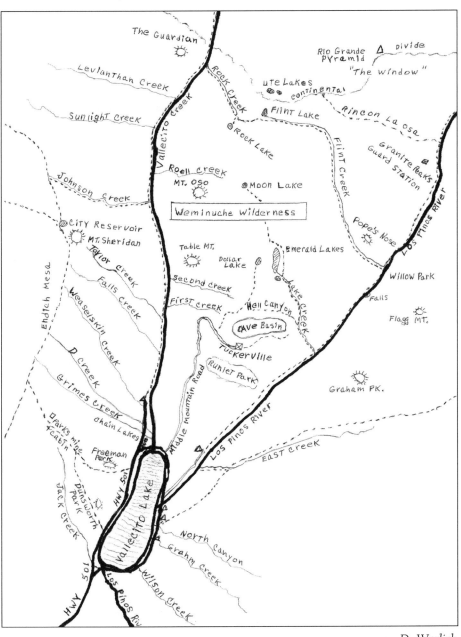

D. Warlick

HOMESTEADERS

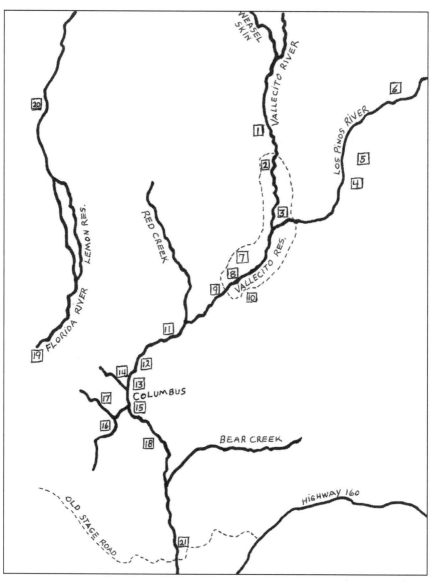

D. Warlick

1 Wit's End	8 Conklins	15 Columbus School
2 Deckers	9 Currys	16 McCoys
3 Sullivans	10 Pearson/Wilmer	17 Richards
4 Wilderness Trails	11 Scott/Marshall	18 Wommers
5 Teelawuket	12 Glovers	19 Burkett/Lissner
6 Granite Peaks	13 Parks	
7 Dunsworths	14 Pattons	

CHAPTER 4

Cabins in Indian Country

J ust as each Southern Ute male received allotments of one hundred sixty acres of reservation land, the Homestead Act of 1862 also gave white settlers the opportunity to file on the same amount of unallocated land if he lived on and improved it ("proved up") over a five-year period. At that time he would be awarded a final certificate and own the land.

After a lengthy perusal of records in the Durango Courthouse and the National Archives in Denver, it becomes apparent that there were sometimes long delays in entering homestead filings or final certificates. Between the late 1870s and the early 1900s a surprisingly large number of white men came to the valley where the Vallecito and the Los Pinos Rivers join. By 1881 the Indians were on reservation land and weren't creating as much fear as they once had instilled in the white men. As the Indians and whites were exposed to one another more frequently, a measure of trust developed between them.

Most of the early settlers found the life that they had to endure at an elevation of nearly 8,000-feet to be too much for them. The beautiful surroundings and plentiful game were not enough to hold them for any length of time, so they left in search of a place where the living was easier.

Some of the earliest recorded homesteaders in the Vallecito area are still remembered because their names were given to localities and other natural areas. John T. Graham and Thomas Wilson had creeks on the east side of the present-day lake named after them. Charles C. Graham homesteaded what later became the Teelawuket Ranch, where his original cabin still stands. George Brawner homesteaded part of the present-day Cool Water Ranch and has a canyon named for him, and Adolphus Germain homesteaded part of the Dunsworth/Warlick Ranch south of Sawmill Point where the Warlicks now live. These hardy fellows were followed closely by a number of others

Sometimes an enterprising person would hire another person to homestead a piece of land; then, when the homesteader had the final certificate or patent, on the land, he sold it to his sponsor. Of course this was against the rules, but it was done nevertheless.

Timber and stone deeds were issued by the government for land that was unsuitable for farming and ranching, but which still might be valuable. Some of the land at Vallecito fell into this category since it was so rocky and steep that it wasn't considered to have enough value to become a homestead.

However it might have worth by harvesting timber or collecting rocks, or simply to have more room between you and your neighbors.

Most of the early folks must have wandered into the valley in the warmer seasons, since travel through the deep snows of winter was almost impossible. Only the hardiest of the early settlers would choose to stay after they had lived through some of the hellatious winters known to strike the Vallecito area, especially with the primitive conditions they must have had to endure.

Vallecito has never been an actual town. It is simply a valley where the Los Pinos and the Vallecito Rivers join. As settlers ventured in, some ranches sprang up along the edges and bottom of the widest part of the valley where the rivers actually join, and other ranches were located up both of the individual rivers. Some people settled down on the area below where the rivers combined, which then was known as the Los Pinos or Pine River. No real boundaries to "Vallecito" have ever existed, but it is presumed, by most, to end a few unspecified miles below the present dam.

The closest thing to a town was in the 1800s, when the tiny settlement of Los Pinos was located about eight miles to the south of present-day Vallecito near the Pine River. This settlement consisted of a stage stop, post office, flourmill, and one house. It afforded the settlers living at Vallecito a place that they could get mail service and flour. The post office began operating at this location in 1877 and continued operations until 1898 when the more populated town of Bayfield was laid out and mail service was moved to that location.

An article in the 1885 edition of *Crofutt's Grip-Sack Guide* had this to report:

> Pine River — La Plata County, consists of a ranch, hotel, and post office, in one building on the west bank of the Rio de los Pinos, surrounded by timber and agricultural land, where stock raising is the principal occupation, and where a little mining is done. To the northward, coal abounds. It is on the wagon road from Animas City to Pagosa Springs, 20 miles east of the former, and 40 miles west of the later. Here, we found the best accommodations for travelers in the whole San Juan country. It is the first and only place where we were reminded of the chicken, and that it laid eggs, and found the meals well cooked, without being "wallowed in grease."
>
> Game is abundant in the vicinity, as well as trout in all the streams. Produce of all kinds raised here brings good prices.
>
> In 1880 on our visit to this locality, we said: This place is only four miles north from the Southern Ute Reservation, but

the Indians are friendly, never giving the whites any trouble. Twelve miles south is situated the Indian agency. These Utes, unlike the northern brethren, are engaged in raising ponies and sheep, principally. They receive rations weekly and their allowance of annuity goods every fall. This reservation, notwithstanding our treaty with the Indians to the contrary, is overrun with cattle and sheep belonging to white men living just outside of the Indian's reserve, which results in great loss and disadvantage to the occupants. We understand the Indians have complained bitterly of these wrongs, but can find no redress. The agent says he cannot expel the white man's stock; certain influences are too strong for him. The result will be, eventually — war.

Our government makes treaties, claims to be civilized, yet Indian rights, secured by the faith of a "civilized" people, are seldom respected, and when the 'barbarian" complains the czar is deaf to his pleadings. We say, "a curse to such civiliza-tion." It is now March 1885. "Civilization" has done its work."

This article expresses the opinion of many in the nation who didn't agree with the treatment of the Indians by our government. However there were many in agreement, who were mainly the ones who would benefit from it most.

The fact that the Los Pinos name was already used at this nearby settlement was probably the reason that the settlement, on the upper part of the Los Pinos River was named after the Vallecito River, which ended here where the rivers joined.

The white settlers discussed in this chapter, almost without excep-tion, either lived in the Vallecito Valley itself, at one time or another, or a few miles down the Pine River, including the families that went to the old Columbus School with the Vallecito children. Some of the children came from the nearby Spring Gulch, Texas Creek, and Lemon Lake areas that lie to the west, so a few families from those areas are also included. Some of these people consider their land as being a part of "Vallecito".

⮜ ⮞

JOHN TAYLOR

John Taylor was a former slave who was born in Paris, Kentucky in 1841, and later served in the Union Army. One source of information claims that he was a scout for the military. Another source places him in the cavalry unit of black soldiers that the Indians called "Buffalo Soldiers" because the texture of their hair reminded them of buffalo hair. This was quite a compliment since they held the buffalo in such high esteem.

After the war was over, John came west with an army colleague to Tierra Amarilla in New Mexico, where he married an Indian girl who bore him several children. Most of the children, and perhaps his wife, died of smallpox. Some old-timers remember hearing that the Indians gave John the option of marrying an Indian maiden or dying. That was an easy choice to make.

John Taylor and his bride, Kitty Cloud in their wedding portrait. John joined the Southern Ute tribe and claimed to be "the first white man in the Pine River Valley." A far cry from his early years in slavery. (Animas Museum Photo Archives)

John Taylor claimed to be "the first white man" in the Pine River Valley, meaning that he was the first man other than the Indians to live here. John arrived in the Pine River Valley between 1871 and 1873. His claim to be the first white man in Vallecito area was rather misleading since John was not white, but he certainly felt more like a white man than he did an Indian. The Indian race was entirely unfamiliar to him before he came west.

John was better known as "Nigger John" throughout the whole upper and lower Pine River valley. In those days, using that name for Blacks was very common and didn't seem to have the demeaning connotation that it does today. John certainly didn't take offense to it, nor was it meant to be offensive.

John later came to the Ignacio area where he met and married a Ute, Kitty Cloud, who was the tender age of fourteen, not an unusual age to marry in those days. John would have been around thirty years old at the time. He became a member of the Ute tribe, and fathered two children, Henry and Euterpe Taylor. Euterpe remembered that John brought his deaf son from his first marriage to live with them in Ignacio.

John first worked at trapping and, later on, as the government continued to press the Utes into an agricultural life, he turned to farming. His previous life as a slave had exposed him to that way of life, so he could accept it more easily than the Utes could. He also carried mail between Bayfield and Ignacio for a time. He was quite a dapper fellow and was said to enjoy a spot of gambling on occasion.

While John never actually lived in a house at Vallecito, he frequently spent time there; and he truly was the first man, other than the Indians, to settle along the Pine River. He loved bringing his family to Vallecito on extended camping trips. They would catch their fill of native trout in the clear mountain waters in no time at all; but being a tribal member, John resided on the designated reservation.

Everyone liked John. With his keen sense of humor and engaging personality, he was one of the most popular and respected members of both the Ute tribe and the white community. He was sorely missed when he died in 1934 at the age of ninety-six.

⊰ ⊱

THE PARGINS

David Warlick, Jr., son of David Warlick, Sr. and Gertrude Pargin Warlick, tells about the Pargin side of his family:

> While my father's family was among the fairly early settlers on the Upper Pine River, my mother's family (the Pargins) had already been in this part of the country since 1877. My great-grandparents, Daniel and Serelda Pargin, had been living in Illinois, but after fighting in the Civil War and returning home for a while, Daniel wasn't satisfied with the flat land they lived on in Illinois. His dream was to go west and live in the mountains, so they decided to join up with a wagon train that was heading west to South Dakota in the spring of 1876. They heard that there was a plentiful supply of wild game in the hilly country there, and this sounded like an ideal setting to Daniel.
>
> When the wagon train reached Fort Larned, Kansas they hit a snag. General Custer was there with his troops, and he told them they could not go to the Dakotas because the Cheyenne and Sioux Indians were on the warpath. He and his soldiers were on their way there to do battle with them. After a

few days they decided that the group would split up. The main group headed to Oklahoma, and the smaller group, headed by Daniel Pargin, decided to continue on west to Colorado.

The smaller wagon train made its way to Fort Garland, Colorado, where there was a small settlement and an army encampment. Here they heard that the Indians had killed Custer and his troops at the Battle of Little Big Horn on June 26th and 27th, 1876, one of the greatest battles of the Indian wars.

By this time cold weather was closing in, so the group wintered at Fort Garland, which gave Daniel enough time to find out that he didn't want to settle in the San Luis Valley. During the winter he received information about the San Juan Basin on the west side of the Continental Divide, an area that included Pagosa Springs, Bayfield and Durango. It sounded like appealing country to him.

At that time, the only way to get to Durango from the east was by a route that went from Alamosa to Monte Vista, then to Del Norte and southwest up Pinos Creek to Summitville on top of the divide. The trail from there went down the west side of the divide and down the East Fork of the San Juan to the San Juan River, and then on into Pagosa Springs.

Daniel's group left Fort Garland and started up the long climb to Summitville, where they encountered a small group of miners living and working in the gold mines. Then they started the grueling descent down the treacherous East Fork of the San Juan River. The terrain was rough and steep. In some places they had to let their wagons down over bluffs and rocks with ropes and block and tackle. The raging waters of the stream had to be crossed a number of times as they made their way down the steep, winding canyon. They all made it safely down the most challenging part of the journey and headed on to Pagosa Springs where the weary travelers could get a much-needed rest.

Daniel scouted around until he found, and laid claim to, a promising piece of land a few miles east of Bayfield on Beaver Creek. This is where he, Serelda, and their four sons, Charles, Ben, Daniel D. (who was called "Doll") and Edward settled and started their new life. They were right in the middle of the feared Indians! The other families moved on and settled in other locations.

The family had a cabin completed by winter, so they were protected from the elements. Since the closest neighbor

Pargin family 1905. Top row: Maude Pargin, Charlie Pargin, Ben Pargin, Jose Pargin, Ed Pargin, Maggie Pargin. 2nd row: Leona Pargin, Daniel D. Pargin (Doll), Tom Reaves, Pearl Pargin Reaves. Front row: Sylvia Pargin (daughter of Charlie and Maude), Serelda Pargin (mother), Mike Pargin (Ben & Jose's son.) Circa 1908. (Warlick Collection)

was miles away, they were still uneasy about encounters with the Indians who came around occasionally, but this soon became less worrisome since the Utes gave them no trouble. The Pargin boys soon struck up a friendship with the Ute boys that lasted for the remainder of their lives.

Daniel Pargin was able to get a hay-mowing machine and a hay rake to cut the lush wild hay that grew in the Beaver Creek Valley. The Indian agent agreed to buy the hay to feed the horses of the detachment of cavalry soldiers stationed at Ignacio. He even sent soldiers to haul the hay on government wagons. Each load of hay was called a ton, and the agent allowed Mr. Pargin sixty dollars for each load. With the money from the hay, the Pargins bought more cattle and some horses and became more prosperous.

But misfortune was soon to strike this family. In 1882 several people saw a big silver-tip bear in the area, and that fall it killed one of the Pargins' cattle. On a cold and stormy day after a big snowstorm, Daniel and three other men set out to hunt the bear. On the second day of the hunt, Daniel shot and killed the bear, which was so big they had to go back to the ranch and get a wagon and team of horses to haul it home. The neighbors gathered at the Pargin place to help dress out the bear and render the fat into lard. They got several hundred pounds of lard, so all the families had enough lard to last through the winters of 1882 and 1883.

During the hunt, Daniel got very cold and wet from the snow. He contracted a cold and sore throat and became so ill that he died in December 1882. This left Serelda alone with her four boys; and then in the spring, she gave birth to a daughter, Pearl Pargin. It was reported that Pearl was the first white baby born in the area. Serelda now had five children to raise by herself in wilderness country. She felt fortunate that she was on good terms with the local Indians.

By 1883 the railroad was extended up the Animas River to the boom town of Silverton, and the smelter in Durango was soon built to extract the silver and gold from the raw ore. The train was running from Alamosa to Durango, as well as the wagon freight line and the passenger stage. During this time Mrs. Pargin was taking in money from the freighters and stage passengers who came by her ranch, which was on the stage line. They stopped by for meals and, occasionally, a place to spend the night. She was also able to sell some butter and cream to help eke out a living for her brood

The freighters traveled in groups of four or five wagons a mile or more apart, so they could help each other, if help was needed. One day, young Doll and Ed Pargin wandered up the road and were about half a mile from home, when one of the freight wagons came along loaded with supplies for Durango. Doll and Ed were sitting on a side hill watching as the freight wagon came down a steep, rocky place in the road, and, as it hit a rough spot, a hundred pound sack of flour fell off the back. Doll and Ed immediately ran to get it. Since they were too small to carry it, they rolled it off the road, over a small bank, and hid until the other wagons went by. Then they ran home as fast as they could to tell their mother the exciting news. Serelda exclaimed that the flour was a gift from Heaven, as they were out of flour at the time.

The Utes and the Pargins became increasingly friendly and Buckskin Charlie, who was now chief, could see that Mrs. Pargin was having a hard time of it. One day in the 1880s, he came to their house with six pair of moccasins and some food for the family. Not only were the moccasins and food appreciated, they were greatly needed.

The boys were getting older and, due to their association with the Indian boys, were becoming quite skilled at fishing and hunting. They contributed fish and game to help keep the family larder filled.

The Indians would often camp near the Pargin house and go hunting north of the cabin, but one time Mrs. Pargin decided that the Indians had stayed too long and it was time that they left. She didn't want them to take up permanent residency for fear that her boys might take on the Indian way of life completely. She gathered all the children into the house, covered all the windows with blankets, and went out where the Indians were camped. She pointed to her face without saying a word. This made the Indians think that someone in the house was very sick, so they left in a hurry. They were deathly afraid of the white man's diseases.

The Pargins and Buckskin Charlie, along with some members of the Indian Council, had become such good friends that it was suggested by the warriors that the Ute Tribe should adopt Ben Pargin. After considerable thought on the subject, Mrs. Pargin finally gave her consent and Ben was adopted through a ceremony in council. From that time on, he was considered a full brother in the tribe.

Ben and Buckskin were lifelong friends. In 1936 Buckskin was near death and he asked to be moved back to his teepee and for someone to send for Ben. Ben soon got the message and came and sat with his dying friend until his last breath. The old chief was ninety-eight years old.

The Pargin boys were a rough and tough bunch and were all crack shots. Their little sister, Pearl, grew up to be just as rough and tough and could ride a horse and shoot a gun just as well as the boys. You had to be tough to survive back then.

David's grandfather was Edward Pargin, the youngest of the Pargin boys. When he was nineteen years old, he decided to strike out on his own. He homesteaded a parcel of land over in Fawcett Gulch (which is just west of the Piedra River) and in 1895 built a sturdy log cabin and some out buildings, many of which are still standing. The Candelerias, one of the early Spanish families, own it now. Ed went on to buy several other ranches, and the family lived at the ranch on Yellow Jacket Pass when

David's mother, Gertrude, was growing up. She met his father when he came to help Ed Pargin build a barn. He wooed her and married her, and then brought her over to Vallecito to live.

Ed's brother, Ben, had some land nearby in Peterson Gulch where he lived with his wife, Jose. Jose's father was the Ignacio Railroad Station operator. The job also included the duties of being the telegraph operator.

Doll Pargin [Daniel D.] bought land near Chimney Rock from the old Ute named George Washington. In the March 25, 1915 edition of *The Bayfield Blade,* there was an article that read: "Two large herds of deer are making their home on the Pargin ranches on the Piedra. Hunting and fishing licenses are needed." Three weeks later the same newspaper had an article that read, "Doll Pargin's herd of semi-domestic deer are all destroyed by wolves."

Charles, the oldest boy, homesteaded southeast of Ignacio, near the small settlement of Tiffany. In May of 1914, lightning killed Charles Pargin instantly. He was plowing with four horses and was riding one of the rear team. The horse under him was also instantly killed. Whoopie Carmack was holding the plow, and for a while he was helpless and couldn't use his hands or arms. His arms seemed to remain in a half folded position. After he came to his senses, he managed to get to the Hott Ranch for help.

The May 22, 1914 edition of *The Bayfield Blade* called the Charles Pargin funeral one of the very largest funerals held in Bayfield. He left a small daughter named Sylvia and his wife, Maud, who gave birth to twin boys soon after his death.

Somehow, most of these old-timers seemed to live through all their trials and tribulations and do whatever they had to do to survive.

◁ ▷

WOMMER

Nicholas and Elizabeth Wommer, and their first son, Jake, came here from Germany in 1878 to homestead on land a few miles down the Pine River from Vallecito. Elizabeth's father, Henry Rich, came with her because he didn't want her to come to this wild country without him. Perhaps he wasn't sure if her husband could provide enough protection, or maybe he really wanted the adventure of the trip to this strange new country with its marauding savages.

Shortly after the couple arrived, Nick built a house that resembled a fort because of the threat of trouble with the nearby Indians. The cabin had portholes on each side of it so that he and Elizabeth could stick a gun out in any direction and shoot. They felt prepared for an attack, but the expected attack never came as the long years of struggles between the Indians and the whites were coming to an end.

Nicholas bought some registered Hereford cattle, and the Wommers began their life of ranching. Soon, other German families settled nearby, which gave them a few scattered neighbors. Five additional children were born in the ensuing years.

When the settlers arrived, they had to make a living somehow, so most of them started clearing land to farm. Of course, crops grow much better with water, so one of the first things these farmers and ranchers did was dig irrigation ditches to transport water from the Pine River to the fields where they planted their crops.

This was a major undertaking. It required communities to work together to accomplish the task. It also called for cooperation regarding the individual amounts of water allocated to each farmer who had rights to the ditches. If disagreements arose, it was usually because someone was not doing his share of ditch maintenance or was taking more than his allotted share of water.

Ed Wommer, a grandson of Nicholas and Elizabeth, was born in 1921, and remembers well the stories handed down in his family from generation to generation. He lived through some of the early, rugged times

1888 home of Nicholas and Elizabeth Wommer. It was also know as the Wommer Fort. There were no windows in the lower level. A stairway at the north end led to the upper story which had port holes cut in the walls to shoot out of in case of Indian attacks. The only known conflict was when the Indians built fires some distance back and danced and chanted all night. Neighbors probably gathered here for protection. (Courtesy of Ed Wommer)

himself. Ed remembers the first local killing over water ditch problems along the Pine River.

> *In 1883 my grandfather, Nicholas Wommer, got into it with Mr. Lignowski, a Russian immigrant, over ditch water. Nick had gone up to the ditch with a shovel, and an argument started between the two men.*
>
> *Nick may have taken after the Russian with a shovel, no one knows, but Ignaski put a tiny pistol up near Nick's head and pulled the trigger and shot him right between the eyes and killed him. Then he dragged him over into the bushes and left him. By the time searchers found him, his body was swollen and covered with flies, and Lignowski was long gone. I reckon the whole Wommer family was too strong of a presence for Lignowski to contend with.*

Haying time for the Wommer family. This picture shows them using the "cable and courage" method with the old "harpoon fork." (Courtesy Ed Wommer)

They buried Nicholas on a hill on family property just east of the present County Road 501. Ed put a plowshare on the grave as a marker and put steel posts around the area to protect it from vandals.

Ed's father, Henry, was killed in a horse accident when Ed was fifteen, so this left him to take over the cattle operations. In the fall the family always shipped their cattle from Ignacio to the sale yards in Kansas City. Since Ed was so young, he had to get a note from his mother giving him permission to ride with his cattle in the cattle cars during the trip. In those days, someone had to ride with the cattle to make sure they were fed and watered along the way.

The train track through Ignacio was narrow-gauge, so the cars were also narrow. When the trains coming from Ignacio reached Alamosa, the cattle had to be transferred to larger cars on the standard-gauge track before they headed on north to Denver and then on to Kansas City. Ed remembers some of his early years:

> *When I was in the eighth grade, Joe Perkins was the teacher. Some days, instead of going to school, I would just take my lunch and go up Bear Creek to hunt and fool around. Nobody seemed to care, or at least didn't say anything about it.*
>
> *I'd been doing this almost steady for about a month when I realized that we had a final test coming up which I wasn't prepared for. So I sneaked back to school one night and got the door unlocked with a wire and went in and found the test answers and copied them. I did okay on the test but didn't try to do too good so nobody would catch on. I just wanted to do good enough to pass.*
>
> *The McCoy boys and I grew up together and were always good friends. There were seven boys in that family and only one girl. They only lived about three miles from me, so we were close enough to hang out together a lot. Most of the time we either fished or hunted together, but we also played a lot of practical jokes on each other.*
>
> *One day we were going duck hunting, but could not find any ducks, so we decided to hunt sparrows instead. Four or five of us each took a different spot. Harold was supposed to stand on the east side of the barn while someone flushed the sparrows out. Well, he didn't give the sparrows enough time to get out in the open and shot too quick and shot a couple of dozen holes in the barn roof. Not a big deal, but a joke on Harold.*
>
> *Another spring day we wanted to create something to do, so one thing led to another. One suggestion was that we hang*

Harold McCoy and take a picture of it. There was an old rail fence about one fourth of a mile up Bear Creek, a pretty spot for a view. We took three of the best and longest of the rails from the old rail fence and made a tripod. Someone came up with a rope, probably off his or her saddle. After tying the rails together, we put the rope around Harold's chest, making it look like it was around his neck. Then we lifted him up and tied the rope off so his feet were about two feet off the ground. His feet were well off the ground, but it didn't look that good in the picture.

Another time, when we all got together and had dinner, the cook put salt instead of sugar in the cake. Everyone but Harold McCoy put the cake aside and would not eat it. Harold ate all of his without saying a word.

Late one night when we were older, probably in the early forties, the Sapp boys and me caught a nannie goat south of Durango. We started thinking about what to do with it. Knowing that Harold was living in a one-room cabin up on the hill next to Weddles, we decided to take the goat there to Harold.

We had a little short rope that we tied to the door knob and left. Later, the goat tried to walk away from the cabin and pulled so hard that he choked down and it sounded like someone was being murdered. Harold could not open the door because the goat was pulling on it. Harold really spooked! He thought someone was dying. He finally crawled out the window and found the goat. He turned it loose and thought that was the end of it, but next morning, when he walked to work, the goat followed him to the REA [Rural Electrical Association] where he worked. The people sure did kid him about shacking up with a goat.

My uncle, Lester Thompson, told me this true story. One day when he was in Pagosa, this sheepherder drove in. He was probably a Mexican or Indian since that's what most of the sheepherders were in those days. He pulled up in front of the barber shop where there was a peg-legged guy sitting on a bench, and the sheep-herder yelled, 'Come over here and see what I've got,' and showed him two gold bricks. The peg-legged guy took out his knife and cut into the brick to see if it really was gold.

It was illegal to own gold in those days. The word got out about it and the law threw the sheepherder in jail. They tried to get him to tell where he got the gold, but he never did tell. I suppose they finally got tired of feeding him and turned him loose, but without the gold of course, of course.

[The gold, more than likely, came from one of the caches from La Mina De La Ventana, the famous Mine of the Window, which lies high on the Continental Divide between Pagosa Springs and Vallecito. The Spaniards had one especially large cache where they smelted their gold from the mine at Pagosa Peak. This isn't far from the present town of Pagosa Springs. One of the families living in that general area came up with sudden wealth some years ago and many locals figured the family had found one of these caches.]

Two local brothers, Bob and Albert Townsend, were riding two young horses up their lane one day when they came to a square turn in the lane. They were going too fast and couldn't hold the horses as they turned the corner, and both of them got their legs cut up pretty bad on the barbed-wire fence that ran along side the lane. Albert treated his legs by pouring coal oil on his cuts, and they healed fine. Bob wouldn't put the coal oil on his legs and waited for the doctor to treat his cuts. He got infection and was laid up for months. He ended up with one leg so damaged it was twisted for life.

Ed and his wife, Evelyn, lived on the old homestead ranch until a few years ago when they moved to Bayfield. At the age of eighty-one in 2002, Ed continues to run his cattle and raise hay on the old home ranch up the Pine River.

If some of these old-timers occasionally appear to be tough and crusty, it may be because they had to be that way in order to survive. Most of them, like Ed, have soft hearts beneath those tough crusts.

☙ ❧

JESSIE PERCELL WOMMER

Emery Percell came to Colorado in 1905, looking for work. He first stopped at his sister's place in Colorado Springs and then somehow heard of the Bartholomew Sawmill that was operating on the Wommer property on the road between the new town of Bayfield and Vallecito.

Emery found employment at the sawmill and lived in the little mill town that had sprung up around it. He met Mamie Myers, who also worked there, and soon the two married. Mamie's parents, Dan and Kate Myers, lived nearby.

Jessie Percell Wommer was one of Emery and Mamie's children. The following quotes chronicle some of the times that she and her family lived through that were still fresh in her memory:

I was born in 1907, at the sawmill that was near Red Creek, where my father worked. It was near the Pine River, about where the present gravel operation is on the Cool Water Ranch. They probably moved the sawmill up there because the trees around the Wommer place were about cut out by then.

My family moved back to Beech, North Dakota when I was about six months old. They homesteaded there and farming was good for a while, but then came a long, dry spell and that all changed. We got starved out there and came back here in 1922 and bought Grandpa Myers' place that he had homesteaded on the Pine River. It was on land now owned by Forest Lakes. We had land on both sides of the road, including the present Forest Lakes Subdivision.

I was fifteen when we moved back in 1922, and I went to the Bayfield School for a while, but I had to quit because there was no way to get to school. There was the Columbus School nearby, but I was past the age for that school. My brothers and sisters went there though.

There were lots of houses down near the Pine River on Red Creek when the sawmill was there. The people working at the sawmill always put up little houses and lived near the sawmill. You can still see signs of their efforts to make their surroundings pleasant. Some of the old, old fruit trees and bushes they planted, and hoped to see to fruition, still remain.

I married Frank Wommer, Jr. His folks came from Germany. I think that Grandfather Wommer first went to California to look for gold before coming here and homesteading in 1878.

Grandma Wommer said she had a baby in the 1880s when the snow was neck deep. It turned out to be twins, and she only had enough clothes for one. In those days, you didn't have things like they do now, and you couldn't just run to the store and buy more, so she didn't know what she was going to do. But here came a man down through the valley on snowshoes, and, of course, he stopped to stay all night with them because that's the way they did in those days. He said he thought he could scare up some extra clothes for the new babies, so he snow shoed on to Bayfield. Mrs. Dean lived there. She and Grandma were the only white women on this side of the river. He went to her place and she gave him clothes for the other baby, and he brought them back to Grandma who was desperately in need of them by this time.

The old stage road was there on Beaver Creek. That's the road people on the Piedra River used to come over here on. Ben and Jose Pargin and Mike and Mamie Pargin used to come over and visit us for a few days occasionally. Travel wasn't easy or fast, so when people came for a visit, they stayed for a while. The Pargins moved to this country in the 1870s, like we did.

When Grandma Wommer was pregnant with her last child, her husband was shot and killed in that dispute over the water ditch. Here she was, expecting a baby, her husband got killed, and, in the same month, her father, Henry Rich, got sick and died. So that left her all alone with six kids to raise. What a predicament!

Grandma also told me that when she was raising those six kids down there in a little log house all by herself, a man came through one day and said the Indians were on the warpath and for her to be careful. She didn't know what to do, so she hid three kids in one place and three in another place. Some were under washtubs. Then she bid them good-bye because she thought it would be the last time she would see them, and she hid in another place.

When morning came, the Indians had never come, and they never did bother her. As her boys grew up, and the Indian boys grew up, they became good friends. They used to go hunting together. The Wommers remain good friends with the Indians to this day.

☙ ☞

PATTONS

George and Cordelia Patton started their long, demanding journey west from Rockford, Illinois in hope of finding a better life. After a long delay, while they were caught up in the Civil War in Missouri, they and their five daughters arrived in Southwestern Colorado around 1878. They first built a cabin where the old Bayfield Middle School is now located. Since George was a blacksmith, he was a welcome addition to the fledgling community.

The Pattons were soon uncomfortable with this setting. Perhaps the proximity to the Ute Reservation made them feel uneasy. The Utes always had been referred to as "savages," and now they realized they were living within a couple miles of their reservation. In 1879 George scouted around and found a place to homestead up along the Florida River that put them a few more miles from the Utes. The family toiled long, weary hours and finally had a rough, but quite livable, home. Feeling entirely satisfied with this new location, they had just begun to gain a sense of security when one of their wildest fears was realized. One day, when the family was away from home, some roving Indians happened by and set fire to the new home they had worked so hard to build, and burned it to the ground. What a heartbreaker!

The Pattons were plucky people, so while it was a devastating blow, they had the gumption to go on and try again. Actually, they didn't have much choice as they had to have shelter. When you had a family of seven, you couldn't crowd into a neighbor's cabin for very long.

It didn't take long to come across a choice piece of Vallecito land, south of the present-day Vallecito Dan, where they could take advantage of the Homestead Act in 1885. The Patton's home remains today on the corner of Florida Road, across from the Parks family's old, red barns. The corner is referred to as "Black Dog Corner" by many old-timers, in honor of an old black dog that used to sleep in the road at this intersection. Florida Road, also known as Highway 240, was called "Spring Gulch" in early times, and is still occasionally called by that name.

Mr. Patton went to Texas and bought a fine herd of cattle, but after the long, arduous journey driving them to Vallecito country, the cattle didn't survive in the deep snows of that first bitter winter. It was another calamity the family had to face!

Once again showing his grit and determination, George bought a young Percheron stallion from France and went into the horse business. The horses thrived on the rich mountain grass and the grain he raised as a food supplement. Life finally got easier for the family.

When Armour Gearhart was one hundred and four years old, he made this remark:

> George raised horses near where the dam is now. The grass always grew so high there that it came clear up to a horse's stirrups. He never had to feed them in the winter until one year when they had a big snowstorm. George fed the horses potatoes to try to get them by, since the grass was buried so far down under the snow that neither he nor the horses could get to it. Apparently this wasn't enough for the horses because they started eating their own manes and tails to replace the hay they normally ate. George finally had to kill them. He undoubtedly learned to keep supplements stored for them after that.

The Pattons were one of the pioneer families who persevered in this beautiful but demanding land. In later years, the family moved to some choice farming land east of Bayfield where they didn't have to contend with the deep snow and bitter cold of the upper country.

⊰ ⊱

THE PATRICKS AND THE WIT'S END GUEST RANCH

The Patricks were the original owners of what is now known as Wit's End Guest Ranch. The "official records" don't place them at Vallecito until 1882, but family stories tell of them arriving in 1879. Building a home to shelter them from the environment in this high mountain country was their first priority. Even in the summer, the nights were chilly at nearly eight thousand feet.

The Patrick clan was from Morocco, Indiana. Their mother had died after the birth of the youngest child, and their father, John A. Patrick, soon married a woman with six or seven children of her own. The older Patrick children didn't feel that they were treated very well after the new marriage, so they started making plans to leave home and head for new country.

Soon, brothers Washington, Levi, William, and Marion, along with sisters, Mary and Melissa, and Melissa's husband, John Moore, left home to start their journey west. The wild country they had heard so much about appealed to the boys' adventurous nature. Levi, called "Lee," and Washington, called "Wash," fished and hunted on the entire journey.

Upon reaching the Vallecito area, the Patrick boys were entranced with the beautiful, game-filled country, and they decided that this was exactly the place for them. After they were reasonably well established, they sent for a younger brother, Milton, who had tuberculosis, thinking that the good mountain air might be beneficial to him. Milton did survive for several years before passing away and being laid to rest in the Bayfield Cemetery. The only members of the Patrick family to actually file on homesteads at Vallecito were John Milton, Wash, and Melissa's husband.

Emerald Flint Patrick was born in 1902 to Rose Allen Patrick and Wash Patrick. Emerald loved to recount the colorful happenings of the old frontier days with all of its trials and tribulations. Actually, they were much easier to tell about than to live through them.

Emerald related these memories of the family's life in the Vallecito country:

> *Lee and Wash were like twin brothers. They were always together. They made big traps out of quakies [the old-timers' name for aspen trees since the leaves seem to quake in the breeze] and trapped and hunted bear. The bears would climb into the trap, hit the target, down the gate would come, and they would be trapped!*

First fish hatchery in southern Colorado was built in the 1880s on Grimes Creek on Patrick Ranch at Vallecito, now Wit's End Guest Ranch. Pictured are: Wash Patrick, Lee and Louisa Patrick, Milton Patrick, Marion and Anna Patrick and George Smart. Hatchery building at left and one of the Chain Lakes in foreground. (Emerald Flint Patrick Collection)

> *In 1885 the two of them started the fish hatchery in the little lakes near their home by taking spawn from Emerald Lakes to put in their own ponds. Emerald Lakes are located to the east, higher up in the mountains. Johnny Kirkpatrick owned that land, and he helped finance a hatchery at Emerald Lake. Dad [Wash] and Lee built a cabin up near the lakes to stay in while they worked at that location. They packed a boat all the way up there on the backs of some burros to use in their work. The boat is sunk now in Little Emerald Lake. When Jack Moss was a game warden up there, he burned the cabin down.*
>
> *There was an article in an 1888 edition of* Fish and Farm Magazine *saying that the Patrick brothers had between 50,000 and 60,000 trout ready for market, so they did quite well with the project. Dad would take a spring wagon at dark of night, and load it with buckets of clean fish and cover them with gunnysacks, and head for Durango. He had to stop at every creek and throw water on them to keep them fresh. He'd get into Durango at daylight, and would sell them at the Strater hotel for a dollar a pound. That was a real good price in those days.*
>
> *Root Creek came down by the Dunsworth cabin, and Dad came down one time and built a pond there with a shed over*

it and kept some fish in there. Charlie Dunsworth kept that hatchery going for a while when he was alive.

Uncle William didn't find this cold country to his liking, so he headed west and settled in Oregon. Mary's husband, Preston Bell, taught school at the Lowell School before the town of Bayfield was built. Later on, he went to Pagosa Springs and ran the bathhouse for a few years. Uncle Marion moved to Denver to run the McKeen Institute. It was a place to dry out the drunks. Aunt Mary and Uncle Preston had a boarding and rooming house up in Silverton in its heyday. I rode that little train from Durango to Silverton for a dollar and a half many times.

Aunt Belle taught school at the Yellow Jacket School over by the ranger station, off of highway 160, near the Piedra River. There was a little settlement there where Ed Pargin had his ranch.

The stagecoach route came over Yellow Jacket Pass and on west to the Bellflower Ranch by the old settlement of Los Pinos. There it crossed over the Pine River on the middle bridge to Moss School, went out Wallace Gulch, and on past Benn Springs before going through Horse Gulch to Durango.

Above: *Levi "Lee" Patrick.*
Below: *Washington "Wash" Patrick.*
(Emerald Flint Patrick Collection)

Dad and Lee homesteaded near Ignacio right around the turn of the century. One year they heard that the Indians were going on the warpath. Dad and Uncle Lee hid on the Pine River below Bayfield, but nothing ever happened.

Dad was always out trapping for the government, so he would furnish a man to help Uncle Lee run the farm. A government trapper caught coyotes or whatever else the government

wanted to get rid of. If the beavers were doing damage along the river, like tunneling in under the river bank so cows could come along and fall through and break a leg, the ranchers got upset and started suing the state. The state didn't allow the ranchers to trap beaver, so the state government had to hire someone to get rid of them. Dad got eighty dollars a pelt for beaver. They would trap martins up on Wolf Creek Pass, too. It was a one-way road at that time.

Dad would also trap mountain lions. One time, a fellow by the name of Joe Carpenter, who was wintering his sheep at Bondad, was having trouble with a big wolf. The hounds couldn't catch it, so Dad was asked over to catch the wolf. Dad wouldn't set his traps until they took the hounds away, then he caught a big old timber wolf in his trap. It measured nine feet long, tip to tail.

When I was old enough, I helped him trap at times. He caught a few grizzlies up in Vallecito. One time, when we were up there camping, Dad had his traps out, and we had pitched the tent in the field about where Virginia's Restaurant is now. There were spruce trees around there then and it was a beautiful place. My

Mary and brother, William Patrick and sister, Mellisa (Millie) Patrick Venatta. Circa late 1800s. (Emerald Flint Patrick Collection)

brother, Harold, who was seven years younger than me, was with us on this trip; and he and I had stayed in camp that morning.

Along about ten o'clock, I happened to look down the field, and there came a big old black bear in our direction. It looked like a grizzly! The wild hay had grown way up there, and that grizzly's back was high out of the hay, and he was headed right for our camp. I told my brother to get out of the tent and shinny up a nearby tree as far as he could go without breaking any limbs. I got the gun and decided if the bear kept coming, I would shoot him. I only had a .22 caliber gun, so that sure wouldn't have done much good. We lucked out because the bear turned and veered off, and headed the other way before he got very close to us. Boy, did I draw a big sigh of relief!

We used to pitch a tent and camp by Charlie Dunsworth's place in late fall, and go up the Pine River to a big rock slide and pick wild raspberries. Sometimes we'd pick a ten-pound lard bucket full and bring it back and divide it up, and Charlie would get us cream to put on the berries. That was long before Vallecito Lake was here.

Right before you made the turn to go to Charlie Dunsworth's place, there used to be the thickest prairie dog town right about where the dam is now. We would sit and shoot them with our .22s for hours. Livestock could break their legs when they stepped in their holes, so the ranchers tried to kill all of them they could.

The smelter in Durango that was used for smelting the gold and silver from Silverton was going full blast then, and belching out smoke. You couldn't hang out clothes with all that smoke pouring out, but nobody thought a thing about it in those days. There was business for everyone in this country then.

We lived off the fat of the land when I was a kid. I never knew what a piece of beef tasted like until I was seventeen years old. We lived on wild meat. We ate muskrat and shot bullfrogs by the gunny sack full, and cooked the legs in a Dutch oven.

The cook over at Uncle Marion's hotel at Pagosa Springs would get drunk now and then, and Uncle Marion would have Dad come over and cook. Dad was such a good cook that the patrons wished the cook would stay drunk for ten years.

When Dad came home from trapping for the government, he would turn Mom out of the kitchen. He would pick dandelions and put vinegar with them and have greens. Every time *it rained, he knew where every mushroom bed could be found. There were puffballs all along the river that we found to eat.*

Durango wanted a fish hatchery and there was a good spring there, so Dad went around to all the merchants in town and collected nine hundred dollars and bought the land that had the spring on it. Then he gave the land to the state, conditional upon them putting in a fish hatchery there. They did, and Dad was appointed superintendent for six years before he moved on to Denver.

Dad and Lee prospected all over these mountains. One day we were sitting at our cabin, and someone knocked on the door. It was an old prospector. He had a bad case of flu and wanted us to take him in to see a doctor. Well, that night he told us about a mine he had up at Vallecito, and showed us his poke of gold nuggets. The way he explained it, his mine was up Middle Mountain. We took him on into town that next morning. We couldn't get it out of our heads, so we hunted and hunted for that mine, but never found any trace of it. The old prospector was so out of his head that he might not have told us the right location.

Sammy Dowell was with Dad and Lee on the Red Cloud Mine up by Tuckerville. It was over the hill from the Mary Murphy mine. We spent a month every summer looking for the old prospector's mine. You go past the old cabin on the edge of the cliff overlooking Cave Basin to get to the mine. Lee and Dad had built that cabin, and when my cousin, Les, and I were kids, we split shakes for shingles to cover it.

We were staying at the cabin one Fourth of July when they were mining up there, and we didn't have any firecrackers. So we didn't know how we were going to celebrate. After thinking about it for a while, we came up with the idea of making our own firecrackers. We got into the dynamite caps and the fuses, got them made, lit one, and pitched it down the canyon. It went Wham! Boom! After about five of them went off with their ear-splitting noises, all the miners in the country were down on our necks.

Dad was one unhappy man! He walked us down from the Red Cloud mine, down through Five Points Camp, and all the way down Middle Mountain. We came out at 'Bruce's By The Pines' and he borrowed a rig and horses from Dunsworth and took us back to the ranch by Bayfield, and told us to stay there. Then he went back up to the mine.

There was Tuckerville, and then Five Points as you went to Cave Basin. Lloyd Sheets ran a store at Tuckerville. He had everything from groceries to candy. One time he had a couple of real nice horses and they came up missing. They hunted and hunted for them with out any luck. Les and I were always out scouting around together, and we went up a canyon and heard a whinny, and we found the horses. They had a rope and halter on and were tangled up in the trees. They weren't stolen at all.

One time when we were older, Les and I went to Silverton to see Uncle Marion. We went over to one of the saloons and sat down at a table and drank a glass of beer. There was a stairway going up on one side of the room and a door at the top. Suddenly, that door busted open, and a woman came out and raised a pitcher over her head and hit this guy standing there over the head. He fell down the stairs, and when he hit the bottom, his six-shooter slid on the floor and came clear under our table. We reached down and picked it up. It was inlayed with gold. We didn't mean to take it, but in a little while the bartender came over and said, 'Let's cough up that boy's gun.' We almost had a gold-handled six-shooter.

Dad used to talk about Weaselskin and Buckskin Charlie a lot. When Bill Sanders had his butcher shop, Buckskin told Dad and him about a place on Cumbres Pass, just over the New Mexico line. The Utes used to go out on raids and steal horses from other Indian tribes down there. They would stop at a place where there was an uprooted tree, and one time he picked up some rocks there and saw some gold in them. My dad and Bill Sanders really perked up their ears. They paid Buckskin Charlie's way on the train to go back there with them and look around and find it. Unfortunately there had been a big slide during the winter, which covered it up. Buckskin couldn't recognize the place again, but he said he knew it was still under there. Maybe Buckskin just wanted a free train ride.

Leonard Burch's boys, Sam and John, told Dad about a place up the Vallecito where there was a gold vein the width of your hand. Those Indian boys took them up to the foot of the draw but then wouldn't go any further with them. They said the rest of the Indians would kill them if they showed them the gold. So they backed out on them.

The ranger station was on the west side of the valley, across from the Pine River. Ralph Shaw was the ranger there. Les and I were camped up there near the station once, and there was a herd of deer that hung around in that flat by the bunch of trees east of the Vallecito river. So I said, 'Let's go get us a deer.' We had Dad's rifle and a shotgun there. I rigged up some shells with some buckshot in them and gave the buckshot to Les, and I took the rifle.

We went up to the head of the herd and weren't over seventy-five feet from them. We had to go through a fence, and I didn't want to make a noise going through it, so we circled down around them. I told Les to get up on the side of the hill, and when the deer come around, we'd get one of them. I crawled up there behind a burnt tree and shot a deer. I had only shot him in a leg, so I had to finally kill him with a knife.

Here we were, right across from the ranger's station, so it wasn't a very good situation, and it was an illegally killed deer! We skinned it out and hid the hide in a beaver pond in the floating sod. We told Dad what kind of a situation we found ourselves in, and he got the team of horses, loaded the deer, and took it in to Durango where we were living then. Boy! We sure got a lecture from Dad that night.

There was a dam between the two Emerald Lakes. Dad and some others built the dam to raise the water level in the upper one. When they left up there, Ben Rivers, who had a big ranch, took it over. Later on, some of the ranchers built the Pine River Canal for irrigation water and got the water rights for the Pine River Ditch. They also built the Emerald Lake dam so the lake would hold more water in the dry seasons. One time when there was a really dry season, the farmers went up to Emerald Lake and blew the dam up so that the water would come on down to the farms. Some of the farmers were from the King, Morrison, and the Government ditches. They never did rebuild that dam at Emerald.

Another time, Dad and Lee went over to the Mancos River and were prospecting for gold. When they went up one of those canyons, they discovered some cliff dwellings. They were camped right there in Mesa Verde. The Wetherill brothers rode by looking for some of their stray cattle, so Dad told them about the cliff dwellings. So, in the end the Wetherills got the credit for the discovery.

Dad and Lee took three wagon loads of relics out of there, but then decided they didn't want anything to do with them because the government would get on their necks for removing them. So they ended up giving them to the Smithsonian Institute, which shipped them to Switzerland.

My family sure did live in an interesting time in history!

CHAPTER 5

More Homesteaders Arrive

S ince the easily accessible land was taken, the next wave of settlers chose their homesteads even farther up the Pine River in a more isolated, but quite beautiful spot. Nestled along the rippling, silvery waters of the upper Pine River, against the towering backdrop of majestic peaks and lush stands of quaking aspen, lofty pines and spruce, the sheer beauty of Vallecito had the same drawing power for the Indians at it had for the whites. Plentiful game was also a factor, but the harshness of the winters caused the Utes to stay down in more friendly climates after their fall hunts. When spring came and the deep snows melted, causing the streams and rivers to run full, they would return to resume their hunting.

The Utes knew this land to be rich hunting grounds. For years different tribes would try to establish their exclusive rights over this favored paradise. After numerous bloody encounters, an agreement was finally reached, whereby one tribe hunted one month and the other would hunt the next month.

With the coming of the first settlers, the Indians weren't dissuaded from their choice hunting grounds. Even after several changes of ownership, stories were still related by white families that Utes, including Chief Buckskin Charlie, had been hunting on their ranches far up the Pine River. However the Indians didn't feel free to hunt over the whole Vallecito area that they once had known, and eventually they gave up hunting in Vallecito entirely.

-岩 岸-

GRAHAMS-TEELAWUKET RANCH

Charles C. Graham and his brother, Joseph H. (who was better known as Howard), were the first settlers to claim the land that the Indians treasured so highly. Later it became the main part of the famed Teelawuket Ranch. They and their father, John T. Graham, left their home in Butler, Indiana, in 1879, to join the ever-growing westward movement that was pushing ever farther to the west.

Like countless others, they were captivated by fascinating stories of the vast, bewitching land with its cascading streams and rivers and majestic snow-capped mountains, which were just waiting for any adventurous soul to claim. The lure of these stories led to the Grahams' decision to join in the journey to the unknown West, where surely they would find a better life.

The trio first settled in Middle Park, in central Colorado, but after a few years they came down to look over the San Juan country. The brothers found the land high up the Pine River to be more to their liking, so they homesteaded on what they named "Graham Park" in 1886. It was re-named "Teelawuket" by the next owner.

Their father, John Graham, also settled on the Pine River, but down lower, in the general area of the Graham Creek Campground on the lower east side of the present lake. The records show that the Grahams bought additional acreage with timber and stone deeds.

Charles built a substantial log cabin on his homestead, close to the present ranch buildings. The cabin is still standing. After years of being used as a tool shed, plans are in place to restore it. It is a very tight building and was put to use by several wintertime caretakers in the early years.

The Grahams didn't stay in the high country for many years. Howard Graham, who was an electrical engineer by trade, went to work at the Tomboy Mine in Telluride for a number of years. Charles Graham ran a hatchery in the Animas Valley and later worked at the hatchery in Durango. They were among the earliest arrivals in the valley to find that living in this high, unsettled country was just too difficult.

Charles Graham's homestead cabin built in 1886 on present Teelawuket Ranch. This cabin has been re-furbished by present owners, Keith and Dianne Graham, and is now used as guest quarters. (Photo by D. Warlick)

Teelawuket Ranch — meaning "Summer Home" in Ute. The ostentatious home was built by skilled European workmen for Johnny Kirkpatrick in 1895 as a place to entertain his wealthy guests. It is located up the Pine River, above Vallecito Lake. Circa 1926. It is now owned by Keith and Diane Graham as a private summer home. (Courtesy Keith and Diane Graham)

⇥ ⇤

KIRKPATRICK

In 1894 John Kirkpatrick took possession of the Graham brothers homestead. Johnny was better known as "Coal Oil Johnny" because he owned the oil concession business for the area. Johnny was so taken with the magnificent setting that he built an equally magnificent home near Charles Graham's original cabin. He named the ranch "Teelawuket," which means "Summer Place" in the Ute language.

He brought highly skilled workmen over from Europe to construct his house, which was said to have no equal in craftsmanship in the Southwest. In addition, a huge log structure was built at the cost of $10,000 to be used as a recreation hall. It was built with perfectly matched, varnished, and oiled spruce logs that were peeled and fitted into place with tongue and grove notches. It was later used as a dining hall.

Johnny was a bachelor and earned quite a reputation for giving marvelous parties at the ranch. Guests would ride up from Durango in buckboards to his parties, which lasted from a week to ten days. Game was plentiful and the grouse were so thick that the guests could walk among them and pick them up with their hands. Members of these house parties also went to Emerald Lake on camping expeditions. A wagon went up first with tents, bedrolls, and food to prepare for the guests who would come later on horseback.

Johnny was not only punctual, but also quite fussy. If you arrived at the dinner table late, you didn't eat. Guests were expected to wear proper attire, which was formal! After dinner, everyone went to the recreation hall where they would gather around the piano to sing, always ending the night with a hymn. Bedtime was at 9 p.m.

Johnny was a very elegant fellow. Helen Frahm described him as always dressed in black, wearing a fancy cape, and carrying a fancy cane. There was a story told about him laying down his cape in the gutter so that a lady wouldn't have to walk through the mud. One would imagine that the lady in question must have been either very attractive or very old and feeble.

One time when Johnny was traveling, he happened upon a place in Syracuse, New York where they made bells. He was shown several bells, but the B Flat bell caught his fancy because of its unique tone. However this particular bell was ten times smaller than what he wanted, and since it was the most difficult to cast, he was told they couldn't make one the size that he wanted. Eventually he convinced them to try, and he got the bell he wanted. A bell tower was constructed near the dining hall at Teelawuket and the bell was installed. It reads: 1903 New York on one side and 1904 Emerald Park on the other. In 1988 the bell had to be taken down for a short time, so that the rather unstable old bell tower could be taken down and replaced with a new, more substantial tower.

Johnny entertained grandly, even having Teddy Roosevelt and Vincent Price as his guests. Rancher Carl Brown heard that Teddy's son's fiancé lost her engagement ring on a hunting trip up Red Creek.

Due to a heart ailment, Johnny was forced to sell and move to a lower altitude in 1917. The buildings he so carefully planned still remain in remarkably good shape. A part of Johnny Kirkpatrick's ranch was transferred to Grace S. Bishop while Johnny owned it. The story that was bandied about was that Johnny gave her this gift of land as an engagement present, but when the engagement was broken off, for some unknown reason, the lady kept the land as her own. Was she a woman scorned? Had Johnny cast his eyes in a different direction and found another lady who was more desirable? Or did Grace have a change of heart and a touch of greed in her soul when she decided to keep the land? We shall never know.

Grace married George Salmon later, and they remained guardians of the land until they sold it, in 1947, to Bob and Mary Venuti. This portion of the Teelawuket Ranch was later known as the Wilderness Trails Ranch.

≼ ≽

PORTER & PALMER-GRANITE PEAKS RANCH

John A. Porter was a smelterman and metallurgist from Connecticut. He rode into Durango in the mid-1870s and joined up with William Bell, Alexander Hunt, and Rio Grande Railroad founder, General William Palmer.

General William Jackson Palmer, center, and John Porter seated with unidentified people at Granite Peaks Ranch which the two men jointly owned in 1909. (Animas Museum Photo Archives)

Granite Peaks Ranch during William Jackson Palmer and John Porter's ownership. Pine River upper canyon in background. Circa: 1909-1910. (Animas Museum Photo Archives)

The leaders of the Animas City community were not cooperating with these gentlemen who brought the railroad through Durango and on up to Silverton, so Palmer and his cronies planned their own nearby rival city. The city, which would be called Durango, soon grew into a thriving community that far overshadowed Animas City.

Porter was instrumental in moving a smelter from Silverton to Durango, where his management ability turned it into a business that smelted more than a million dollars in gold, silver, copper, and lead.

These prominent men started the Durango Trust, which bought land for the new town and coal mining properties to fuel the smelter and the trains. In 1884 the holdings of the Durango Trust were turned over to the Durango Land and Coal Company with Palmer and Porter as president and vice president of the enterprise. However these two gentlemen had other interests besides their business projects. In 1895 they purchased two adjacent properties high up the Pine River at Vallecito, which they named "Granite Peaks Ranch" because of the sheer granite cliffs that form the backdrop of the spectacularly gorgeous ranch. The Pine River and the Pine River Trail run alongside the ranch as they angle upward towards the Weminuche Wilderness and all the wondrous sights that it enfolds.

General Palmer was a Civil War hero from the Union Army, as well as a pioneer railroad builder. His Rio Grande rail lines ran throughout Colorado. He was also quite a philanthropist, perhaps best known for starting Colorado College in Colorado Springs.

John Porter, who was now known as an industrial leader in the San Juan region and considered to be an extremely attractive man by the ladies, was also a fishing enthusiast. It was most likely his idea to buy the mountain retreat. Porter was known for his exceptional ability at fly-fishing and he also loved hunting ducks and other game. They used the ranch as a personal hunting and fishing reserve, but General Palmer wasn't destined to use it for long. In 1907 he passed away, leaving Porter as sole owner until D. McLean took possession in 1921. A few years later Kelley Wells from Bayfield bought it to use as a fishing camp.

In the early 1900s, Palmer and Porter added to their holdings when they bought adjacent land from several homesteaders who were ready to give up the struggle to survive the harsh winters of the high country.

Wells' enterprise lasted for ten years until a prominent oilman and real estate magnate from Ft. Worth, Texas, C.F. Corzelius, and his wife, Ann, bought it for a private residence. During their residence, the barn, guest cabins, and other outbuildings were built. Corzelius' ownership wasn't destined to be long-lived. In 1944 the property, along with six other ranches (including Pine River Ranch) was transferred to his wife when she divorced him.

🌣 🌢

PARKS

Samuel Parks came to Colorado from Kentucky when he was seventeen. He said he always had a hankering to come out West. He first went to Denver and worked in a mill near Cherry Creek, where gold mining operations were still going on, and then decided to come down to Vallecito country. He stopped in Pagosa Springs where he joined his cousin, John, helping him set up a sawmill just south of Pagosa Springs.

Sam then found a place on the Pine River that was particularly appealing to him, and filed for a homestead in 1896. After a few years he decided to take a trip back to Kentucky and came home with his new bride.

Sam's grandson, Henry Parks, goes on with the family story:

> *Grandad always told me he got "the old lady" from the Cherokee Indian Reservation, which he may have, since she was half Cherokee. Her name was Lydia Ann, and she was a quiet, poised lady.*
>
> *My dad, Calvin, and his brother, George, were born while the family was living at Colorado Springs. My granddad*

Sam Parks 1896 homestead on east side of 501 and Spring Gulch (Florida Road) intersection which is known as "Black Dog Corner" by locals. (Courtesy Henry Parks)

was going back and forth, trying to get everything moved down here, and the two kids were born in the meantime.

Granddad had homesteaded six hundred and forty acres. In 1903 the Glovers, another family of settlers, moved onto property that our family thought belonged to them. The survey had a gap in it, and it seems that where the old orchard was, was left clear out.

Granddad Parks' place was on the east side of the road near the intersection of Highways 501 and 240. The present road is a little higher along the hillside than the old one was. The road used to have an 'S' curve and it curved around the yard and the well of the old place. There used to be big old pine trees there that they had to take out when they straightened out the road to bring in the big machines to build the dam. My family used to live in the old Patton house, which is still there, on the west side of the road, at that intersection.

Granddad was always a great hunter. We have a picture of him standing in front of a building with a mountain lion stretched out in front of him. It was nine feet from his nose to the tip of his tail. They put the lion in the shed to freeze so they could keep him to show people. It was a great conversation piece! He killed that lion right across the river from where Glen Glover's place cornered on the Parks' place. Granddad Parks was also known as the 'potato king' hereabouts, according to an old Durango newspaper article.

My Grandpa and Grandma Knight, on my mother's side, traded the place they had down on the LaPlata River, near Farmington, for the forty-acre place the Dunsworths had by Columbus School, and they lived in the old remodeled school house. I stayed there with Grandma Knight for two school years so that I'd be able to get to school.

They have done away with the old fairgrounds. It was in 1925 when I went there for the first time. My Uncle Ivan was roping, Uncle Cecil was riding broncs, and Dad was team-tying with Norman Payson. Norman used to rope, too. I remember when Norman used to go up the road in a little horse and buggy delivering mail. He was a real rough character.

Uncle George Parks and his son, Irvin, worked the old mine up on Parks' Hill for years but never struck it rich. That is the mountain to the west that they call 'West Mountain' now."

There are still remnants of the old Parks' cabin and mine that bear witness to the Parks family's efforts in their mining endeavors.

☙ ☞

LISSNER

Helen Lissner Burkett's father, Louis Lissner, came from France in the late 1800s, and worked on a farm in Canada for his room and board. He wanted to learn all he could about farming before he attempted to engage in the occupation himself. After he thought he had gained enough farming knowledge, Louis left Canada and came to Durango with a friend. By this time they were broke, so they got jobs at the smelter.

Louis' friend went back to Innsbruck, Austria, to get his wife. When he came back, he brought not only his wife but also her sister, Anna. A romance developed between Louis and Anna, and soon they married. They took a horse and buggy up the Pine River to Vallecito on their honeymoon trip.

In 1897 Louis bought one hundred and sixty acres from Mr. Griffin at the present Helen's Store location on Florida Road, and later bought some additional acreage. Helen, one of Louis and Anna's children, was born at the ranch on April 28, 1905. She had five brothers and a sister, but Helen outlived them all.

The six children went to school at the Lissner School, which was about a mile up the road toward Lemon Reservoir. The school was named after Louis Lissner, who most likely donated the land for the school so that his children could get an education close to home. Nearby neighbors, who also wanted a school for their children, helped in the construction. Helen later related:

> *School started around April. We had four months of school for a while, and then, later on, it went for six months. We would have to feed the pigs and chickens and do our other chores before we went to school. We rode horses to school when it was stormy; otherwise, we had to walk. My dad didn't like horses to be tied up all day.*
>
> *I didn't get to go to high school because my mother had passed away, and I was needed to keep house. I liked to brand and rope, and I broke horses. I would always rather be outside than in the house.*
>
> *We went to dances at our schoolhouse and at Columbus School. Sometimes we would have dances at our house. We had eight rooms, so it would hold quite a few people. Ben Turner played the fiddle and his wife played guitar. Lloyd Knickerbocker played or called the square dances. In those*

*days, when you were courting, you still went to the dances with
your parents.*

*I married Dave Burkett in 1925. He worked at John
Nelson's sawmill on the other side of Durango. I stayed over
there with him during the week, and then would come home on
weekends to help my dad. I baked bread, washed clothes, and
cleaned up for my dad and brother. Then John Nelson moved
his sawmill up the Florida River, which was near our ranch, so
we got to move back over here. By this time, we had four hundred and eighty acres of land. In 1936, I started my store here
on the ranch.*

*AI Glover and my dad built a lot of the chimneys
around here. They built the one still standing near the
Columbus Bridge. Don McKee, the brand inspector, was living
in that house when it burned down. I just happened to be
passing as it was burning, so I helped him get some silverware
and guns out. The fire was burning so hot, that's about all we
had time to save.*

*Our own house also burned down. It happened in the
winter of 1934. The men at the sawmill were out of work at
that time, so we got them to help build our new house.*

The men around here considered Helen to be the "Belle of the
Valley" in her younger days. She must have been a real knockout according
to the comments of several men. She and the oldest Glover boy, Carl, were
always close friends.

Helen's daughter, Anna Marie Schilling, and her husband,
Clarence, are living on the family ranch and running the store that Helen
started so long ago. The store, located where the Florida Road splits to go
to either Lemon Lake or Vallecito Lake, is a great place for tourists who
need to purchase small items or a soft drink, or just to stop and visit for a
while. Anna is still keeping up her mother's tradition of lending out frying
pans to unprepared tourists.

Helen is in an Aztec nursing home at this writing, and no doubt
charming the other residents with her incorrigible wit and spicy stories.
She is a lady who lived a hard, but interesting life.

⊰ ⊱

WILMER

Harold Wilmer's great-grandfather, Louis F. Wilmer, came from
Redcliff, Colorado to southwest Colorado in the 1870s. About 1901
Harold's grandfather, Tony Wilmer, and Will Pearson bought 320 acres of

land on the lower east side of what is now Vallecito Lake. They ran their cattle on the mountain above the Teelawuket Ranch.

They built a cabin on the land, but only used it in the summertime when the cattle were up in the high country. They brought the cattle down to lower ground to get them through the winters. Not long after they built the cabin, Tony Wilmer built his house near Bayfield where the family lived for the biggest part of the time. The Pearson place was right next to it.

County records show that Pearson and Wilmer first bought their Vallecito land from Edmond Trusler, the man who had homesteaded it in 1900. They bought additional land from the J.M. Graham Estate, but in 1938 they had to relinquish all their acreage when the U.S. Government took over ownership in preparation for building the dam.

The following are memories of Harold's earlier years:

> *My father was Joseph Newton Wilmer. He was born up Wallace Gulch in 1894. He married Grace Bertner. Dad worked for Tony Boyle. They logged up in the Vallecito area in the winter months when they didn't have to watch the cattle.*
>
> *Us kids used to have to pick raspberries and strawberries every week to sell in town along with chickens, eggs, and butter. We didn't need a peddler's license either. When they butchered in the fall or early winter, they would cut the pigs or cows into pieces and wrap the pieces in either flour sacks or gunnysacks to keep the magpies out. Then we would hang them and let them freeze to preserve them. In the warm months, they would have to bone the meat and can it. They used salt to cure the ham and bacon.*
>
> *In the old days, everyone would gather their cattle to ship at the same time, and then all of them would drive the cattle down to the railroad at Ignacio to ship them to market.*
>
> *When they were building the dam, my older brother, and about everyone around here that was old enough, went to work on the dam project. I wasn't old enough, so I took care of the cattle herd in the summer.*
>
> *Around 1931 or 1932, my mother had ordered the family's Christmas gifts by mail, but at the time that her order should be arriving, it just so happened that a big snow-slide hit on Cumbres Pass. It pulled down part of the mountain, and it took weeks to re-open the pass so the trains could get through to Ignacio. Therefore, at Christmas time, our whole family was left sitting around looking at our candle-lit tree, but there were*

no presents in sight. They finally came about the end of January or first of February. Christmas sure came late that year!

It was that same winter that we had a big snowstorm hit at Thanksgiving time, and we had to cut through five feet of snow to get up to Vallecito to get the cows out and down to lower pasture. We cut through the lower part of the Dunsworth place to get to our cattle up there. The Dunsworths were real good neighbors, so they didn't care.

I sure had a bad experience in the cattle business. When I went to the Production Credit Office for a loan, they convinced me that if I paid more and bought real good cows as dairy animals, I could get more for them. So I ended up paying nine dollars a head more for them than I got paid for them after putting them through the winter. That's when I graciously got rid of all my dairy equipment and started to work in the oil fields and on big construction projects.

⊰ ⊱

GLOVERS

The Glovers were another family of early settlers. Jasper Glover and his family were living in Chepota, Kansas about the time of the Cherokee Land Rush in 1893. Jasper and his wife had malaria, and the doctor thought it would help if they moved to Colorado. It was hard to think of leaving the familiar setting to head for unknown territory. After much thought, the couple decided to take their son, AI (named for the biblical city of AI), and move to Colorado in hopes of regaining their health in that climate.

When it was time to depart, their good friends and neighbors, the Trone family, decided to try their luck in Colorado also. The group first stopped in Colorado Springs, where the ailing Mrs. Glover passed away. In 1903 the two families arrived and settled a few miles below the present Vallecito Dam on the Pine River.

AI Glover was still single at this time. He homesteaded where the old Glover house was located for so many years before it was razed by the new children's camp in the year 2000. AI's land included part of the mountain to the east of the river.

His father, Jasper, homesteaded directly north of AI's land, where it met the southern boundary of the Cool Water Ranch. Jasper's property continued across the river and east to the mountain. The George Trone family homesteaded in nearby Wallace Gulch. AI built his house in 1904, and married Lenta, one of the Trone daughters. They had seven children.

First barn on A.I. Glover's 1903 homestead. (Warlick Collection)

Glenn Glover related memories of his early years on the Glover ranch:

> The road ran closer to the river then, and the whole area was boggy and full of willows and cottonwood trees. We called it "Willow Springs." Dad cleared off the brush and drained the land by digging a ditch from the spring. He used the water to irrigate other nearby land. He put in a pipeline to the horse tank and had a hose coming down close to the house, and so we only had to carry the water inside from there. Dad made his living working at the sawmill.
>
> In the old days, Warren Mullen lived on the Patton place at the corner of 501 and Florida Road. When Dad first came here, and was proving up the place, Mullen was living in a "dugout," which is now our root cellar. He thought this was on his property and hated finding out he was mistaken after a survey was done. His property started just to the south of ours.
>
> Sam Parks bought the old Mullen place, and the McClains had a ranch near the present bottom end of the dam that Hugh Currie bought from them. Hugh was said to have been knighted by the queen of England, so we may have had a Sir Hugh Currie in our midst.
>
> We had several bad floods over the years before the dam went in. In 1911 the floodwaters raged so far into Mullen's

field that it washed away Dad's hay equipment that he was using there on a field he was leasing from Mullen.

We kids all went to Columbus School through the eighth grade. The Daltons lived up at the north end of the valley before the Deckers came to take over the ranch, and then the Daltons moved out. My brother, Lloyd, always said that the Dalton boy that went to school there was "one rough rider." He had a real good horse and outfit. It was much better stuff than the rest of us had.

Lloyd worked at Granite Peaks Ranch, which was a girls' camp in 1922 and 1923, while Ray Duffy and Wells were running it. He milked the cows and was a horse wrangler between Granite Peaks and Emerald Lake. He had to take the girls from the camp up to Emerald Lake to fish, as they were so inexperienced they couldn't be trusted to ride alone.

When we were growing up, I took on the job of supplying meat for the family, so that meant I got to fish and hunt much of the time. That suited me just fine. Johnny Farrell used to turn people in for shooting deer out of season. He told on my dad once to the game warden, but the game warden sent a messenger to warn Dad he was coming up to check our place for deer. So, of course we didn't have any deer in sight by the time he came to check.

Glen, who was a bachelor, lived on his family ranch all of his life. He was a long standing member of the Upper Pine Fire Department, ran his ranch, and had one of the best gardens in the area. He is remembered as a quiet, gentle man with a heart of gold and a sense of humor.

⅔　⅔

DUNSWORTH/WARLICKS

Dave Warlick, Sr. had many tales of the "olden times" to relate over the years. Don't confuse Dave Sr. with his son, Dave Jr., who with his wife, Dottie [the author], presently reside on the last remnant of family land on the shore of Vallecito Lake. Being a daughter-in-law gave me the advantage of having many enjoyable hours to collect Dave Sr.'s bountiful memories. Ten-year-old Dave, Sr. and his family arrived in Vallecito in 1917, and spent both winters and summers up here.

Dave Sr. was born in 1907, in the small town of Jet in Oklahoma Territory. His father was Commodore Warlick and his mother was Addie Betis Warlick. Addie and her brother, Bill Betis, had acquired land in the

1893 Cherokee Strip Land Rush. Bill raced as fast as he could on a pony, while Addie followed as fast as her team and wagon would take her in the rush to stake out the most desirable land. The land had been Indian land until the government opened it up to settlers for homesteading.

Addie was, therefore, the proud owner of land when she met and married Commodore Warlick. They had three sons, George, Dave, and Sam, and three daughters, Faye, Jessie, and Nora, before Commodore contracted typhoid fever and died. This left poor, widowed Addie in a difficult situation. However she did have a good wheat farm and some of the children were old enough to help her.

She eventually married Charles Wesley Dunsworth, who was better known as C.W. or Charlie Dunsworth. Charlie was a prominent wheat farmer in nearby Texas, and was also known for the fine Morgan horses he raised and trained for surrey racing. His wife had passed on and his children were grown by this time. The couple later had four other children, Laura, Lucy, Edith, and Charles, Jr.

Charlie's oldest daughter, Nettie, was married to Clelend Brown. Nettie and Clelend, together with Charlie's brother, George, moved near Vallecito on a place up Texas Creek. It was probably due to George's ravings about the country that Charlie came up to see if it was as wondrous as he had been told. Charlie and Addie left all the children at home, except

Some of the Dunsworth family: Charlie Dunsworth at left. Back row: Clelend Brown, Nettie Dunsworth Brown, Lucy Dunsworth, Laura Dunsworth. Front row: Addie Dunsworth, unknown woman, Edith Dunsworth. Circa 1930. (Dunsworth Collection)

for seven-year-old Sam, the youngest, and set out for Vallecito. George and Dave Warlick, the oldest boys, were left in charge of running the farms.

Sam Warlick related what happened many years later. "When The Old Man [the name the Warlick boys always used for their stepfather] saw the land at Vallecito, he knew that he had found his dream ranch. He put one foot up on a stump, peeled out some cash, and paid John Root for it right there on the spot." This was in 1917.

Charlie and Addie went back home, harvested their crops, sold the farm at Jet, and left the farm in Texas under the care of young George and Nora Warlick. Tragedy soon struck! Teenaged Nora developed diabetes and died before ever seeing the beauty of her intended mountain home.

Dave remembers their trip to Vallecito. "We came here in a blue Buick touring car and came over Wolf Creek Pass, which wasn't much more than a trail in those days. The road was so narrow, and had so few turn-outs, that Sam and I had to get out and walk as we approached each corner to see if anyone was coming toward us from the other direction. Our household furnishings and livestock were shipped by rail to Ignacio, and from there we had to haul them up to Vallecito in a wagon."

John and Candace Root built a cabin on their property in the big upper meadow that later took on the name of "Dunsworth Park." It is located just above Lake Vista Estates at the southwest end of the lake. The Dunsworth-Warlick family needed quarters larger than the small cabin that the Roots had built, so they chose to build a house down on the edge of the big lower valley, closer to the Pine River. Unbeknownst to them, this spot was destined to become a reservoir.

From the porch of their two-story log home, the lush pasture in the bottomland with the Pine River snaking along its edge, made a beautiful scene. The house was on the north side of Root Creek, and a little to the south of the present day Shoreline Restaurant, right along the high water line of today's lake. There was an enclosed porch with a portion of Root Creek running through it. The creek served as a refrigerator, since the water was always icy cold. Charlie also had a small fish hatchery next to Root Creek above the present-day highway. Dave said:

> The barn and pasture were down the hill and to the east of the house, and then the land leveled out as it went on toward the river. It extended south from Sawmill Point to about where the dam is now. The Conklin family lived to the south of our place, down on the river. They were isolated and had no legal access to the road, so The Old Man gave them a right-of-way across our land. Mr. Conklin died and Mrs. Conklin

*started teaching school at Columbus School. She was my
teacher. Later on, Mrs. Morris was the teacher.*

*Dan McLain's place was below the Conklin place,
below where the dam is now. He was there when we came and
was just building it up. He had several nice big outbuildings. He
had money, so he hired a caretaker. There was a road that went
around there and to the east of Jack Creek. Sam and I used to
sneak over and fish at the Conklin place. They had a nice pond
that was fed by springs, and they kept it well stocked.*

*Hugh Currie bought McClains out. His place sits right
below the dam and to the west at Jack Creek. Pearsons' and
Wilmers' place was on the other side of the river.*

When the family got settled in their new surroundings, Charlie
Dunsworth bought fifty head of purebred Herefords, of which he was
mighty proud. Unfortunately, he didn't anticipate the ferocious winters
they would face at Vallecito. The cattle were soon lost to the dreaded deep
snowdrifts that accumulated in the long, treacherous winter months. After
that he switched to raising sheep, and Dave remembered when his father
bought a new ram to add to the flock:

*The Old Man sent to Europe for this real expensive
Merino ram to upgrade his flock of sheep. When it arrived, we
put it in with the rest of the sheep where it was immediately
challenged by this old, raunchy ram we had. They squared off,
and when they met, head-on, the new ram was killed deader
than a doornail.*

*One winter, my brother, George and I stayed and
looked after the ranch all winter while the rest of the family was
on the place near Farmington with the sheep. This particular
winter the snows were so heavy that the roof of the barn caved
in. It was a real nice big barn too. We sure hated to be around
when The Old Man came back home and saw it.*

*One night that winter, we woke up to a loud racket and
saw a big old mountain lion on the porch, chewing on some
empty tin cans we had put out there. We figured that it was a
hard winter for that lion, too, and he must have been pretty
hungry. He was no stranger. We would often see him standing
on the white rocks way above Sawmill Point and letting out
those God-awful screams.*

Dave and George watched the Teelawuket Ranch one winter for Pete Scott. This was about 1919, right after George got out of the army. George was ten years older than Dave and mature enough to get hired for the caretaker job. Their main job was to keep the snow shoveled off the barn and other buildings. They stayed all winter with Pete Scott snowshoeing or horse-backing in to check on them when he could.

Since Dave, George, and Sam were Mr. Dunsworth's stepsons, they were a little ornery and resentful. Charlie only had experience raising girls, so things got pretty rough at times, especially as the boys got a little older. Charlie could be a rigidly stern man. He didn't believe that children should have toys that could divert them from their assigned work, and he wouldn't put up with any childish foolishness. At times, it got so hot between them that the boys would hop a freight train and head out to California where their older sister, Jackie, lived. The boys would stay with Jackie for a while to let things cool down. Dave shared some of their encounters:

> One time when we were branding calves, Sam, who The Old Man was always picking on, had the job of bringing the hot branding iron from the fire to The Old Man where he was branding the calves. On this particular day The Old Man wasn't in the best of moods, and at one point he went over and kicked Sam in the rear end and told him to move faster. Sam let out a yell and turned around with the hot branding iron in his hand, and chased The Old Man to the house. Luckily Mama stood in the doorway and stopped anything dreadful from happening.
>
> One time instead of going to California, Sam, who was just a teenager, took the train to Silverton where he got a job sweeping floors and cleaning up in a cathouse. Prostitution wasn't really legal, but it wasn't illegal either. It was a way of life in those times. Most of the girls were a generous, kind-hearted lot and they sort of adopted Sam. One of the better-known girls was Diamond-Tooth Lil, who got her name because of the diamond fillings she had in her teeth.

As The Old Man got older, he mellowed a lot, as old men do, and the boys matured also. Their mother, Addie Dunsworth, was a sweet, good-natured woman who must have been "plumb tuckered out" after raising so many children under such difficult conditions. She was quite a successful gardener, relocating her garden every year to the spot where the sheep were penned the year before. Frontier women had to be tough to survive. Many died young, but many women and men alike seemed to live to very old ages.

Dunsworth family fishing party on big Emerald Lake. Circa 1930. (Courtesy of Laura Dunsworth Petri)

Charlie's sheep range was around City Reservoir and Mt. Sheridan that was reached by driving the sheep up through Dunsworth Park, up the old government trail that goes up Park's Hill, and on up through Carbonate Basin. From there the trail went to Endlich Mesa, and then northward across the high mesa to the Mt. Sheridan and City Reservoir area where the sheep remained all summer. They were driven back down to lower country before the start of the heavy winter snows. This was a steep, arduous trip for the short-legged animals, so it would take several days.

Dave related some of his shepherding memories:

> We usually had a Navajo herder stay with the sheep. One time, I rode up on horseback with The Old Man to check on the herder. We found that he had deserted the sheep, so The Old Man had me stay up there with the sheep while he went down to find the sheepherder. There were next to no supplies in the camp, so when The Old Man didn't come back, I killed a lamb so I would have something to eat.
>
> No one showed up with supplies for a couple of weeks, so when I woke up one morning to two feet of snow on the ground, and not a trace of the sheep, I headed down the trail for home. When I got there I saw the sheep, which must have

followed their instincts and beat me home. I had left two burros up there that we never did find. I don't know if they died up there or found another way out.

When I was about seventeen, I stayed up there and herded for The Old Man for a while. I never saw a sign of another human being, except when Sam came up to stay with me from time to time. We always set up our camp on Mt. Sheridan. There are lots of minerals in the rocks up there, and they are often hit by lightning. I used to sit and watch the lightning blast holes in the ground. The rocks would kind of explode when they were hit, which accounts for all the dug out places you see up there. A guy didn't feel too safe, but I didn't have much choice.

I had a little dog named Fanny that was just a real good little dog. One morning, just after daylight, she came tearing into the tent just a'whining. Then I heard such a commotion outside that I jumped out of my bedroll and looked out. There was a bear standing up on its hind legs. He had an old ewe in his paws and was eating her milk bag. He looked about seven foot tall to me at that time, so I grabbed my old .38 six-shooter. But realizing that I only had about three or four shells, I looked at the bear and thought, "No, better not."

The old Root cabin set on the south side of Dunsworth Park. It was a nice one-room cabin until The Old Man took the door off and started to bait marauding bears in it. The bears were a terrible problem because they would come down and kill the sheep. One day I went up to check out the bait with The Old Man. We found a huge bear in the trap — and mean, boy was he mean! The Old Man pulled down on him with his old 30-30 and made a streak across the top of his head, but that's all it did. The old bear really faunched then, being livid with rage. I guess he placed the next shot better because that one killed him. We rendered the fat out of the bear, and it made the prettiest white lard. We'd use it for biscuits and serviceberry pie.

One time we had a big cub in the trap, and The Old Man decided to keep him awhile; so he kept him chained up down by the house. He and the chickens had quite a game. The chickens soon learned just how far the bear could go on his chain and would peck around, just out of his reach, until one day the bear figured out how to handle this. He wouldn't go out as far as he could on his chain, so eventually the chickens *started to get a little closer, until finally, he could lunge far enough to catch one.*

That bear fooled my sister, Lucy, once too. Lucy had a habit of teasing the bear with a long stick on her trips to and from the outhouse. She got a little too close to him one day. The bear made a lunge, took a swipe with his paw, and tore a big piece of her dress off. It scared her almost to death, so she didn't try teasing that poor bear again.

As he got larger and more dangerous, we had to destroy him. He wouldn't get over wanting to fight with anything or anyone who came near him. We didn't dare turn him loose to kill sheep again.

Dave shared some of his other experiences whiling living around Vallecito:

Every summer, the family went into Bayfield for the big Fourth of July celebration. This usually lasted two or three days. There would be calf roping, baseball games, and all kinds of other things. Then evening would be the time for the big dance. This was always held at the Woodsman of the World building. The Indians from the reservation would all come, too. About ten to fifteen of their wagons would be parked up on Worrell's Hill to the west of town. They would string a line from one wagon to another to hang their meat on. It would get pretty thick with flies. The squaws would come down and sit in full dress on the edge of the old board sidewalks in town, and the kids would tease them pretty bad. Those Indians would really celebrate!

One time, when I was only ten or so, I remember seeing a gunfight in Bayfield. Two men were behind separate wagons, shooting at each other with rifles. I don't know what it was all about, but it sure impressed me! I got out of there in a hurry.

The Old Man bought a house in Bayfield that Sam and I batched in while we were going to school in Bayfield. Us kids used to hang around the old livery stable. Sometimes we would go up in the loft and lie on our stomachs watching, and when the freighters came in, we would reach down with sticks and knock off their hats as they went by us. All of us kids had great times sliding down Worell's Hill on our sleds in the winter, too.

Sam Lane and I worked as skinners, with four head of horses each, on the old stage road that came out onto Highway 160, a few miles east of Bayfield. This was around 1923.

Money was tight in those days, so we worked at any kind of a job we could pick up.

The first winter after Gertrude [Pargin] and I were married, we spent as caretakers of the Dunsworth place while the rest of the family was down on the lower ranch with the sheep. That was in 1933. We had brought up a lot of supplies for the winter, but pretty soon we noticed that our prunes were disappearing. We finally traced this thievery to a pack rat's nest. He had hidden them in the pockets of an old coat that was in an unused part of the house. We finally caught the rascal.

That New Year's Eve, a big storm came up and the lightning was really getting scary. I had a box of dynamite stored on the porch to blow up stumps to get the rich wood for our fires. Well, when that lightning got so bad, I decided I had better get the dynamite away from the house. I grabbed up the box of dynamite and ran out into the night as fast as I could to the outhouse, where I dropped it, and left it for the night.

I did a lot of trapping that winter. One day after I took the trail out of Dunsworth Park and climbed up the ridge to the red cliff overlooking Jack Creek, I spied this beautiful Canadian lynx, which almost reluctantly, I shot and killed. Trapping and selling hides was about the only way to earn a living up here in the winter, and we sure could use the cash.

Sammy Dowell visited us a lot that winter. I used to visit him when I was near his cabin trapping, even spending the night sometimes; but this particular winter, I really became acquainted with him. He would come down about once a month with two or three martins that he had trapped. He would make his headquarters with us for the worst part of the winter. Sometimes he would go into Durango. We would see his tiny figure come around the corner of Sawmill Point, walking with his stick in his hand, and know we were about to have company.

Sammy Dowell was a long-time familiar figure around Vallecito. He could be seen as he came along the road from his various mining claims to get needed supplies. A burro accompanied him at times. Sammy would stop at different homes and trade his mining stock for whatever food he might need. He was described as a "little bitty guy." He was already at Vallecito when the Dunsworths and Warlicks arrived on the scene. He had a cabin up on the mountain near the north side of D Creek close to one of his biggest diggings. The cabin is still fairly intact.

In the winter of 1936 Dave and Gertrude and their two young sons, two-year-old Monte and one-year-old David, were caretakers of the Teelawuket Ranch. They lived in the old Graham homestead cabin. It was a winter of isolation in which Dave spent a good deal of the time trapping. East Creek was his main trapping area while he was living up at Teelawuket. He set his trap lines for miles around, all the way east to Mosca, Little Mosca, and Cold Creek areas.

Dave had a homecoming ritual. When he got close to home, he would set his rifle sights on the old dinner bell, which hung in the bell tower by the main house. This would start the bell ringing to tell Gertrude that it was time to build up the fire and put the skillet on. There was a hungry man coming in. When the bell was taken down in the late 1980s to replace the old bell tower, it still showed the dings made from the bullets.

Dave's main trapping would be done in the late fall or early spring when the pelts would be at their best. In the worst of the winter weather, it was too dangerous to go far from home, for the snow reached treacherous depths. Dave and Gertrude took turns snowshoeing down to get the mail at Red Creek. It was quite a trip on snowshoes!

One summer, about 1933, the family looked across the valley and saw the mountain to the east covered with smoke where the CCC (Civilian Concervation Corps) crews were cutting and burning pine-beetle infested trees. Now and then a fire would get away from them and really put them under pressure to get it in hand. The fifty or so teenagers working on the project were housed in barracks that would later be moved to the Vallecito Resort area, where they were used to house the dam workers.

The CCC was the brainchild of President Franklin Roosevelt. During the Great Depression in the early thirties, he started the program to help the unemployed youths who were in desperate need of work. At the same time, it was a way to accomplish needed work in the forests throughout the country. It proved to be a very successful program and certainly benefited Vallecito in getting rid of the beetle infestation.

In 1937 Charlie Dunsworth took Gertrude up to Dunsworth Park on horseback and told her to pick out a parcel of land where she and Dave could build a house. She chose a piece of land just east of the big park on the bank of Root Creek. Dave bought the rights to the old lumber that remained from the small sawmill that had been located nearby and used some of the wood to build a house, a shed, and a chicken house.

The two-story home that Dave Sr. built still stands, along with an addition. It was owned by the Goshorn family and others before it was bought and refurbished by Dave Jr. and Dottie in 1999. The Goshorn family claims the house is haunted. Their family had a reunion in 1986 at

Vallecito, and Lorene Atancio and Elaine Goshorn Roth related a story about the house. "Our parents, Carl and Emma Goshorn, bought the house in 1946 and lived there in the summers. One time, years later, we had a family gathering up there and everyone had gone outside away from the cabin but us two women, who were in the kitchen cleaning up from dinner. Suddenly we heard Aunt Emma's distinctive voice talking to us. The problem was, Aunt Emma had been dead for years! This left us with a very uneasy feeling."

The Albertson family, the next owners, said they had heard trunks stored upstairs, sliding across the floor and banging around. But when they went upstairs to check, no one was around. Perhaps this mysterious ghost is at peace now that the original family owns the house once more.

When the government wanted the land for the dam and reservoir, they offered to purchase it from the owners. All of the landowners, with the exception of Charlie Dunsworth, agreed to sell their land to the government. Charlie loved his land and refused to sell. The government confiscated his property, and, of course, gave him a far lower price because he hadn't cooperated with them. This meant that many of the Dunsworths' holdings would be gone, since the lake would cover their best pasture and farmland, as well as their home and outbuildings.

Charlie realized he would have to find another way to support his family. A tourist camp or lodge seemed to be the logical solution. The old ranch house was torn down, and from it they salvaged enough lumber to start the Pine River Lodge. Charlie also decided that if there was going to be a lake, there would surely be a need for boats. He hired Scottie, who later built Scottie's Store, to help him build cabins and boats to rent.

There seemed to be work for everyone during the dam preparation and construction. If you didn't work directly for Wunderlichs or the government, you could sell produce, meat, or whatever to feed the crews. George Warlick worked as an inspector and Dave worked as a diesel operator. Housing was scarce, so Dave and Gertrude took in a couple of boarders. They had to sleep in the attic, but at least it was reasonably close to work.

For entertainment, there were illegal slot machines in the commissary as well as many other places, but the law never seemed to bother the owners of the machines in this part of the country. One night, two well-known locals, who shall remain nameless, went over to the hot spot in the county, Trimble Springs, where there was a big gambling party going on. They walked in as big as you please, completely unarmed, and walked out with the guests' money and the loaded slot machines.

Not satisfied with this, the same two brazen characters went into the Chimney Rock Store, which was owned by Brayton Cooper, and while one walked out with the slot machines, the other told Brayton to sit tight, which Brayton didn't hesitate to do. They couldn't report the incidents to the law since their illegal slot machines were involved. These thieving scoundrels just wanted the money, not the machines themselves.

Dave also reported problems with the KKK:

> There was lots of trouble over the clan. The clan was against Catholics more than anyone else in Bayfield. They burned crosses in the grass, and that sort of thing. One night Tad Morrison, who was against the clan, and Frank Bosky, who was rumored to be in the clan, got into it at a dance that was held in the dance hall above the garage that George Warlick and Bosky owned, and they vowed to fight the next day to settle their differences.
>
> The big fight was set for noon and the whole town had heard about it, of course, along with half the people in Durango. Sam and my sister, Fay, worked at the telephone office in Bayfield and were swamped with calls from people in Durango the next morning. Everyone wanted to know if the big fight had taken place yet. Along about noon, the two met on Main Street and went at it. They were really whaling each other for a while, but Frank ended up winning the fight amidst cheers from the horde of by-standers. The crowd didn't much care who won; they just enjoyed seeing a good fight. It was a rough kind of living back then, but I sure enjoyed most of it.

Dave's younger sister, Laura Dunsworth Sower, used to help her dad take horses loaded with cream cans full of tiny fish to plant in the upper lakes. He raised them in his hatchery on Root Creek. They would start at Dunsworth Park, go up to Endlich Mesa, and plant the fish in the little lakes up there.

Laura married a Bayfield boy, Kenny Sowers. While Kenny worked on the dam construction they lived in a small cabin at Red Creek amidst the dam workers and the gaming activities that went on there.

Charlie Dunsworth was also a contributor to Durango fund-raisers that collected money to bring elk into the Western Slope. Like so many other ranchers, he was a conservationist at heart and did his part to make this place what it is today.

⊰ ⊱

THE SCOTTS

Peter Scott was born in Las Animas, Colorado in 1877. His mother died in childbirth, and his father was killed when his horses were frightened by a train whistle and ran away with him, leaving behind Pete, his two brothers, George and Jim, and sisters, Tina and Ann.

They stayed in Las Animas until Pete was able to buy two ranches about six miles east of Ignacio on Spring Creek near the Charles Pargin Ranch. About this time, he married Maude James, a Canadian girl. In 1917 Pete and a man named Cooper bought Teelawuket Ranch from Johnny Kirkpatrick, whose health forced him to sell.

The Scotts used Teelawuket for a summer sheep ranch. Their summer sheep range was around Emerald Lake, which was close to the ranch. They would drive the sheep south to Aztec before winter set in, since sheep couldn't survive in the bitter winters of the snowy high country. In the spring they would drive them right through the town of Durango on the route back up to their summer range at Vallecito.

Helen Frahm's father, an older Presbyterian minister, ran the lodge as a fishing camp during the Scotts' ownership. He had health problems, and everyone worried about his health at the high altitude, but he found his health improved so much in the clean, cool mountain air that he also spent some winters there.

Pete Scott's son, Sandy Scott, tells about the Scott family's life at Vallecito:

> The Indians no longer hunted very often on Teelawuket when we lived up there, but they would come up to the ranch to take off for their own cattle camp. Tony Buck, Guy Pinnecoose, and Buckskin Charlie [all Utes] ran their cattle up on East Creek. Guy was an exceptionally good-looking cowboy.
>
> Mr. Gansky was our winter caretaker up there most of the time. Dad snowshoed all the way in once to check on him, but he always seemed to make it in and out okay. The rest of the year Mr. Gansky stayed up at Emerald Lake and took spawn from the fish hatchery. There used to be two nice cabins up there. One had two rooms and was real nice, but people chopped wood off them for campfires and the Forest Service came in and burned them down.
>
> My sister, Alice, and I caught a bear once. It was getting to the sheep, so we went up, set a trap, and caught the bear. We

took a mule up with us to carry the salt to the sheep and thought we'd put the bear on the mule, but he wouldn't cooperate with us. But we could lead our horse right up to the bear that we had all roped and tied, so we put the bear on him. We called that horse "Jack" after its owner, Jack Moss, the Forest Ranger.

I told Alice, "I'll ride the mule down." I got on the mule and when we got down to the ranch, the gate in the drift fence was closed, as usual. I thought that I'd get down and open it. Before I could get off, hell, the mule jumped over the fence and ran down to the barn. It went around it two or three times with me still on it before I could get off the damned thing! Buckskin [Charlie] was there delighting in the spectacle that mule and I made, and we took pictures of the bear.

Buckskin would come up to the ranch two or three times during a summer with his two squaws. This had been their hunting ground. The squaws came in the wagon and he rode behind on a little pony. They camped right by the barn on East Creek while they took salt up and checked on their cattle.

We had this Mexican named Velasquez who worked for us but who couldn't talk good English, but he would try to interpret for Buckskin. However Buckskin could talk a lot better than Velasquez. Dad and I both knew some Mexican since we sometimes had Mexican hired hands.

Buckskin told us this story: "The Utes used to come up on East Creek and camp, and there was a grizzly that used to come down into their camp and pick up a kid, then kind of back up a ways and sit down and eat the kid. So the people thought they'd catch this bear. They got all the warriors on their horses and took off after the bear, but the bear turned and started chasing the horses. There was one horse that was a lot slower than the others, so the bear caught that horse by the tail with his paw and held it. The Indians had a saying, "One hand hold it" since the bear could hold the horse with one paw." Buckskin would chuckle and say, "One hand hold it!" now and then and laugh as he thought about the old days.

Sandy Scott continued with his remembrances:

The Indians would hunt groundhogs together. They would dress them out and wrap them in water-soaked burlap, and then when they had a big fire going, with a lot of good coals, they would put them in the fire and roast them. It was just as good as rabbit.

When we went to Durango, we generally went the long way, through Bayfield. It was a long trip. We didn't go through Wallace Gulch like some people did because it was usually too muddy.

Teelawuket was never a very good ranch. It only has one big meadow, and we could only run around a thousand sheep on Forest Service land up in the Cave Basin area where the old mines were. We had Cave Basin, Emerald Lakes and Porcupine Ranges, all that country for our sheep range.

Once we were going through the mining town of Tuckerville with about three hundred head of sheep, and we had six or eight Navajos with us. We discovered that the people had just walked out and left everything just sitting there. They left clothes on the line and dirty dishes on the tables. The storeroom was full of groceries and there were three big Majestic ranges left sitting in the kitchen. I believe I know who got away with those.

Anyway, we went in the storeroom and there was RJR tobacco in these sacks, and a lot of Horseshoe and Star chewing tobacco in flat boxes. Of course, my Navajos packed home a couple of burro loads of tobacco, and they just smoked and spit all summer.

The word got out that there weren't enough minerals left at Tuckerville to bother with, so everyone suddenly decided to leave and go back home. They never did come back to try to mine in Tuckerville. Most of the miners were from Bayfield and Vallecito, so they went in search of a better way to make a living closer to home.

The log cabins at Tuckerville were in beautiful shape. I used to take hunters and put them in the cabins and hunt out of that area before I went to the service during the Second World War. We sold part of the Vallecito land to Bruce Sullivan. The Sullivans first built a house and a shearing shed down on the bottomland, and then they built some cabins.

My dad, Pete Scott, had Dr. Pollack, an Easterner, as a partner for the last few years of his tenure. Then in 1927, Dad sold his half to Dr. Pollack's group. Dad's brother, Jim, bought what we know now as Cool Water Ranch. After Jim died, his wife, Susan Scott, married Tom Crowdis and they continued to live there on the ranch until Dad bought it in 1935. The ranch was known as the Bar Y at that time.

Tom Marshall was married to my dad's sister, Tina. He built the big house that burned down at Cool Water Ranch before Dad bought the place. It burned, and then another house that Crowdis built burned down.

Our family lived in the little store that used to sit about where Tommy Beutens' garage is now, while Tom Crowdis helped my dad build the house that Beutens still use. My sisters, Ethyl and Alice, were schoolteachers and lived in the little white house east of the Browns' big barn.

When Dad bought the place, it had three barns on it. We had a hired hand named Augustine Velasquez, and with his help, we tried to remove the many years of accumulated manure in the barns by hauling it out on the manure-spreader. When we finally reached the five-hundredth load, we decided it was a hopeless task, and just burned them all down. They had evidently never been cleaned before.

Our family always lived in Durango in winter and we went to school there. Dad's brother, Jim's son, was named Jim, Jr. He was a big husky guy about six foot three or four, and they hired him as a Marshall when they were building the dam.

Jim disappeared in Colombia in the early forties. He had gone there with a friend, and they were stuffing alligators when he called from Colombia for ten thousand dollars he had in the Burns Bank in Durango. He wanted to invest in a rock quarry. The bank mistakenly sent him eleven thousand dollars. When they realized their mistake, they sent someone down there looking for him. Judge Bradford was a real good friend of Jim, and he traced him to a certain hotel, but there was no trace of him after that. The best guess was that someone waylaid him and took the money. Jim's friend wasn't successful in his search either. It will always remain a mystery. About ten years later, the government of Colombia finally turned over the body to the family.

When we were running our sheep in Carbonate Basin, I remember seeing Charlie Dunsworth riding up by our sheep camp on a large Shetland-like pony and leading one or two packed ponies. He'd head up the old government trail and go past our sheep camp on Mt. Sheridan when he took supplies to his herders. Sometimes, if it was chilly, he'd be wearing his old bearskin coat.

When our family had land at Red Creek, we leased the land for a sawmill to a man by the name of Nelson. The loggers came and took out trees for power poles, then peeled them before they trucked them to Ignacio and put them on railroad cars to be shipped.

When I got out of the service I borrowed four thousand dollars from Dad and bought my own sheep outfit. I had fifty sections down near Aztec and we have lived there since, but Vallecito sure was an interesting place to grow up.

CHAPTER 6

Ranching Prevails

he 1920s and 30s brought a few more into the area. Vallecito was observed as a wonderful place to live in the summer, but not a place that you would want to live in year round. The early pioneers were hardy, but they lacked many of the conveniences that we take for granted — like four-wheel drive vehicles, snowplows, and good roads. Who could blame them for seeking an easier place to live. However people like the McCoys, the Deckers, the Sullivans, the Paysons, the Lemons, the Hammonds, the Carmacks, the Browns, and many others did come to stay.

THE MCCOYS

Fred McCoy was one of those who stayed. He was born and raised in LaPlata, New Mexico in the late 1800s. As a young man he went to Oregon looking for work, and there he met Amy Zadell when she delivered milk to his house in Cottage Grove, Oregon. They married and eventually went to New Mexico where they ran cattle.

In 1918 Fred and Amy came to the Vallecito area to take advantage of the Homestead Act. There was still unsettled land available for home-steading, and they found some choice land on Texas Creek. The McCoys went on to buy additional land, until they had accumulated eight hundred acres. They would need every bit of this hilly land to support their growing family of nine children.

Their baby Herbie died at a very early age, like so many frontier children. He succumbed to whooping cough a few months after his birth, leaving eight children in the family. Fred and Amy's sons, Chet and Harold McCoy, were born in 1914 and 1921, respectively. One day in 1993, when the two brothers were in their seventies, they shared the McCoy family's early life at Texas Creek:

> *Granddad Conrad built the house we are living in now. The house is where the Richards family used to live. Our family lived a little ways up the south branch of the road in the early years. The house was just a box, and it's over one hundred years old now.*

When we added on to the house, there were newspapers pasted up on the walls, which is how they insulated the houses in those days. That's all they had. We found dates on some of them that were in the 1800s. Abe Conrad had just finished building this house when he fell off the porch and broke his arm. We don't know if you would call that good luck or bad luck.

We always went to Bruce Sullivan's Sunday rodeos. They barbequed beef for a whole crowd at those events. We used to have the big Fourth of July picnic at Bruce's Bridge, as they called it. Doc Oschner did some real good shooting tricks with a mirror at the rodeos. We McCoy boys really enjoyed watching him.

We used an old chicken wire screen to dip fish out of the water the first year after the dam was built. That snowmelt water was so cold we should have died of pneumonia. They were the darnedest looking fish, with little bitty heads and great big bodies. We'd get up in that shallow water where it was easy to wade, and just scoop them out. If they had caught us, we would still be in jail! The biggest one we caught was eleven pounds. It was like a holiday for us when we went fishing. We would go up there and eat our lunch and catch those fish and laugh at how funny looking they were.

Guy Shupe said he used to go down there on the lake and throw them out on the bank with a pitchfork. At that time, the fishing season opened on May 23rd. That was right after the lake filled and they got it stocked, in 1941 or 1942.

One time Harold stole a chicken and was afraid to take it home, so he gave it to Melba and me. It was an old white hen. Melba always said that it was 'a good old hen.' We remember when Dad was going to take old Charlie Wagner home once, and they backed into the chicken house and scattered all the chickens. As he was backing, he kept saying, "Whoa now, whoa!" You know, one of us kids could have been standing there just as easy as the chicken house. It broke Mom's setting hen up that was just about to hatch. It was the first car Dad ever had, and he kept it in the buggy shed. Even after the buggy shed was the permanent home of the car, it was still called the buggy shed.

Dad could sure scare you with his driving. The car only had one gear, and if he changed, he would back right into the house. Years later Carl Brown also got kind of dangerous with his driving once. He was chasing a coyote on a snowmobile, and ran

*right into a barbed wire fence. It caught him right across the
neck. He was very lucky that it didn't take his head off.*

*I wonder how our mother had the patience to put up
with all of us. Seven boys and a girl; we must have about drove
her crazy sometimes. Our mother used to make homemade
bread, and it wouldn't be long before it was all gone.*

The Bayfield and Vallecito area still has a good representation of
McCoys to assure that the name will be around for many years to come. It
takes people like the McCoys to help keep this a friendly, lively community, and to occasionally add a little spice to life.

⊰ ⊱

DECKERS

The Dalton and the Decker families were partners in ranching near
Bluff, Utah. The Daltons came to Vallecito in 1919 and stayed for just a few
years before returning to live in Utah. The three Decker brothers, Elmer,
Claude, and Jim arrived at Vallecito and put down their roots in 1922.
They first operated as the Vallecito Livestock Company and, in 1936,
changed the name to Decker Livestock Company.

The Decker brothers were running cattle and farming in Utah. To
build up their herd, they would chase, catch, and brand the wild cattle that
were running loose. By the time they were ready to leave for Vallecito, they
were driving 3,200 head of cattle.

Elmer's eight-year-old son, Austin, was along on this long, hard
cattle drive. Driving cattle over the terrain they encountered was no easy
feat, so it didn't take long to be mighty saddle-weary. One night, the cattle
were getting very restless. Thinking the cattle were about to stampede,
Elmer picked up Austin and threw him, bedroll and all, over a fence. The
cows did stampede, but Austin was safe on the other side of the fence,
sleeping peacefully!

The three Decker families owned the whole upper part of the
valley, but they all lived in houses that were in close proximity to where
Grimes Creek and Vallecito Creek came together in bottom land.

This is the way Elmer Decker's son, Mutt, [James W. Decker]
remembers those years:

*My mother had a very bad case of arthritis, so she had
a lady called Ida who came in and helped her with us kids.
When I was little, Ida would always say to me, "You little mutt,*

get out of the way," or "You're in the way, you little mutt." That's how I got this nickname, and it stuck to me ever since.

When I was young, I went to school in Durango and stayed in a house the folks bought in town. I went to Vallecito in the summers. Hardly anyone stayed up there in the winter. Dad took us out of school in May and we would go down to New Mexico and brand, and then drive the cattle up to Vallecito. Cattle would string out for ten to fifteen miles. In the summer we would put up thousands of tons of hay.

We rented pasture from below Kirtland, New Mexico from the Utes in the winter, and then drove the cattle up from New Mexico into Colorado in the spring. We brought the cattle up through Mexican Flats [the old southern part of Durango] and on up Horse Gulch to get to Vallecito. On one of the trips, there were about 1200 strong in the herd we were driving, and an old Mexican woman sat in her doorway and counted the cows as they went by. She was only off two or three in her count.

There are a lot of poisonous weeds around that can kill a cow. The only remedy we had was to catch the cow and turn her head up hill and cut her tail so she would bleed. I remember one time I found a sick cow and I didn't have a pocketknife with me, so I pounded the tail off with a rock and saved the cow. The vet says that doesn't have a thing to do with saving cattle, but we saved a lot that way.

When I was about ten years old, we went up to Tuckerville. That place was loaded with chipmunks, and I found some old metal chipmunk traps. They were about one by two inches long, had a lid, and you put bait in them. We picked up a few of the traps and took them back to the cabin and started catching chipmunks. We rigged up a wire apparatus to go around the chipmunk's head so we could hold them. We heated up baling wire and branded them, and then we ear marked them. We caught about fifty of them that summer, and branded them X-O and turned them loose in Runlett Park. For two or three summers the Forest Service would come up there and see the strangest thing —- chipmunks running around with brands on them.

By the time the U.S. Government bought part of our land in 1938 for the dam and water storage, Jim had already moved on. This left Dad and Claude with around three thousand acres of land at Vallecito. Then the government took eighteen hundred acres from us for the dam project. The

Sullivans were over on the east side, and when the dam came in, they only had four acres left by the Pine River. It was all Dunsworths' land from Sawmill Point south, and they took his best land.

This is when the big change of ownership happened. Dad [Elmer] took the upper part of the remaining land, our family moved up to Wit's End, and Claude and Sally took the lower part. There used to be a fence dividing them, down below the Chain Lakes and fish hatchery that the Patricks had started when they owned the property.

The log cabin on the south part of the Wit's End Ranch used to be our house. Our old homestead ranch, in the bottom, is now underneath sixty-five feet of water. Our land went clear up to the Vallecito Campground and up into Freeman Park, so we were still left with a good-size piece of land.

The Bureau of Reclamation wanted everyone to get the old buildings and such out of that lake bottom. We put the old ranch house on skids and moved it clear up to Wit's End. When we were living in the bottomland, there was a bridge we crossed

Decker family ranch house that sat at upper end of lake bed. It had to be moved before the lake came in and covered it. Circa 1935. (Courtesy Fort Lewis Southwest Studies Center)

to get to our place, and I got the job of tearing the bridge and all the fencing out. But the water started coming in, and the lake was filling up before they anticipated it would, so I didn't get all the fencing out, or the barns torn down, before they flooded us out.

The two-story hatchery and the Chain Lakes set where D Creek came down off of the hill. When we first moved to Vallecito, Jim Decker tore the hatchery down and took some of the lumber to build a home in Kirtland. The big barn, that is now a restaurant was already there when we came. We had an icehouse where the dining room in the barn is now. Dad put up ice, which we cut from the lakes in wintertime, and we used sawdust as insulation to keep the ice from melting.

The spring came down through the yard, and we had a trough all the way through the milk house that we stored milk and butter in. It wasn't a place to milk cows, but a place to keep milk and butter cold.

My family built four cabins north of our house near D Creek, two by Grimes Creek, and two by the rock quarry, and we ran "dudes" when we had Wit's End. Claude and Dad built eight cabins near the present-day Buffalo Gap Restaurant, and they also built a cabin for Claude and Sally to live in by Dobbin Shupe's present house. Sally ran a little store there, on the west side of the road, for a long time and rented her cabins out from there.

Lake Eileen is up a mountain that was on our land and is supposed to be a bottomless lake. The Forest Service was up there and dropped a five hundred foot rope, and it never hit bottom. There is no inlet or outlet to this lake. It is a warm lake, with water lilies growing in it, and stays at a constant level. It is just full of leaches and water dogs and is supposed to have underground streams coming into it. There is a steep trail going up to Lake Eileen now.

My dad was a real horseman and owned some fine horses when we lived at Wit's End. We put on a few rodeos when we lived there, and people would come from miles around to participate or just to watch. The locals and the tourists all enjoyed them a lot.

Vera Decker, the wife of Austin Decker, remembered the Decker's Vallecito life:

One winter, Claude and Austin stayed in one of the cabins they had built, by what is now the Buffalo Gap

Restaurant. They were snowed in most of the winter, and they would ride in a sled down to the big yellow house at Red Creek, where they had a car parked, and use it to go into town to a dance or get groceries.

In the early 1990s, Austin and his brother Jim's sons, J.B. and Webster, went on a pack trip up the Pine River. Our family had moved out of Vallecito years before, but the guys all wanted to camp out and fish, like they did in the old days. Our sons, Kennon and Johnny, took them up there to a favorite camping spot and left some kid to help with the camp chores.

This kid happened to be a city kid, and the crazy little nut got up the first morning and went to the corral to put the bridles on the horses. He was carrying all the bridles with him but couldn't find the horses. He was probably thinking the horses had left for home, so carrying the halters and ropes with him, he walked out of camp and on down the Pine River Trail, looking for them.

The four men, all in their seventies, got up that morning and the horses were where they should be, by the corral. So they kept thinking this boy would walk back into camp. They didn't know he had walked out. Craig had got sick the first night. He had a heart condition and the trip was bothering him. Probably the elevation was getting to him in that high country.

Austin, Webster, and J.B. were eating breakfast and looked at each other and said,

"What in the hell are we three dumb so and so's doing up here? We may just as well walk out." Then they decided they could make halters for the horses out of belts, so they wouldn't have to walk the fifteen or so miles down the trail. They left the camp there for someone else to bring out later, and started down the trail. When they got almost down, they met Kennon coming out of Teelawuket with a horse trailer. The kid had made it clear down the mountain carrying all that horse paraphernalia and notified Kennon about the predicament they were in.

That was on Monday, and Austin had his heart attack on that Wednesday. J.B. died that winter after a heart attack. They were lucky it didn't happen when they were all up there at the campsite. It was their Waterloo trip. Their wish for one last camping trip sure didn't turn out very well.

Little by little, the Decker families all sold their land at Vallecito, but Austin and Vera Decker's son, Kennon Decker, still has the Decker family cattle range allocation at Vallecito. You can still see Kennon occasionally, as he takes his cattle to or from their high summer range on Middle Mountain. He is quite distinguishable in his black derby hat and devilish smile.

◃ ▹

SULLIVANS

Bruce Sullivan was born in New Mexico on the south side of the San Juan River near Bloomfield. His wife, Marguerite, was from Missouri. After their mother died of TB in 1899, Marguerite's father brought her and her sister to homestead south of Aztec, New Mexico.

After the two married, Marguerite taught school and Bruce worked as a timekeeper on the railroad on Soldier Summit. Every payday Bruce would send his paycheck, and any other money he had made, to Marguerite, and she would buy female sheep for the herd. He was a left-handed pool shark and made extra money shooting pool to pay his living expenses and to build up their herd of sheep.

Soon it became apparent that he needed more grazing land for his expanding herd, so he bought part of Pete Scott's land at Vallecito in 1926. They would bring the sheep up to Vallecito from their New Mexico ranch in the spring and shear them before taking them up on the mountains for summer grazing. Then they would take them back to their Bloomfield ranch before winter.

Earl Sullivan is the son of Bruce and Marguerite Sullivan, and the following is his story of the family's years at Vallecito:

> When we moved to Vallecito, my folks started a dude ranch. Our land went way out into the valley along the Pine River. That is where we built our house and eleven cabins. The cabins sat right alongside of the river, so they were ideal for the fishermen that came up to stay a week or two. We would also take people on pack trips into the mountains, and then in the evenings, we would cook for the whole bunch. That ranch was a playground for my sister, Bonnie, and me. Bonnie and I were twins. We were both adopted, but we had the same birth date. [Bonnie was the baby that was left in a box at the Sullivan's mailbox.]
>
> In the 1930s my family put on a rodeo about every Sunday and a really big one on Labor Day. You had to cross the

bridge right below the ranger station to get to our place, which was between the Vallecito and the Pine Rivers. Everyone going up to the Pine River had to cross at the bridge and was charged twenty-five cents for the big Labor Day rodeo. The bridge was on our land.

People camped all along the river. There were usually around two thousand people that came to this event. They fished, hiked, swam, and played baseball games. They even had boxing matches and, of course, we had rodeos and horse races. My folks were excellent singers, so they entertained sometimes.

Elmer Decker would furnish horse races, and Granite Peaks Ranch would bring down cattle to ride and rope. My Uncle Frank would drive broncos clear from Bloomfield for the bucking horses. We never knew what horse trailers were in those days. They would start with the horses four days early to get from Bloomfield up to our ranch. They just let them walk all the way so they would still be fresh for the races. We cooked two beefs and a half dozen sheep and enough beans to feed the Navajo Tribe. All that for only twenty-five cents!

When the dam work was starting in 1937, we had to move everything from the lake bottom up to the hillside, where Elk Point Lodge is now. We called it "Bruce's on the Pine." We moved the house on logs, and a big caterpillar drug it up on that hill.

We skidded the rest of the cabins up there, then built four more before the lake was completed. Later, we bought one big cabin from the commissary down below the dam. We also bought their outhouses, and I was the chairman of the out-house committee and had to dig the holes. That part wasn't too much fun!

The store at Elk Point Lodge is our original ranch house. That was moved up and set in the same direction as it was in the bottomland. My dad always kept plenty of help to build the cabins and do a lot of the work. Mom usually had two girls to help her in the summer when the tourists were there, and they washed all the wash in a gas Maytag washer. They would hang it all on the lines, then here came a horse through the clothesline, and tore some of it down.

The three Decker brothers came here from Utah and bought Tony Boyle's place. They had Runlet and Freeman Park for their cattle range. Our range was north, around Cave Basin and Flint Fork. That's where we ran our sheep.

Sheriff Bruce Sullivan. Circa 1939. From cattleman to lawman after Bureau of Reclamation made his ranch part of Vallecito Reservoir in 1938. (Courtesy of Earl Sullivan)

Marguerite Sullivan was the "backbone" of the Sullivan family according to her son, Earl. (Courtesy of Earl Sullivan)

Charlie Dunsworth ran his sheep on Miller Mountain. He still had sheep when I was a kid.

We could drive our sheep up East Creek and hit the old stock driveway, and go clear up over Flag Mountain, then come down into Pope's Nose, another mountain. It's where Flint Fork and the Pine River come together and it's beautiful country up there.

The west side of Flag Mountain was terrible. One man lost eight bulls up there. They rolled down the side of that steep hill. He had to go back down and re-stock and get a new camp. Their territory went down off Flag Mountain into Flint Fork, then up to Flint Lake and Rock Lake. That can be some rugged country.

My dad came off of Flag Mountain one night, and a mountain lion followed him all the way down. He could hear the lion howl behind him, so he was a little uneasy. We also went up to Runlett Park and Cave Basin by the back way, by Teelawuket Ranch to Table Mesa, Dollar Lake, Emerald Lake, Moon Lake, Horse Canyon, and around Porcupine [between Lake Fork and the Pine River]. It was real good range. That is almost all part of the Weminuche Wilderness now.

We would hit the forest with the sheep around the first of July and bring them out the last of September. We had Navajo herders that stayed up with the sheep. We would take up supplies and move camp every so often. We ran eighteen hundred head of sheep just *before the ranch was taken over to make way for the lake. Then we bought a ranch and moved over on the Florida River where we could run two thousand head of sheep. It was a better working ranch, but we didn't have all the fun activities that we did on the Vallecito and the Pine Rivers.*

There weren't very many people who lived at Vallecito in the 1920s and 1930s. Our neighbors were the Deckers, Dunsworths, Scotts, and Hugh Curry. Carl Brown was a tow-headed guy and was just a year older than I was. In 1945 the Browns had a sawmill where the old Meadowlark Bar sits, by the foot of Middle Mountain. Leonard Brown would go up and bring logs down off of the mountain with his rattley old trucks. And they had another guy working for them that was a real cowboy, Lee Rector. Lee had polio in one leg, but if he had two good legs, he would have charged everybody a quarter a day to live. He was tougher than hell!

Lee was one of the best teamsters I have ever seen. He pulled logs for the Browns, skidded logs. He had six of the best workhorses you ever laid eyes on. He would go up there and start a log down the mountain and get them rolling. And he could jump those logs, even with his crippled leg, and bring them right on around. He had a feed trough that he always kept full of oats for those horses. If anybody got stuck, they would call Lee to get him out.

I think Helen Burkett started her store on the Florida River when she had a big sawmill there around 1935. She was a real cutie! They have a pretty nice little ranch there that she inherited, since she took care of her handicapped brother all his life. He would scare the hell out of me when I was a little kid and he came riding by.

When I was still running sheep up above Vallecito, there was a snowstorm, and some hunters came down from the Lake Fork Bridge up the Pine River. Somebody called me and said they had found eighteen head of sheep up there. My count had come out right, so I was sure they weren't mine, but I could have been short somehow, you never really know. Anyway, someone needed to get those sheep out of there since there was a storm coming in.

I took a horse and started out, and as I went up looking for the sheep, a buck came out, and I shot it. About twelve miles on up the mountain, some hunters came by. I asked them, "How's the hunting?" and they said, "It's not worth

Earl Sullivan, son of Bruce and Marguerite Sullivan. (Courtesy of Earl Sullivan)

a darn." So I told them I was going after some sheep, and if they would stay there and help me get the sheep across this bridge, I'd let them have the buck. So they waited there and helped me get the sheep through the gate, and then picked up the buck on their way down the mountain. I took the sheep on down through Granite Peaks Ranch, even though I hated to, because Gordon Schillingburg owned Granite Peaks Ranch at that time, and he was tougher than hell. He wouldn't let anyone on his ranch, but I rode in there anyway since the storm was getting so bad. This time he was okay about it, and we got to be pretty good friends after that.

I had this three-quarter-ton truck, and I loaded all those sheep by hand. There was no loading chute, so I had to lift each one of them up into the truck. I went back to my ranch and turned them into a little pen, so they were separated from mine. Then I went to the house and called Mr. Perry, who they belonged to. The next day, he came over and accused me of stealing his sheep. I said, "Mister, I wasted a whole day, and about killed myself, loading those sheep. If I were going to steal them, why would I call you? That's a lot of appreciation you show me."

My parents divorced, and my mother kept the ranch at Vallecito for quite a while after the lake went in. I was up there until 1946, and then I told her I wasn't going to be a dude rancher because I wanted to run sheep. So I raised sheep on the Florida and she stayed at Vallecito. I believe she had fourteen cabins and thirty-some dude horses at the time. She legally adopted two boys from an orphanage after that. She adopted

Joe first, and then when his friend, Lewis, who was from the same orphanage, came to visit, she ended up adopting him too.

Dad stayed in Durango, and I stayed up on the mountain with the sheep. I had three different sheep camps, so I had to haul salt and groceries to them. I built a cabin up on East Virginia Creek, which is up the Florida River a ways. I hauled cement, the stove, and everything else on mules to the cabin site. It is still a real sound little cabin to this day.

Dad went on to be County Sheriff from 1939 to 1948. He looked the part of a Hollywood western sheriff. After that, he went on to be a state senator. It was during his time as a senator that he was instrumental in moving Fort Lewis College from the Mesa to its present location in Durango.

One time when Dad was campaigning for an election, he was at a precinct up on the Florida. He was eager to get out the vote although there was a blinding snowstorm. He went to pick up a voter, Mollie Ryder, who lived alone and ran cows up above where Lemon Dam is now. He brought her in to vote and later learned that she cast the only vote in the precinct against him.

Everything my dad touched turned to money, but behind every man there is a woman. My mother was the backbone of the family.

⊣ ⊨

PAYSONS

Norman Payson was born in Telluride in 1902, and his family came to Bayfield in 1906. Norman relates some of his experiences:

My dad bought a ranch three miles south of Bayfield in 1907. I started school that year in the Missouri Center School, out on what they now call Road 516, and then I went to high school in Bayfield.

I had the P.U.C. Truck Line in 1929 and 1930 and hauled cream to Durango. Mr. Addington, the man who promoted Tuckerville mining in 1928, was one of my customers. I delivered coal to him. I hauled about anything that needed to be hauled to about anyplace it needed to go.

I started to run the mail route from Bayfield to Vallecito in 1927. I did mail on Monday, Wednesday and Friday and did my truck line on the other days. In 1930 I started running the mail every day, so I sold the truck line to

Elmer Spenser. I had an old mail route book with everybody in it. There were about one hundred-fifty families in it when I started. My route was only thirty-two miles long, but by the time I retired in 1968, it was about eighty miles long.

Tom Marshall had a sawmill on the east side of the road by Red Creek, and that was the end of the mail route. All the families that lived above there had to come down there to Red Creek for their mail. Most of them would come down about once a week. Granite Peaks Ranch had a big mailbox at Red Creek. It was about half as big as a kitchen table and had a big lid with hinges on the top, because they only came down once a week to check their mail. One time when I drove up to deliver mail, there was a girl sitting on the top of the mailbox. When I drove up, she slid down off of the box, but in the process, she caught her dress on the hinge of the mailbox, and her dress was pulled way up over her head. I didn't know if I should help her or not, but she got up and ran away. She was a girl who worked at Teelawuket, and was about sixteen years old, but I'm not going to tell who it was.

It was snowing hard one time in the winter, and when I pulled up to deliver the mail, I heard someone yelling. Mr. Smyth, who was seventy years old, had come down to meet me and had gotten his foot caught in the cattle guard he had to cross. When I went over to him, I managed to get his overshoe off, which was caught under the cattle guard. Then I could pull his leg out. He was so thankful that I had come along; otherwise, he might have frozen because there was no traffic that late in the day. He was so happy to be freed from that predicament that he broke down and cried.

Another time, I was delivering a registered letter to a house. A little boy answered the door and told me his mother was at home, so come on in. I went on in so the mother could sign for the letter, and to my surprise, I found her sitting in an old fashioned washtub in the middle of the room. She grabbed a towel and signed for the letter with one hand and held the towel with the other. Boy, I got out of there pretty fast!

The thing that shocked me the most, was when I found a baby in a box next to the Sullivans' mailbox. It was a little girl. Margarete and Bruce Sullivan never had children of their own, so they adopted her. There was lots of speculation on who the mother was, and why she would put it by Bruce's mailbox.

I seldom had to do the route on horseback. I had an old Model T Ford that I used. Sometimes when I had to go up Texas Creek in the winter, I would go as far as Wilbournes' place, and then I'd take snowshoes and go on to the Vinton and Tule places. Then I would snowshoe back to where I left my car at Wilbournes' place.

If somebody didn't have groceries, they'd phone down and I'd bring up whatever it was they needed, along with the mail. My route ended at Scotts' place for years, and then, with the influx of people when the dam was being built, it was extended to Red Creek.

Bayfield had three bars, two flourmills, and a bank at one time. Tom Weston, who had the sawmill by Sawmill Point, had the contract to cut the timber on the land that would be flooded when the dam was completed. His sawmill was right in the middle of the dad-burned lake.

One time a bear came down through East Creek and was scaring the horses and cattle at Teelawuket. Sam Carson, Fred Frahm, and Steve Elkins, who was well known for his skill at lion hunting, got a couple of hounds and were going to track the bear down the next morning. They spent the night in the hay barn at Teelawuket. There was a ladder for them to climb up to the hayloft, and also a trap door at the top of the ladder. They slept in the hayloft and during the night Steve Elkins had to get up and go down through the hayloft trap door. On the way down the ladder he evidently missed a step, and fell down, and broke his neck. When the others got up the next morning and started down the ladder, they were met with the gruesome sight of Steve's lifeless, twisted body sprawled at the bottom of the steps.

One year, up above Teelawuket, two guys had killed an elk and loaded half of it on one packhorse, and the other half on another packhorse. One of the horses stumbled and went over the cliff. Fred Frahm helped get the horse back up to the trail, but the rider and elk were mincemeat.

Fred had a mining claim at Cave Basin up around Emerald Lake. Like a lot of the mines, he might have broken even. Cave Basin got its name from all the caves, or cavities, in that basin made by snowmelt water that ran through them from the surrounding heights.

Norman married Sophie Coon in 1933, and they had four children. His friendly manner and colorful language made him a well-remembered character in both the Bayfield and the Vallecito communities. When he passed away in 1998, one of his last wishes was that his and his late wife's ashes be scattered over Cave Basin. As much as Norman loved the wildness of these mountains, this was a fitting end to his long, adventurous life.

⊰ ⊱

LEMONS

Henry Lemon's family was living in Crawford, Colorado when he decided to come to Durango, where he met Vivian Slack. Her family came to Durango from Missouri. Henry and Vivian soon married, and around 1930, they moved up the Florida River and homesteaded land that would later become the Lemon Dam and Reservoir.

Henry and Vivian were fortunate in coming to the Vallecito area when they did because it was becoming more civilized, although it still had a long way to go before the roads were upgraded and living got easier.

When the couple's daughter, Hazel, married Archie Bodo from Durango in the winter of 1931, the young couple had an immediate problem. Hazel and Archie went back to the Lemon ranch, after the ceremony, to pick up some of Hazel's clothes. They intended to leave immediately and go to Arizona where Archie had a new job waiting for him. That day a snowstorm dropped enough snow that they couldn't get out of the valley until March. The two remained in the Durango area for the next seventy years.

One story has it that Lemon Dam was named after Henry Lemon because he owned the land under it. This "story behind the story" tells the rest of the tale. The Lemon family didn't part with its ranch willingly.

Henry Lemon put up a good fight for their ranch, but the Bureau took it anyway. Lemon fought them so long and hard that his son, Charlie, bitterly joked once, "My father gave the Bureau workers so much trouble, and they called him 'that damn Lemon' so often, that they decided to give the dam that name.

It was extremely difficult for the men and their families, who had worked so very hard to build up their ranches, to have them suddenly yanked out from under them. They had endured hellatious weather and faced countless obstacles as they spent years fighting to build, improve and civilize the demanding land. It just wasn't fair, but most of these people understood that their sacrifices helped many people by providing water to the dry land and by providing flood control to the people below. It was really a matter of a few sacrificing for the good of the multitude, but it was still hard to take.

⊰ ⊱

THE HAMMONDS

David Hammond was the son of Lucy Dunsworth and her husband, Reed Hammond. He, his brother, Derwin, and his sister, JoAnn, are therefore cousins to Dave and Gertrude Warlick's two sons, Monte and David. The cousins had some rip-roaring times in their younger years at Vallecito.

David Hammond is married to Eileen Richards, who is one of the Richards' family from Texas Creek. He lived at Vallecito from the time he was a small child until he started high school in Durango. His summers were spent working or visiting with his grandmother and grandfather Dunsworth and other relatives.

The following is David's recollection of his time at Vallecito:

> *Our house was one of only three cabins that were on the upper side of the road between the point and where Sawmill Point Lodge is now. It set just south of the little canyon that led up to the old still. We got our water from a small spring by our house that was fed by this little canyon and creek bed. We shared this water with our neighbor, John Ball. Ed Canterbury was the owner of the third cabin, but when the dam was coming in, he moved further north and started Bear Paw Lodge.*
>
> *Granddad had a fish hatchery beside Root Creek, or as the old-timers called it "The Spring Branch." Granddad had a building where he kept the troughs used to raise the fish, and outside there were two ponds that he kept the larger fish in, according to their size. When they were large enough, he would take them up to the mountains above Dunsworth Park, to stock any of the little lakes where he thought that fish would survive. The State Fish and Game Department furnished him with the eggs and fry.*
>
> *When the government took Granddad's lower land away and they started Pine River Lodge, Grandma Dunsworth had a small store and ice cream parlor in the front of the new house. Granddad built some cabins and a fleet of twelve boats, which was later enlarged to eighteen, and he started a boat-renting business. He had been allowed to keep the main part of the land that the old ranch house had been located on. He was able to use the old cellar for a boathouse, and he could launch boats near the mouth of the Spring Branch, which is fairly flat.*
>
> *Since my grandparents' youngest son, Charles, was gone in the service, they needed help. Scottie, the man that helped them build the cabins and boats, took care of boat rentals and fishing tackle sales, and Granddad took care of renting the cabins. This worked for a couple of years until they had a parting of the ways.*

Scottie left, got some land from the Deckers, and built a store near where the Rocky Mountain Store is now. He rented boats out of there. Sally Decker also started renting out cabins, so competition was starting at Vallecito.

When the grandparents were building the Pine River Lodge, they built the road from their lower old place to where they were building the lodge on the hillside above by using mules and a scraper. They would haul the materials from the old house up in wagons to use in the new building. When the roads got so they were good enough, they would drive the pickup up and down this steep, narrow road.

One time, Granddad was up at the top in the pickup and was coming down the steep road. He was turning a corner and starting down the steepest part yelling, "Whoa, whoa, you son-of-guns." He was so used to driving the mules that he was yelling at the pickup like he was driving the mules. When the pickup wouldn't stop on his command, it ran over the bank and into the oak brush, and stopped against a tree. As steep as that hill is, it could have been much worse. I helped him hitch up the trusty mules and pull the pickup back up the bank. I had to steer the car while the mules were pulling it back up. Every now and then Granddad would revert back to trying to drive the pickup like it was the mules.

While the grandparents were still living in their old ranch house, the grain field below was level enough that a meat packer used to fly up and land there in his plane. He would then try to talk the farmers and ranchers into bringing their livestock to him. I remember that Granddad told him he wouldn't bring him anything unless he would give him a ride, so the guy gave him a ride.

Some of the family were unhappy with my grandfather because he donated quite a bit of money to the foundation that was trying to get the elk started back up. His goal was that there be enough elk that he could get a license to hunt them.

When this actually happened and he finally got to kill his first elk, there was almost a killing over it. Another hunter came down and argued that he had killed it. It was a nice big bull and the other hunter kept insisting that he had killed it. He said that Granddad's old 30-30 wouldn't kill anything. Granddad maintained that "your 30-06 would just go right through him and my 30-30 slug would just kill him. We'll just skin him out and see whose slug got him." So they skinned him out and discovered that it was Granddad's slug that had done the job. So he got to keep his long-awaited trophy.

Edwin Green and Kenny Sower had the first boat on the lake. J.W. Sower had a cabin and a private boat dock on land just south of the present-day Lakehaven Lodge. Other cabins soon sprang up near the new lake.

I built the first platform boat dock where you could actually pull up and park your boat alongside. It was anchored about where Shorty's old dock is now, where there is a big cut in the ground. It was about thirty-six inches wide and about thirty feet long, so it was big enough to park a couple of boats on each side.

George Warlick brought a big boat up and we used it to give tours for a couple of summers. We would charge twenty-five dollars for a tour around the lake. We ran it out of Grandma Dunsworth's house after the lodge was sold. That was the gray house just below where the burger place is now, on the lower side of the highway. She had her little store and ice-cream parlor there at that time.

It was about this time that Granddad and Grandma Dunsworth had a disagreement, and Grandma took a stick and drew a diagonal line through their property and told Granddad that one side was his and the other side was hers. This separation was done legally because there is a map on file in the La Plata County Courthouse showing the property split, which, ironically, was called a Pre-Nuptial Agreement on the county map, for lack of a better name I suppose. A Property Division Line would have been more accurate.

They soon discovered there was money to be made in selling off lots to the people that wanted cabins near the lake; so Grandma started selling her lots and Granddad sold some of his lots. They started several small subdivisions that quickly sold out and, of course, there were a number of offspring that ended up with lots.

Ed Canterbury's two brothers, Vern and Jessie, bought land right across from where Virginia's was built later. The boys used some of their veterans' benefits to build a shop and a big house. They had only been in the house for about a week when it all burned down.

We all thought my grandparents' old ranch house was haunted. When the family had been gone awhile and came back, they could hear the old player organ playing, or see lights on in the house. But when they went in, there was no sign of anyone, and no tracks in the snow around the house.

I still remember some really odd things about the Teelawuket bell when Dad was caretaker up there. On some real still, cold nights when not a breath of air was stirring, the bell would ring. Nobody was around, and there were no tracks in the snow. It happened several times. It was kind of spooky, and it gave one an eerie feeling. Dad happened to be out there one night and saw this big old white owl that was sitting on the bell, and when he flew away, he would give a push on the bell to get himself going, which would cause the bell to ring. Dad had finally solved the mystery of the bell ringing in the middle of the night.

⚔ ⚕

THE CARMACKS

Georgie Carmack Fahrion still remembered her cowgirl days in her older age and delighted in telling these stories:

My dad was Syl Carmack. He left Texas in 1880 and came to the Bayfield area to live. I was born at home in 1907, with Dr. Newland delivering me. When I grew up, I married Cliff Fahrion and we had two boys, Donnie and Howard.

In the summers, Cliff and I rode the summer range, watching cattle for other people. We lived in a cow camp east of the Sullivan place and across the Pine River. We got fifty to seventy-five cents a head for the job, depending on how big the permit was.

1933 was the first year we started riding cattle up at Vallecito for Dr. Newland. He had a range permit to run cattle up above Teelawuket. Bob Venuti was managing Teelawuket at that time. If a person didn't have enough cattle to fill their Forest Service permits, they would pool their cattle and run them together.

George Thompson, an Indian, ran his cattle up past Vallecito, by East Creek, and clear up to Mosca Creek area. The Indians branded their cattle with an "ID" brand for Indian. They all had their individual brand on the side, and the "ID" brand on the hip. George used to say, "Well, my mother was an Arapaho and my father was an Indian." The Indians always took their mother's name.

We stayed in a little old cabin with a dirt floor. The loose dirt was a foot deep; so I would shovel the loose stuff out the door and then water the floor down to make it pack hard. The cabin was below East Creek in the flats, on the far side of where the lake went in. It had barbed wire on the windows to keep the bigger varmints out. We had a swinging bed made out of quakey poles so the rats and mice couldn't get into it. Everything had to be hung up in the air so pack rats and mice couldn't contaminate them. The cabin had a thatched roof. When you sat at the table the dirt would come down on you and everything else. The kids slept on army cots, and the chipmunks would come in and run all over them in the mornings. Boy! I tell you, we were really hard up.

When we rode with the cattle, I would take the kids with me. I had a long seat saddle and I put a pillow in front, and one kid would ride on the pillow in front, and the other one rode in back of me. It wasn't easy living by a long shot! We took the cattle down to lower country for the winter, so we didn't have to stay in the cabin. It was snowed under for most of the winter.

We would brand in June before we took the cattle up to the higher country. We could brand around two hundred fifty head a day, and the best we ever did was five hundred in one day. Later on, we had cattle of our own, but we quit taking them up to Vallecito in 1948. When the lake came in, we didn't even try to move that old cabin. We just tore it down.

Cliff was real good at rodeos, so we did a lot of that for the biggest part of our lives. It's a good way to get busted up, but once men start, you can hardly stop them from it as long as they can still climb into the saddle.

My grandmother lived on Beaver Creek. She was afraid of the Indians and they would come around and beg, so she always gave them something; otherwise, she was scared they would take her kids. She hid the kids under washtubs when the Indians came around. By the time I was born, we always got along fine with them. We got to know them better when we were running cows on the same range.

The Deckers lived up there, too. One time Austin Decker broke his leg and crawled a mile to get help. He even had to crawl across the river before someone found him and took him in to a doctor.

Lucy Dunsworth's husband, Reed Hammond, was one of the best cooks around. He cooked for the Dude Ranches and *at the Strater Hotel in Durango, and he would cook at hunting camps for special friends or relatives occasionally. It was a whole different kind of life back then.*

⊰ ⊱

DAVID WARLICK, JR.

David Warlick, Jr., the youngest son of Gertrude Pargin Warlick and Dave Warlick, Sr., remembers his early life at Vallecito:

> *I was actually born on the Trimble Springs Bridge when my father was driving my mother to the hospital in Durango. He was in a hurry to get her there before I was born, so he was driving too fast when he hit a bump on the bridge, and I was born right there on the spot. My dad stopped at the first house he came to and asked them to keep my brother, Monte, while we continued on to the hospital. He didn't even know these people, but in those days people helped each other in whatever way they were needed.*
>
> *My earliest memories are from when my family lived up by Dunsworth Park, where my dad had built a house around 1937. Our house was close to the head of Root Creek and overlooked my Grandpa and Grandma Dunsworth's ranch house, pasture, and barn until the lake came in, and then we had a view of the lake.*
>
> *I was quite small when we lived there, but there is one experience there I'll never forget. My mother had me sitting in a high chair outside the back door of our house so she could cut my hair, when we saw a big bear come in sight just across the creek. It was heading our way. My mother ran into the house to get a gun, but I thought she had deserted me and the bear would get me. I was petrified! She was back in a flash with a gun, but by then, we could see that the bear was ambling off in another direction. I've seen that bear in my dreams many times since that day.*
>
> *My mother would pack a sandwich for my older brother, Monte, and me, and let us go out on the point overlooking the dam and watch the work that was being done. They had some really large equipment they used down below us, so it was fascinating to us, especially since Dad and my uncles, George Warlick and Kenny Sowers, worked on the dam.*

One Fourth of July, my dad rigged up a trough made of boards and propped it up on a big rock to shoot sky-rockets from. He sent them in the direction of the lake, but, of course, some of them probably landed down by Pine River Lodge that my grandparents were building at that time. It's a wonder that we didn't set the whole mountainside on fire!

My grandparents also owned a place right by Columbus School. One time when Grandma was at the Columbus house for Christmas and all the women were busy cooking Christmas dinner, my cousins, David, Derwin, and JoAnn Hammond, and my brother and I were all playing outdoors. My cousin David, who was the oldest and the one who always came up with these wild ideas, thought it would be a thrill to take the toboggan up on the big snow covered sawdust pile at Enyards' Sawmill across the road from the school, and come down that steep hill. None of us younger kids wanted to do it. It looked too high and scary, but David really wanted someone to make the run with him, so I finally decided to go with him so I wouldn't be a "chicken."

I hadn't noticed what was at the foot of that slope. It was nothing but a thick tangle of brush. Everything went fine on our run down the hill until we crashed into the brush at the bottom. We got ourselves so scratched and banged up that we were a pitiful sight! I think I may have had a spanking for that caper.

Another time, the same bunch of cousins wandered down from where we lived, close to the dam, walked down the road to Columbus School, and then started back up the road towards home. We stopped by the Parks' place and 'borrowed' a few potatoes, which we ate raw, and continued on up the road to Red Creek. David Hammond, the oldest, and the ringleader, suggested we go up Red Creek because we could catch fish up there with our bare hands. This sounded like fun to all of us, so we went up the creek a ways and fooled around trying to catch fish until the clouds moved in and it started to rain.

About this time, we realized we needed shelter, so we built a shelter out of sticks and bark and stayed in it until it quit raining. Then we decided to explore a little farther up the creek and got up there a ways when we suddenly realized it was starting to get dark and we had better get home before we really got in trouble.

Cousin David said that he knew a short cut to get back over to the Government Camp, so, of course, we followed him and headed cross-country through the forest. We were starting to come down the hill across from the entrance to where Deertrail Lane is now, when we met a search party with lanterns coming to look for us. Our mothers were frantic since we had been gone for so long, especially now that it was dark. It's easy to get lost in this mountainous country, especially after dark. Boy, did we get a talking to!

Later on we acquired a ranch on the east side of Yellow Jacket Pass. I went to school at the nearby Yellow Jacket School, but we still came to Vallecito to visit Grandma and the cousins often.

When I was about eleven and Monte was twelve, Mom and Dad went to Carbondale to look for a ranch. My dad thought he wanted a change of scene. Monte and I stayed with Grandma and got a job working for Ma Heller at her boat rental operation. Most of the time, we had to bail out the row-boats that she had buoyed there. One day my cousin, Derwin, and I were out in one boat, bailing it out with coffee cans, and it was leaking so badly that we couldn't keep up with it. We thought we were going to drown for a while until Ma Heller finally rowed out and rescued us

One time my folks had to go to town and they made us boys stay home because it was at the height of the polio epi-

Dave and Gertrude Warlick with sons Monty and David Jr. in 1944 at Vallecito. By this time the family had started ranching near the Piedra River but visited relatives at Vallecito often. (Warlick Collection)

demic around 1945. Everyone was trying to keep their children away from groups where they might be exposed. Of course we had been taught gun safety and had our own guns by the time we were ten, so we could wander the woods to shoot at will. My dad had put feed out for the wild turkeys all winter long to help them survive, so he thought he had a right to use one of them to feed the family.

When he left for town, he told us that if we saw a wild turkey around the place to shoot it. It just so happened that when we were roaming around with our guns, we saw some turkeys, so we decided to sneak up on them and try to kill one. We slithered through the brush as silently as an Indian until we got to a good position, and then fired away! We only had single-shot .22s, but when the dust cleared, there were four dead turkeys lying there. The fun was over. Now we realized we had a big job ahead of us. The turkeys had to be plucked and gutted, and that couldn't wait until our parents got home. We carried them all back home and put water on the stove to heat, since we knew we would need hot water to dunk the birds in before we could try to pluck the feathers.

When the folks got home, they found us desperately trying to finish plucking the feathers out of all the turkeys we had in the old washtub, in water that had soon gotten too cool to help release the feathers. We had a terrible mess! But they were so proud of us that they pitched in and helped us finish the job.

My claim to fame in these parts came when I was ten years old and we were living on the ranch by Yellow Jacket Pass. I had taken my gun and two dogs and was hiking around the swampy land that was near our spring when I spied a bird nest among the cattails and tall grasses growing there. I reached in it to see if there were any eggs, and was promptly bitten by a rattlesnake that was lurking there and was feasting on bird eggs.

This scared me to death since I knew how dangerous it could be. I had read in a Boy Scout book that you should put a tourniquet on above the bite, and then cut across the bite with a knife to suck out the poison. Since I was scared almost out of my wits, I yanked the lace out of one shoe and tied it around my arm. Then as I ran across the mile-long field of sharp-as-knives wheat stubble I lost a shoe. I slashed my bitten arm twenty-one times and tried to suck out the poison. By the time I got to the house I had blood smeared all over my face, arm, and clothes and looked a frightful mess!

When my mother saw me, and heard about the snakebite, she was absolutely terrified. My dad and brother were away driving some cattle, so Mom, who hardly knew a thing about driving, pushed me into the car. She drove right through the closed wooden gate and on down the lane until she got to where my father was with the cattle, and then he took over. Then the whole family was in a panic!

We drove west towards the hospital in Durango, but when we reached the Cooper Ranch, we stopped to see if Mrs. Cooper could help since she was a nurse. All she could do was send us on our way and call ahead to the hospital to explain the situation and make sure there would be a doctor waiting.

Dad held down on the horn going through both Bayfield and Durango, and we finally reached Mercy Hospital. When we got inside, a Catholic Sister kept asking my dad all kind of questions that were delaying me from seeing a doctor. Dad finally exploded and was just about to choke the frightened Sister, when she decided that she'd better let us see the doctor immediately.

The hospital didn't have a drop of anti-venom serum, so they called Denver to fly some down. Of course, this would be too late, but the doctor was very concerned with all the nasty cuts on my arm where I had slashed myself so many times. He was especially concerned after I told him that I had shot a groundhog and had used this same knife to cut it in two pieces for my two dogs just before I was bitten.

Penicillin had just become available, so they gave me a shot of it every few hours to keep infection from setting in. I got deathly sick, but survived the bite and cuts in good shape. The Durango newspaper had an article about it in the paper, which the people who owned the Gardenswartz Store saw. They sent word that when I got out of the hospital I could come to their store and pick out any knife in the store. The minute I got out, that is exactly what I did.

Later, Dad was able to find where I had dropped my gun and bring it home to me. I still meet old-timers who, upon hearing my name, ask me if I am the boy who was bitten by a rattlesnake. And me, I stay as far away from snakes as I can!

⊰ ⊱

THE BROWNS

During the time of the construction of the dam and on into the forties and fifties, the pace of life quickened a little at Vallecito. More people were moving in to join the little community that had gained some recognition. The Brown family entered the picture at about this time.

Carl Brown was born in 1927 and has lived around the Bayfield and Vallecito area all his life. His father, Leonard Brown, worked at the smelter in Durango and then went into the sawmill business. This is the way Carl remembers his early years:

> The first time I went to Vallecito was around 1938, and I saw where they had just dug the test holes to build the dam. I still remember all the big, beautiful pines up there by Aspen Point, where the road turned off to the east towards the Sullivan place. There was a bridge there then. Now when the water gets low enough, you can still see the abutments and the foundation of the old ranger station. It's where Grimes Creek came into the Vallecito River.
>
> My father had sawmills. The first one he ever owned was up on the mountain, above the house that my wife, Freda, and I live in now, on Cool Water Ranch. That was in 1939. Sawmill people lived in shacks and moved around like Gypsies. When they ran out of trees close to one place, they would move on to another place. They would cut a little lumber, and take a roll of tar-paper and cover it, and you had a new house.
>
> My Dad's second sawmill was over at Forest Lakes, and the third one was over at Beaver Creek. He bought timber from landowners and paid by the stumpage. They could figure the board feet in a tree pretty well by looking at it, and estimating how much lumber was in it. They have a way of scaling logs to see how much lumber is in them, but they can estimate pretty close. They used crosscut saws for many years, then Dad got the first chain saw around to use in his sawmill operation.
>
> Dad also had sawmills where Virginia's Restaurant is now, and one over by the old Cowboy Bar, on the east side of the lake in 1945. Roscoe Hammond and Lee Rector logged for us. Lee had a limp as the result of polio when he was a kid. One of his legs was terribly shrunken, but he made up for that deficiency with the size of his shoulders and his lightning speed.
>
> Tom Marshall had the sawmill down by Red Creek. His saws were steam driven. He put some wooden rails up on the mountain, so he could slide logs down the hill to the sawmill. One story I heard says that when they first tried it, they had a problem. When they put the first load of logs on it, and slid them down, there wasn't a braking system. The logs

picked up so much speed that when they got down to the sawmill, there was no stopping them. They went right on through the mill. I think Tom Marshall's sawmill later burned down.

There was a sawmill at Sawmill Point owned by Widemans, and one on up the lake towards Aspen Point in the lake bottom. They were both taking the trees out to make way for the water when the dam was finished. The Sowers boys had the sawmill up Bear Creek, and one in Bayfield. The name of their company was "Great Scott Lumber Company."

Once this valley started filling with people when the lake came in, there was a big demand for lumber. People were building houses, stores, and all kinds of buildings, both here, and all around this country. All the lumber the little sawmills turned out was needed.

Norman Payson seemed to get by delivering mail in either his car or on horseback. However the old mail carrier over on the Florida Road had big, high buggy wheels with spikes on his Model A, so he could get through the mud. He could go where nobody else could. That road could be a nightmare in those days.

From what I know of Tom Marshall, who ran the sawmill at Red Creek, he was a very colorful guy. Tom was Pete Scott's brother-in-law. He was well up in years when I knew him, and us young guys used to enjoy buying Tom drinks just to hear him talk. He'd tell us some of the darnedest stories. As long as people put drinks up there in front of him, he'd drink them. He would sure get intoxicated. When he came up the road in that old car he had, he'd drive right up the middle of the road. He was an ornery old devil! Tom was ninety-six when he died.

After I married Freda Beuten, I started raising cattle and a few horses here at Cool Water, but I still keep my sawmill up one of our canyons, and use it from time to time.

CHAPTER 7:

From Ranching to Tourism

I n 1940 the Vallecito Dam was nearing completion, and the scenery in the valley changed drastically. There were no horses, cows or sheep in sight. People were hurriedly trying to get the last of their buildings and fences moved out of the bottomland before the rivers were dammed and the water would rise to cover them.

Farming in the upper Pine River Valley was a thing of the past, but soon the farmers and ranchers of the lower country would be able to use the irrigation ditches they had been frantically digging, which would increase the use of their land tremendously. The whims of nature would no longer mean parched ground and ruined crops.

⇥ ⇤

LAVENIA MCCOY

Lavenia Morgan was born in 1919 and came to the town of Bayfield in 1939 to teach high school after obtaining her teaching degree at Colorado State College in Greeley. She was from a small town, so she felt quite at home in the friendly town of Bayfield with its mixture of farmers, ranchers, and business people.

When she arrived in Bayfield, the basketball games and dances were still being held in the Akers' Hall, which was over what is now the automotive repair shop. This was before the school had a gymnasium.

She met Dee McCoy, and they decided to get married in 1940. They went to Aztec, New Mexico, to get married, as many of the young couples did in those days, because it was the cheapest, easiest way to do it at that time. There was no need to pay for a fancy wedding.

Lavinia McCoy tells about her days at Vallecito:

> Dee was working at the dam site, helping to con-
> struct the new dam when we married. We gathered up our
> things and moved onto an eighty-acre parcel of land on the
> hill on Florida Road, just east of Helen's store. Dee didn't have
> far to drive to work.
>
> We pitched a sheepherder's tent and set up house-
> keeping on the property. We barely had room for our big wood
> cook stove, a bed, a table and two chairs. We were buying the
> land we were living on from the Maynes' Estate, and we had

put down earnest money on it. But the family was having a hard time coming to an agreement on the deal. Every time we were supposed to sign the papers, there was another delay.

We had cows to take care of on our property, and Paris Engler had sheep on the adjoining property. The girl taking care of Paris' sheep and I had a lot of fun trying to keep the sheep and cows separated that summer. We just had a battery-powered electric fence around the place, and it didn't work too well.

Uncle Fred McCoy and his family lived a little ways down the south branch of the Texas Creek Road, and they came to visit us often on Sundays. Grandpa Hartley came up and stayed off and on with us all summer and started building a fence for us. Dee made a little "dog house" extension on the backside of our tent for him to sleep in.

I tended cows, cooked and kept house while Dee worked up on the dam. I had this big stove with a nice oven, but I didn't know how to make bread. I had to learn real fast.

We had a wonderful spring there with the best tasting cold water, so Dee built a cream-house over it, and we kept our

Sunday gathering at Lavenia and Dee McCoy's tent home on 240 in 1940 while Dee worked on dam construction. Standing L to R: Aimee McCoy, Audrey McCoy, Grandpa Hartley, Early McCoy, Peggy McCoy, Jim Hartley, Lavenia McCoy. Sitting L to R: Earleen McCoy, Fred McCoy holding Donnie McCoy, Teddy McCoy, Kenneth McCoy. (Courtesy Lavenia McCoy)

milk separator in there. The place had one little old building on it that we used for storage. We had to carry our water in buckets to the house. We washed clothes in a tub, and scrubbed them on the washboard like so many others did in those days. We used that same tub to bathe in.

I've been told that when Hugh Curry had his little resort down by Jack Creek, he had two little boys. He would put one boy in the pannier on one side of his horse, and the other boy in the pannier on the other side. He would ride all over these mountains with them. Melba McCoy and Grace Green both worked for the Currys at their resort for a time. Working at the resorts was about the only way for young people to help make a living.

When the Wunderlich Company finished the dam project, they moved to Panama to build locks for the Panama Canal. Dee didn't want any part of the tropics, so he opted not to go with them. It wasn't long until the war started and Dee went to the service. He had to spend the next three and one-half years in the South Pacific, so he had to go to the tropics anyway. I was pregnant then, and I went home to stay with my mother in Arkansas for the duration of the war.

We never did get to buy that eighty-acre place on Florida Road that we wanted so badly, since the Maynes family could never reach an agreement on it. When Dee came back from the service, we settled in Bayfield on our seven acres. Dee went to work for the REA [Rural Electric Company], and I started teaching school in Bayfield.

Lavenia McCoy can still be found living in her Bayfield home. She continues to raise her yearly garden and enjoys her active social life.

☙ ❧

SHADDENS

Jimmie Shadden shared some of his memories of the earlier years on one of his Vallecito hunting trips. Jimmie and his family are Texas residents, but their family still enjoys coming to Vallecito for the fall hunting season. They stay at the familiar Pine River Lodge.

Addie Dunsworth had a sister living in Texas who died at a fairly young age, leaving her six small children motherless. From time to time, Addie, being the good Christian woman that she was, had the children come and stay with her at Vallecito. One of the boys was named Otey, better known at Vallecito as "Runt" Shadden. He was Jimmie Shadden's father.

Runt decided he wanted a place of his own at Vallecito. In 1943 he obtained a lot from his Aunt Addie Dunsworth and built the house that sits across the highway from Pine River Lodge (where the Warlicks live now). He and his family used it only as a vacation home since they had a large wheat farm in Texas.

Since Runt had several children, he decided to build an addition to the house about 1950, so he would have enough room for his growing family when they had gatherings. Runt brought in Bill Garrett, a stone-mason friend of his from Oklahoma, who built three stone fireplaces and other stone work in the new addition. Since the house sits on a hillside, it has two levels; so he added a large room on the lower level that was totally made up of stone on both the inside and outside.

Now these weren't from ordinary stones. They were special stones. Some came from an old gold mine in Silverton and supposedly have real gold in them, and some came from above Granite Peaks Ranch. There were large pieces of rose quartz from an unknown location, and stones from Arkansas embedded with blackish-colored Arkansas diamonds. Garrett hired two local young fellows, Dobbin Shupe and Jerry Newman, to help collect the stones.

When the stones were all collected, it took Garrett a week to study them and decide how to go about the project. Then he started with a rounded corner fireplace in the lower level. From there, he built the solid stone room around it and the rounded fireplace on the main level, which is just above the lower fireplace. Then he added another fireplace to the old part of the house.

Garrett also built fireplaces at Wilderness Trails Ranch, Teelawuket Ranch, and in several other homes; so quite a few folks made good use of Bill Garrett's talents during his stay at Vallecito. Dobbin Shupe said that Bill was a perfectionist and working with his critical demands was quite an experience.

Bob Echols owned the house next door to Runt's house. The two families wanted a deep water line to their homes that would come from the spring and water system that Charlie Dunsworth had set up above Pine River Lodge. The Canterbury, Shadden, and Echols boys dug the line from the first spring on the hill by the lodge, making sure it was down deep and wouldn't freeze in the winter. Jimmie remembered the experience: "When we crossed the highway with it, we had to blow it with dynamite. This blew out some windows, and the lodge owners at that time really raised hell! When we got it all connected, we turned it on, and Mama had a fit! There was such a drop in elevation that the water had so much force that it just came gushing out and drenched everything around, including Mama. We learned real fast about water pressure. We had to put in a reg-ulator valve to cut down the pressure and eliminate that problem."

≼ ≽

THE CAVIGGIAS

Pauline Heller and her husband Pearl were living in Gallup, New Mexico, when they met Johnny Cavigga. Johnny was from a large Italian family in Gallup. Pauline Heller, who wanted desperately to go to California to see her daughter, Doris, asked Johnny to drive her to California.

Doris was living out there, playing her saxophone and singing with a band. Johnny obligingly drove Mrs. Heller, since he wanted to see that country anyway. When he met Doris, the two of them really "hit it off," so Doris went back to Gallup with Johnny and her mother. Soon Doris was playing her saxophone, and Johnny was bartending at the Silver Moon Night Club in Albuquerque.

It wasn't long before sweet-talking Johnny convinced Doris that she should marry him. Doris' mom fought the marriage, but Johnny was persistent. Pauline thought Johnny was wild, since she knew he had been running a little bit of illegal whiskey.

"If she would have known how it would turn out, she never would have hired me to drive her to California. She didn't like me until the day she died," Johnny said.

Johnny and Doris came to Vallecito for the first time in 1942. Her mother and stepfather accompanied them, and they all stayed in the Dunsworths' cabins at Pine River Lodge. They paid the grand sum of $1.50 per night for lodging. The dam was finished in 1941, and the lake filled up soon after, so the tourists were beginning to come visit the new lake.

Johnny remembered,

> Vallecito Lake was called the "Pine River Dam" in those days. We were really impressed with the place, but since we didn't have any money or job prospects, we didn't think of staying. But Ma [Pauline Heller] liked it so much that she and her husband, Pearl, decided to stay. I guess she saw the possibilities.
>
> Ma bought the shack just below the road, north of where the Warlick house now sits. Later on, she bought another lot from Charley Dunsworth, and built a house on the new lot.

Doris' half-sister on her father's side, Burdella, and her husband, Mac McCaslin, also moved to Vallecito and lived in a house near Saw Mill Point. Doris and Burdella's father, George Root, and Pauline's first husband lived with the McCaslins. So "Ma Heller," as Pauline Heller was called at Vallecito, had her ex-husband, George Root, and her present husband,

Pearl Heller, as well as her daughter and her husband's daughter, all living in close proximity. Luckily it was a friendly situation with all of the parties in the rather complex family. Johnny remembered those days:

> *Ma had rental boats that she kept on the lake shore. She ran the business out of her house. She didn't even lock her door. She'd leave a note on the door saying, "If you want to rent a boat, go down and take the one you want, and leave the money under the door." We'd come home, and here would be all this money under the door. She had two cabins across from Shoreline Inn. It was quite steep down to the lake and the boats. When we sold Shoreline Inn, she kept her cabin for a couple of years and sold a little tackle out of it.*
>
> *Doris and I could never get Vallecito out of our minds, so in 1944, when I got my military*

Pauline "Ma" Heller. She was known as a tough business lady. Circa 1945. (Courtesy Lorene Wheat)

This picture takes in most of the Sawmill Point area with several boat docks, including Ma Heller's, in foreground. Circa mid 1940s. (Courtesy Lorene Wheat)

induction notice, we decided to come back and build a cabin. I thought that I would leave Doris at Vallecito while I was in the service, and she could live on my government checks. We came with fifteen hundred dollars, and bought the two lots on the hill, and the strip of land where Shoreline Inn sits. We paid one hundred fifty dollars for each of the three lots. Then we built our cabin. It damned near broke me!

Then we were in for a rude shock! The government passed a law that twenty-eight year-olds were exempt from military duty. Here we'd come and bought

Johnny and Doris Caviggia facing their "Shoreline Inn" restaurant and the lake. Ferber and Dene Wright's home and first liquor store in background. The sign reads: Whiskey, Beer, Wine. Circa 1950. (Courtesy Lorene Wheat)

the land, and we almost used up all our money thinking that our military checks would keep us, and now we were really in a bind.

If it wasn't for Steve Newman, the Lake Superintendent, and Leonard Brown, Carl's father, I don't know where the heck I'd of been. But I got a job with Newman, and then a job with Leonard Brown. Then Steve Newman got me a job with the Forest Service, so I never lost a day's work. I just lucked out, period!

Our little cabin was just twelve by sixteen, and that's where we had our three kids. We didn't have any water to the place. We had to haul it from Root Creek. Dunsworth wouldn't sell the land to us, but he liked Ma [Heller] so he sold it to her. Of course, it was our money she used to buy it. We started building Shoreline Inn about this time. We knew that a restaurant, close by the boat rentals and lodges that were starting up here, should go over good.

Shoreline Inn was built and operated by Johnny and Doris Caviggia frm 1944 to 1955. It was built in three stages. This picture was taken in early fifties after the third section was added. (Courtesy Lorene Wheat)

> I bought lumber down at the sawmill across from Columbus School. I went down and helped the guy cut wood. It was so damned green! That's what I built Shoreline out of. Our cabin was the same way. All we had was a handsaw in those days. We didn't have peanuts! The lumber was old, rough boards, and when they dried, there were big cracks between them. We never had any footings. We just put it on rocks. But it didn't cave in; it's still standing.
>
> We built the place, and we didn't have money to buy windows and doors in that first section. Mama [Doris] and I went down to J.C. Penney's and bought canvas to put over the windows and the door. It was always left open, and we never lost a dime.

Doris added her thoughts:

> When we weren't there, they'd leave more money than if we were. They'd feel sorry for us, I guess. We rented out our

cabin and lived in a tent just south of Shoreline in the summers. When it got cold, we'd move back to the cabin.

When we first opened, we had four stools. Some of our customers wanted breakfast earlier than we opened. Since there was no way to lock it anyway, we would leave some change out when we left in the evenings. The early customers would fix their own breakfast and make their own change, and leave their payment when they left.

Johnny was running punchboards up here in '44. Marguerite Sullivan still ran Bruce's at the Pines. Fred Frahm was caretaker at Teelawuket, and the Currys owned the place below the dam, on the right. Wit's End had two or three cabins, and there was the Safari Lodge, Lost Creek Lodge, and the Pine River Lodge. I think there were only eighteen winter residents at that time.

When we had Shoreline, we'd walk down the hill from the cabin every morning, and there was a mountain lion on the mountain by the old Dunsworth still. He was a screamer! Boy, he'd just stand up there on the rocks and scream! But it disappeared and I haven't seen it since.

Dad Dunsworth had an old wooden boat that always lay down on the lake shore. One day my sister, Della, and I wanted to go fishing, so we got the boat and took it clear across the lake, over there by the islands. We were fishing, and the thing started leaking. I had a can and was bailing and bailing, and Della was rowing and rowing, and we finally got back to Shoreline. Steve Newman came down when we reached shore and said, "Doris, that boat has been condemned for years." We had hit a stump over there, and I guess that did it in.

Johnny added,

In our early days at Shoreline, we would see Sally and Claude Decker coming down the hill. I'd spot him, and I'd pull out two cans of Mirro Beer, and here they'd come. Claude would reach in his jeans and pull out a pack of cigarettes. I'd open the two cans of beer, and down they'd go, while he smoked his cigarettes when Sally had her back to him. He really liked those cigarettes.

Doris commented,

We ran Shoreline from 1944 to 1955. Ma Heller helped to run it for a couple of years. Then in 1953, we bought

*the land where we built our Valley of the Spruce Lodge. Johnny
and I had gone up to that area for a picnic under a big tree
once, and that's when I decided I wanted that land. We had
been looking at land around the Meadowlark and Silver
Streams as sites for a lodge, but I decided I liked this better.*

Johnny tells how the purchase came about,

> *I came home from work one day and Doris said, "I
> bought that land." And I said, "How much did you pay for it?"
> And when she told me, "Ten thousand dollars," I said, "Oh, how
> am I going to pay for it, a dollar at a time?" I was only making
> a dollar a day at that time.*
>
> *We sold a couple of pieces of land off of it to pay for
> the twelve acres that we kept. We moved an old cabin over to
> our land, and built a lean-to on it, and moved in. Then we
> started building the other cabins. We let Della [Burdella] and
> Mac take over Shoreline Inn, but that didn't work out.
> Somehow we managed to build more cabins and make a nice
> resort out of the lodge, and get our family raised.*

Doris must have gotten her skill at water witching from her father,
as she helped him witch wells before drilling them. Part of her legacy was
leaving a valley with a number of good wells with pure, sweet water. She
was called on numerous times to witch a well for people.

Drilling wells in the rocky Vallecito land was tricky and also very
expensive. The service of a good water witch was an important factor in
finding the exact spot where you had the best chance to hit water. And
Doris was a good witch.

Doris used this method to witch for a well: She would cut a forked
green willow branch, and cut any extra branches off of it. Then, by taking
a fork in each hand and pointing the main end ahead of her, she would
walk around until the end of the branch dipped down and pointed to the
ground. This showed that there was water down below.

Some people have this skill so refined they are able to tell how
deep the water is from the surface. Other water witches use metal rods
instead of green willow branches, which may not be available at all times
of the year. Many people don't believe in witching, but many, who have had
good wells located and drilled by this method, are believers.

The Caviggias raised their three children at Vallecito. Their home
was always a gathering spot for their children, grandchildren and great-
grandchildren, as well as a multitude of friends and lodge guests. Their

daughter, Lorene, married and raised her three daughters in her nearby home. Johnny and Doris are gone now, but their daughter, Lorene, still welcomes the lodges' guests to one of the most beautiful spots in the upper Pine River Valley. The Valley of the Spruce Lodge, on the banks of the Vallecito River, is a place where guests come to enjoy peace and beauty year after year.

⇥ ⇤

SHUPES

When the Guy Shupe family was living near the little community of Carson, New Mexico, Guy made a living raising horses and driving teams on road jobs. The country was so sparsely settled, and visitors came by so seldom, that when someone did stop for any reason, the children were terrified and would run and hide under the house. Guy's wife, Leola, decided she was not going to let the children grow up that way. At her insistence, Guy started looking for a more "civilized place" to bring up children.

It was in 1944 that Guy came to Vallecito, which was at least an area well on its way to being civilized. The lake was in and people were arriving and settling along the valley all the time. Guy thought it looked like an ideal place for his family, so he bought a place just west of Dale Patton's place on Florida Road.

When the family came, they drove their cattle with them, but when he arrived, Guy had to think of a way to make a living. The only thing he could figure out to do was to go into the outfitting business. Since the lake was established, there were quite a number of people coming up to visit, and many of them were quite interested in riding into the high country and camping. The lakes and streams were reported to be thick with fish.

In the spring of 1945, the Shupes spent seven weeks in Texas looking for horses. When they got back with the horses, Guy was able to find a job outfitting out at the Teelawuket Ranch (this was during the time that the Pollacks were running it as a boys' camp).

In 1948 Guy started outfitting out of Wit's End Ranch, which the Deckers owned at the time. However the outfitting business wasn't a year-round job. It only ran from sometime in late May when the snow melted in the high country, to the end of hunting season in the fall; so an outfitter had to find another way to supplement his income during the rest of the year.

For one winter Guy helped Claude Decker. The Chain Lakes were empty, the ditches had to be cleaned out and repaired so they could once more be filled with water, and other repairs were needed around the place.

This gave Guy work for one winter. Then he started driving the school bus since this fit in well with his outfitting schedule.

Wit's End came up for sale for thirty thousand dollars. Guy wanted terribly to buy it, but it was more than he could manage. In 1949 Guy's son, Dobbin, heard the place next to the Buffalo Gap was for sale. Guy bought that land and they started living and running the outfitting business out of there.

Dobbin and Gary, Guy and Leola's sons, were old enough to be of some help when they started the "Big Corral." They took tourists on hour-long horseback rides on the mountain, on breakfast rides that took several hours, or for week-long camping or hunting trips into the Weminuche Wilderness.

Guy was quite the picture of an old-time cowboy with his silvery hair and battered cowboy hat and gear. He passed on in 1992, and his body was carried to the cemetery in a carriage drawn by matching horses in a style that befitted this weathered old cowboy.

⊰ ⊱

BEUTENS-COOL WATER RANCH

In their earlier years, Fred and Alta Beuten lived in Western Colorado on a ranch that sat in the middle of nowhere on Ragged Mountain. Paonia was the nearest town. They sold the ranch and Fred worked for the Atomic Energy Commission during World War II. When the war was over, Fred was ready to get back to ranch life.

In 1945 Fred and Alta looked at several ranches and eventually came to look at the old Scott Ranch near Vallecito. When they saw the nearly three thousand acre ranch with its wide valley and the Pine River running through it, the decision to buy was made almost instantly. The fact that both Jack Creek and Red Creek ran through the heavily forested land was an added benefit. You couldn't find a more picturesque place.

When Fred, Alta, and their two children, Freda and Tommy, got moved in, Alta decided the ranch needed a new name to signify the family's new beginning. After a little time and thought, she came up with "Cool Water Ranch."

Freda Brown remembered the Beuten family's time on the Cool Water Ranch:

> *The ranch had been used as a sheep ranch before we bought it, so my dad decided he would make the switch to raising sheep. He had only raised cattle before, so it was quite a change.*

Only three years after we moved here my father came down with an illness and passed away. After that happened, Mother leased the ranch to J.W. Tubs, who ran his band of sheep along with ours. He bought a small piece of land by Red Creek, where Bob Niggli now has his home and put a trailer there for his family to live in.

Tubs later sold his sheep and started running the place as a dude ranch. He built a cabin on Red Creek, near the Forest Service boundary, for his hunters to use. That cabin is still in use during hunting season.

Mother sold the sheep not long after my dad passed away and started teaching school in Bayfield. She found herself in need of transportation, so she bought a car and taught herself to drive. When they started running a school bus to Vallecito, after the school consolidation in 1949, she rode the bus with us kids on most days.

After a few years, Mother married one of the local fellows, Shorty [Ivan] Parks, and he moved in with us on the ranch. Old Mrs. Parks, Shorty's mother, was in poor health, so she lived there with us, too. Shorty and I soon became buddies and went riding together sometimes. But after a time, the marriage fell apart, and Shorty left for Arizona.

As I was growing up, our biggest way of having fun was getting together and riding like wild Indians up and down the mountains. When we got old enough, Margaret Newman and I got jobs working at Vallecito Resort in the summers. We washed and ironed clothes, cut wood, ran the store, or did about anything else they could find for us to do. Sometimes I had to come home after working there and help Mother clean her cabins down by the River.

When we had a chance, Margaret and I would ride our horses up to Wilderness Trails Ranch to meet Juanita Shupe when she got off work. That's when we went on our exploring trips and rode all over these mountains. My stepsister, Donna Parks, came to stay with us at times. She was a city girl, but she was tough. She kept up with us mountain girls, and never complained.

Melba McCoy was our 4H Club leader. We would either go to her place on Texas Creek or to the Columbus School for our meetings. She taught us to sew, so that meant I had to load my sewing bag on the horse with me when I went to the meetings.

The first time I saw Carl Brown was when he was racing cars with Jack Huntington. When they came to Black Dog Corner, they almost ran into a bunch of us girls on our horses. Of course, that was when I was a little kid, and he was a big, older guy.

The time I actually met him was when a bunch of us kids took our horses on a porcupine hunt in the hills one evening. Dobbin Shupe joined us and brought Carl Brown along with him. At the end of our excursion, Carl asked Margaret Newman and me to go to a movie with him the next night. We told him yes, but he never showed up the next night, so we hunted him down and made him take us to that movie.

Things just kept escalating after that. After I finished my first year of college in 1956, Carl and I got married — much to my mother's chagrin. We spent the first year of our marriage in a trailer, down by the river, during the summer. Then we lived in Mother's home in the winter while she was living and teaching in Bayfield. In the summer, she planned to come back to live in her house again.

That next summer, which was after our daughter, Carol, was born, we had pulled the trailer back down to the river and were preparing to move in, when the flood of 1957 came along. Carl got down to the river and pulled our trailer out of there in the nick of time, but one of Mother's rental trailers floated down the river for a little ways until it hit a wire we had across the river. That held it from going any farther, so that we could still pull it out and save it.

The Pine River Bridge down by Columbus School was washed completely out, and the Florida Bridge was damaged so badly it wasn't usable. The only way people from Vallecito could get to either Bayfield or Durango was by going through Wallace Gulch.

We moved the trailer up to Red Creek, where it was safer, and lived there until we could move into the ranch house where we are living now. Carl bought some cattle, and we became cattle ranchers. We started raising cattle and horses along with our two children and all their assorted pets.

My brother, Tommy Beuten, became a musician. After years of traveling, he came back to live in Mother's house just down the road from us, so Tommy, Carl, and I are all still enjoying our Cool Water Ranch.

⮜ ⮞

SCHILLINGBURG-GRANITE PEAKS RANCH

The following is Gordon Schillingburg's story of his family's life at Vallecito:

> My dad, Con Shillingburg, was running a trading post on the Navajo reservation by Chinle, Arizona, when he came to southern Colorado looking for a fishing place to escape to from time to time. When he ran across the Granite Peaks Ranch in 1927, he thought he had found the perfect spot. Every year after that, we packed up our bags and fishing equipment, at least once a year, and headed to Vallecito to fish. The ranch that was originally owned by John Porter and General William Palmer was being run as the "Pine River Camp Company" at that time.
>
> We would notify the owners what day we would arrive, and someone would meet us at the Pine River and tow us across the river with a team of horses. Then we could drive the rest of the way up the mountain on our own.
>
> This worked out fine until the Corzelius family bought the ranch in 1936 to use as a private residence. This put us on the spot since we liked the Granite Peaks area so well. After that we had to fish at either Teelawuket or the Wilderness Trails Ranch during our annual trips.
>
> In 1946 my dad heard that Granite Peaks Ranch was for sale, so he bought it from the former Ann Corzelius, who was now Mrs. Ann Oliver after her divorce. Perhaps my folks were tired of life on the reservation and longed for a change of climate and the quieter lifestyle the ranch at Vallecito had to offer.
>
> We bought the ranch as a home. It covered two hundred acres in Hinsdale County, and four hundred eighty acres in La Plata County. At one time, the ranch property extended up the Pine River to the Lake Fork, but because of Mother Nature's tendency to keep blowing down snow-laden trees, it became increasingly hard to maintain the boundary fence. This made me decide to sell off a small upper portion of the ranch to the Forest Service in 1977 — the portion that adjoins the Pine River Trail that is used by hikers and horses going up to the high country of the Weminuche Wilderness.
>
> The most remarkable thing about this ranch is the number of structure fires on the premises, none of which were

caused by forest fires. The bathhouse was the first to burn down in 1929 or 1930. Then, in the early thirties, the main house, which was down by the river, burned to the ground. Next, the dining hall burned in the late thirties and was never rebuilt. Corzelius had built a house above the river on the hillside out of square logs, and it also burned down in 1946, which was not long after we bought the place. We thought that a defective flue was the culprit this time.

My parents and I had arrived home at about ten in the evening, and built a fire before going to bed. At around two in the morning, I woke up having difficulty breathing and was surrounded by smoke. I was pretty groggy, but I managed to get up and get my parents out of bed, and out of the house. There was no water available to fight fires, so we had to just stand by and watch the whole house go up in smoke.

After this catastrophe, we moved into a house just across Indian Creek, which was the one that Corzelius had built for his accountant (according to one story). Five years later, we built a large frame home on the same foundation that remained from Corzelius' big log house.

I decided to start ranching up here years ago, and I went into the horse business. I started raising thoroughbred horses as part of a horse-breeding program, and that has been my life for over twenty-five years now.

In 1987 another fire started. It happened on the day that the annual Octoberfest was being held at the Vallecito Chamber of Commerce Building. Activities were just getting under way, and the crowd was pouring in, when the firemen were paged out from Central Dispatch. The volunteer firemen were engaged in a wildly competitive volleyball game with a crackerjack team of Southern Utes. Of course this game had to be hurriedly interrupted, and the firemen then heard about yet another fire at the Granite Peaks Ranch.

The firemen took off with their sirens screaming, as they barreled up the road to the distant ranch. The ranch was on the other side of the lake and up a long steep canyon. It was the most distant ranch up the Pine River, so the firemen knew it was essential to get there before the fire had made too much headway.

They arrived in time to save the house, although there was some structural damage, and they kept the fire from spreading into the surrounding forest and developing into a major forest fire. Then the exhausted firemen rushed back to

*the volleyball tournament where they found they still had
enough adrenalin pumping through their systems to win the
interrupted game.*

Gordon Schillingburg passed away in the winter of 1997, while he
was at his winter residence in Arizona. After waiting until the snow melted
enough to gain access to the ranch the following spring, his widow, Leslie,
brought his body back to be laid to rest on his beloved high-country estate.

ᛉ ᛃ

VENUTI/ROBERTS-WILDERNESS TRAILS RANCH

Bob Venuti had been looking, longingly, at the ranch that Grace
Bishop Soloman owned for years, so when the opportunity arose in 1947,
he bought it. The ranch had been a part of the Teelawuket Ranch when
Johnny Kirkpatrick owned it and was given to his betrothed as an engagement present. The marriage never happened, for some undisclosed reason,
but the lady kept the ranch.

When Bob and Mary Venuti bought the property, their idea was to
start a dude ranch. Since trees were in abundance all around them, they
had their main building material on hand. It was just a matter of spending
long, weary hours of backbreaking labor to construct the log lodge and
cabins. They spent the snowy winters working on the finishing touches
inside the cabins, and opened the ranch to tourists in the summers. The
Venutis ran the ranch until 1960, when they decided to move on.

Mickey and Mary Craig purchased the ranch. Mickey was a well-
known and respected businessman around Vallecito and Durango. He had
a wonderful wife and six children by this time and was involved in the
movie, "How The West Was Won," that was filmed, in part, on the ranch.
Life appeared to be going well for him.

A happenstance meeting with "Do," the leader of the Heaven's Gate
religious cult, changed everything for the Craig family. Somehow "Do"
convinced Mickey to join him and his cult, and Mickey left with them and
was never seen around here again. His family and friends found it unbe-
lievable that a person as down to earth and respected as Mickey could leave
his family and just take off like that.

Mickey followed this cult for years before he joined them in their
mass suicidal exit from their California home to supposedly meet up with
the Hale-Bop comet on its way to Heaven. His family saw him for the last
time, on the television, when he gave his farewell speech to the world.

Mary was left in dire straits, with six children to raise, and a dude
ranch to run. She did what other women before her had done. She simply

Wilderness Trails Guest Ranch, once a part of Johnny Kirk Patrick's Teelawuket Ranch. Bob Venuti and wife built the lodge and operated it as a guest ranch. Now owned and operated by Gene and Jan Roberts. (Photo by D. Warlick)

kept on going. She managed to hold on to the ranch until 1970, and then she sold it to Jan and Gene Roberts.

The Roberts have run the ranch since, as the now famous, "Wilderness Trails Ranch." It has been featured on several television shows such as "Hello America," and in several magazines, as well. Entire families come from their eastern city lives to enjoy the ranch experience together. It gives them the opportunity to stay on a real working ranch with wonderful food and accommodations and a great variety of activities and entertainment.

Guests can go on horseback trips up mountain trails, enjoy water skiing on the lake, hike in the woods, or engage in many other activities. Some, no doubt, spend time just relaxing with a book under the enormous spruce trees in this peaceful setting. Here in this fresh mountain air and surrounding beauty, they have the time to enjoy life away from their stressful lives and have the graciousness of the Roberts and their staff to see to their every need.

Sometimes their hosts take them out for an evening to learn what cowboys sometimes do after a long, hard day in the saddle, gathering and driving cattle down for roundup. They are introduced to Vallecito's nightlife at Virginia's Restaurant or, perhaps, The Buffalo Gap. They can let loose, kick up their heels, and wet their whistles with "good old mountain firewater" like the real cowboys do.

⮜ ⮞

SAFLEYS-WIT'S END RANCH

Martin and Maxine Safley were the ones who really started the Wit's End Ranch on its way to being known as a guest ranch. Martin was tired of the dairy business. The hunting and outfitting possibilities were the reason for buying the place. He had one problem, though. He couldn't swing the deal alone, so he talked his brother into going in with him on the purchase.

Martin repeated some stories of his days on the ranch:

We originally lived in the south but came to Colorado and settled over on Thompson Creek, west of Durango, where we were in the dairy business. We bought Wit's End and moved over on it in 1952, since I was turning into an avid hunting enthusiast. My brother, Harris, and his wife, Ada, went in on the deal with us.

Elmer Decker and his wife had lived up here before us. He had racehorse fever and had a stud horse pen because he always had one to three studs. The double-decker cabin that sits to the east of the D Creek Café was built so you could put hay in the top and throw it out to the stud horse. You didn't have to go near his pen. I guess they could be pretty violent. The barn was just an ordinary hay barn. It used to have hand-hued shakes on it, but it had so many holes in it that the water would just pour in, so we put corrugated iron over it. When you see it now as a high-class restaurant, you can hardly believe the change.

There was only one livable building on the place when we moved here. It was an old log house where we could sort of set up camp. It had a fireplace, and there was a big spring outside with a pipe coming into the kitchen, which is all the water we had in the place. There was also a pipe that led to the washhouse and also to the horse tank. It was the only house that had water to it, and it didn't have much pressure. The house did have electricity, which Deckers had just put in.

There were two cabins when we arrived, and we put up two more for rental units. The logs for the cabins were from Gunnison. As soon as we got the logs up here, it started raining cats and dogs. We had built concrete slabs to put the cabins on. We'd stay up all night and put tarps over the slabs at night so they would cure.

We built a new house to live in after the first two sum-mers. The way they built the old houses, they would start on the ground and lay some big rocks for the corners, then they would lay a log, and then come up to where the floor was and fill it underneath with sawdust. This made the most perfect home for skunks, rats, and badgers. The skunks would go under the house to winter, and they'd eat the rats. Then the badgers came in to eat the skunks. The smells and noises from under there were something else!

Hank and Bob Snow with the Forest Service were our closest neighbors when we first came. Their daddy had a big pack outfit out of Pagosa Springs.

Most of our outfitting customers liked to fish at Flint Lake rather than at Rock Lake, because the fish would bite better there. You had to be real cagey to hook one in Rock Lake. They were both pretty close to the "window" in the divide, and about twenty-three miles from the Vallecito Trailhead.

One year, when I was still in the outfitting business, I had packed up all my hunters to the high country when a huge snowstorm came in and just about buried everything. I got the hunters out before the snow got too deep, but by then the snow was too deep for the horses. The only way we could pull the camp, with its four or five tents, was to go in on snowshoes and fold all the tents and pack all the other gear to bring out.

Martin and Maxine Safley's lodge guests as they head out on a trail ride. Old Patrick family homestead barn in background (Presently "Wit's End Guest Ranch"). (Courtesy Martin Safely)

Winter time at cabin on Safely's Dude Ranch. Circa 1950. (Courtesy Martin Safely)

Finally, with my rear bumping out of my tracks, I got every-thing back to the ranch.

We had the place for ten years and worked the longest hours I ever did in my life. There were three partners in the place, but we were doing ninety-five percent of the work. The others were never there in the rush seasons. I didn't mind hard work, but you couldn't make a lot of money in three or four months on a dude ranch.

We started with two forties on the north end, and we didn't know whether we'd sell one lot. There eventually were some two hundred lots, eight subdivisions, and forty or fifty tracts. About this time, my brother decided to leave. He had had his fill of this whole deal.

We never did make much money, but we made a good living. There are a lot of people living on land that was Wit's End land that I developed. We kept thirty acres for ourselves, and developed Blue Spruce Trailer Park and built our house, which was all a part of the Patricks' homestead and then later, the Deckers' Ranch.

*Life sure wasn't easy! We've seen some awfully good
times and met a lot of good people up here, but we've seen our
share of hard work and hard times too. I guess that's just how
life is.*

⊰ ⊱

PENNS, POLLACKS & GRAHAMS-TEELAWUKET RANCH

Pete Scott owned Teelawuket from 1917 to 1926. While Pete was
living there his genial personality reflected the true western spirit of hospi-
tality, and he threw his home open to a host of friends, or anyone else who
had the good fortune to happen by. During this time, some of the Ute
Indians, including Buckskin Charlie and Washington, still would come up
to hunt occasionally and were made welcome.

During Pete's tenure, many improvements were made. During the
latter part of his ownership, an orthodontist by the name of Dr. H.C.
Pollock and his son, Carlyle, from St. Louis, happened upon the ranch. Dr.
Pollock was in rather poor physical condition and was advised by his
physician to take a leave and get back to nature. So, he and his son came
out to spend some time in Colorado.

Once when they were roaming around the mountains, they were
caught in a drenching thunderstorm and stopped at Teelawuket to ask for
shelter in the barn. Pete Scott, being the sociable fellow that he was,
absolutely would not hear of them staying in the barn. He brought them
into his home and insisted on feeding and lodging them in his true hos-
pitable way.

Dr. Pollock couldn't forget the place, and when he went back home
and showed the numerous photographs he had taken while at Vallecito,
some of his colleagues were so impressed that they wanted to buy the
ranch so that their sons could also be exposed to this type of life. The colleagues formed a partnership and bought Teelawuket in 1927. They started
a boys' camp, which was called Rancho Mesa Verde at Allison and was run
in conjunction with Teelawuket.

Bill Penn, present owner of a parcel of land that used to be part of
Teelawuket Ranch, related some of the happenings on the ranch after Pete
Scott sold it:

*When Teelawuket was used as a boys' camp, Dr.
Pollack and his son, Carlyle, managed it. Since they didn't
know a thing about running a ranch, they hired locals to help
run it and act as wranglers to take care of the horse operation.
He knew Sandy Scott from when the Scotts owned the place, so*

it was logical for him to ask for Sandy's help, along with other locals including Fred Frahm.

They would bring these kids from the city, to Allison on the train. Cowboys who had never worked with kids met the greenhorn boys, who had never seen a horse before, at the train station with horses. And here came the kids, with bags and hats and all this stuff, and the cowboys were trying to get the kids on the horses and get the bags all tied on. One time, when someone blew the train whistle, they had forty horses with forty kids going in forty directions with bags scattered all over the ground. What a hilarious scene that must have been! Total bedlam!

Then came the bottom-busting, forty-five mile ride up the mountain to Teelawuket, where they had many other rides in store for these poor, worn-out city kids. They were taken on pack trips to Willow Park, Lookout Mountain, and on up to the far reaches of the Continental Divide. The wranglers also staged rodeos to help keep the boys entertained. Many of the parents of the boys would also come to the ranch for varying stays.

During this period, Dr. Pollack placed advertisements in newspapers back East, which attracted professional men to the ranch for hunting trips. Fred Frahm, the ranch foreman, was in charge of the bear hunting trips, which were mainly up East Creek. They had a bear trap up there that was sort of a log

Dr. H. C. Pollock, pictured here, and his group of dentists bought the ranch in 1926 and used it as a boy's camp before the Graham's present ownership. (Courtesy Keith and Diane Graham)

cabin with a narrow entrance. They would put a bunch of meat in there to attract the bears. When the bear went in, he would be caught, and then they would rope him and pull him out. Then they would take him down and chain him to the barn.

One time, they had a very wealthy man from back East as a ranch guest while his wife was traveling in Europe. He got very involved in the bear hunting endeavor, and it was getting closer and closer to the time he was supposed to go back to pick up his wife when she arrived back from her European trip.

Now, this old gentleman was having the time of his life, and he just couldn't bear to tear himself away from all this fun and leave. Finally, the day came when his wife was supposed to arrive in New York, and he managed to break away long enough to go down to Durango and send her a wire saying, "Unnecessarily detained. See you in a month."

My dad, William Y. Penn, bought the Teelawuket Ranch from the Pollocks in 1953. My wife, Lucinda, and I tried to run it as a dude ranch. We weren't very successful at that, so in 1965 we sold the lower two-thirds of the ranch. It was the main part of the ranch, which has all the buildings on it. We sold it to two gentlemen by the names of Mr. Audis and Mr. McClure. I can't recall their first names. These men were very close friends at the time, but trouble soon developed and they ended up in a bitter fight. There were lawsuits and court battles ending with the sale of the ranch. The two close friends were now bitter enemies.

Summertime still finds Bill and Lucinda Penn residing in a home they built on the part of Teelawuket that they kept. Here they can still enjoy life on their share of this beautiful ranch.

The main part of the ranch is still known as the Teelawuket Ranch. It is now owned by Keith and Dianne Graham, who use it as a summer home and a place to entertain guests. After the Penns sold it, things were allowed to go downhill amidst all the legal entanglements, so the Grahams had their work cut out for them. They have done a wonderful job of restoring the ranch, including the rebuilding of Charles Graham's original homestead cabin. This cabin, which now has been modernized to include a bathroom, is in high demand as a lodging place for some of Graham's summer guests. The buildings look very much as they did many years ago as they preside over the ever serenely beautiful "Summer Home Ranch."

⇥ ⇤

CRANE

Claude O. Crane was born in Texas in 1899. When he was forty-six years old, he and his wife, Ivy May, decided to travel around the country to find a beautiful spot to retire. After three months, they decided that Durango was the place where they wanted to spend the rest of their lives.

Of course, they hadn't seen Vallecito yet! When they did, they decided it was an even more beautiful place and moved there five years later. While Claude was a relatively latecomer, not arriving in Vallecito until 1952, he did have a lot to do with the development of it. Claude, along with Martin Safley and Don Wheat, was one of the main subdividers in the north end of the valley. The three of them caused the population of the community to grow by leaps and bounds.

Claude and Ivy May opened the Lost Creek Lodge at the south end of the Wit's End ponds, once called Chain Lakes. Later, Claude and Clarence Black started the Dam Real Estate Company, a mortgage loan business, and then went on to help found the Vallecito Baptist Church. Claude took a very active part in church activities as well as all other activities in the growing community. He was sometimes referred to as "Vallecito's self-appointed honorary mayor" and was a very well liked and respected gentleman, as well as being a dedicated community leader.

Claude also had a wonderful sense of humor, which is illustrated by the story he loved to tell:

> *Guy Shupe, who lived next door to the church, had a gray mule at his place. One morning the church was packed, and we were having fellowship. It sounded like a bunch of geese in there. The preacher came to the pulpit and made a few announcements, so by this time the crowd had quieted down. Then he said, "Let us pray," and bowed his head.*
>
> *About this time, Guy Shupe's old mule brayed, "Hee haw, hee haw," just as loud as he could. Well, I thought we'd have to dismiss church for a while there, with the roar of laughter that thundered through the crowd.*
>
> *Claude passed on just short of reaching a full century of life, but he left his distinct mark on his chosen part of the world.*

⊰ ⊱

BOB BURCH-MEADOWLARK INN

There is hardly an old-timer living around Vallecito that doesn't recall the colorful owner of the Meadowlark Inn, and the good times they had at Bob Burch's establishment. Whether it was Christmas, a birthday, or any other excuse to gather for a good time, people got together at Bob's place to forget the rigors of everyday living.

Bob Burch and his wife, Betty, showed up at Vallecito in 1956. While he wasn't one of the earliest arrivals, he was well known in the community after a very short time. Bob came here from the glittery world of California, but was a cowboy at heart. He was born in Cripple Creek, Colorado, and had lived in Wyoming for a number of years, so he was well acquainted with horses and ranch life.

Bob and Betty acquired some of the old Decker ranch on the northeast side of the lake. Their plan was to start a restaurant and outfitting business, and they proceeded to do it in record time. They first built the large, rustic restaurant and bar with living quarters upstairs, and then they built cabins to house their lodgers or employees. Bob "borrowed" the name "Meadowlark Inn" from a place in Jackson Hole, Wyoming and opened the door for business.

Bob mainly took care of the outfitting part of the business, leaving Betty to keep the bar and restaurant running smoothly. Some years the proceeds from the restaurant kept them in the black, and some years it was the outfitting end of the business that made money. But it was Bob who would fall for somebody's line that "they would pay tomorrow," and those tomorrows sometimes never came.

On Saturday nights whole families would come, and if there wasn't a musician playing, the jukebox was soon put into action. When the children tired, mothers would put them to bed on the benches along the walls, and the grown-ups would be free to dance or visit. Most people couldn't afford the luxury of a baby sitter.

Many times they would have potluck dinners, since the cost of a meal for the whole family was beyond most people's means. Each lady would bring her best dish, so these events would usually end up being a meal "fit for a king."

Bob hired both male and female wranglers to take people on camping trips, and of course, one of them would be expected to be camp cook. A wrangler who could play the guitar and sing was always in high demand by the outfitters or owners of the horse operations.

In the summers when the guest business was at its height, the guests enjoyed the colorful mix of wranglers and local people at the Meadowlark. Many a dirty, smelly wrangler, just in from the trail and sitting at the bar clearing the dust out of his throat with a cold beer, was invited to dance with a single lady guest, who just needed a warm body to dance with. The female guests seemed to always be fascinated by the cowboy types. Of course the lady wranglers had the same effect on the male guests. There were more than a few romantic episodes in the business.

Around 1964 Bob decided he needed a big barn for the horses, so he cut down trees from the side of the mountain behind the inn. Then he took his old white horse, Diamond Jim, and harnessed him to the log. Bob would go down the hill, and pretty soon here came Diamond Jim dragging the big log behind him.

Once Bob's ex-wife showed up at the ranch, and one night she had some sort of disagreement with a man sitting on a bar stool. She went back to the powder room, and when she came out, she had a gun in her hand and shot him right off of his stool.

She also did some legal maneuvering to gain possession of the cabins and a portion of the land. Bob didn't have cabins to rent out, so he

The Meadowlark corrals and outfitter's barn. Bob Burch built this from trees growing on his property in 1956.

couldn't really call the place an "inn." That's when the restaurant was unofficially re-named "The Cowboy Bar." The place had a large dance floor and plenty of room for socializing. It was the gathering place for cowboys and locals alike over the years.

It was a sad day when Betty passed away, and Bob finally decided to sell the place. The locals still remember the good times they had there and sorely miss its friendly atmosphere. The old Cowboy Bar is part of the Wit's End Ranch property now and is off limits to the locals nowadays.

PART THREE

❧ *Changes* ❧

Caption for picture on reverse page: Sawmill Point area showing marinas, Shoreline Inn, Sawmill Point Lodge and surrounding homes. Circa 1995 (Courtesy Bureau of Reclamation)

CHAPTER 8

The Children

 settler's first concern, after staking a claim or establishing a homestead, was to find or make a shelter for himself and his family. He would immediately start building a home and perhaps a barn to shelter his animals from the bitterly cold Vallecito winters.

As soon as the more necessary tasks were complete, his next concern was usually for the education of his children in this wild, unsettled territory. It was a monumental task to set up schools in a country where there were absolutely none available for many miles. Transportation on the meager roads and trails was also a time consuming and sometimes dangerous proposition. There were blinding snowstorms, six-foot snowdrifts, or knee-deep mud to try to make your way through and at times the roads were totally impassable, so schools had to be located nearby.

To get to Durango from Vallecito was quite a journey in the late 1800s and early 1900s. Therefore a new school system had to be set up, one school at a time. When enough people, with enough children, moved close enough together to help build a school and hire a teacher, a school would be established.

Columbus School and Teacherage on 501 and Texas Creek (502) corner, near Columbus Bridge. This was the one Vallecito children attended. (Courtesy Ed Wommer)

Columbus School Class of 1929. Back row: Mrs. Morse, Clem Knight, Rex Mccoy, Dayton Percell, Chester McCoy, Earl Blackmore, Orville Mccoy, Elsie Blackmore, Laura Dunsworth, Esther Percell, Melva Wilbourn, Harold McCoy, Henry Parks and Johnnie Richards. Front row: Dale McCoy, Archie Blackmore, Clyde Wilbourn, Ruth Richards, Edith Dunsworth, Rosie Blackmore, Charles Dunsworth, Harlan Blackmore, Frances Wilbourn, Audrey McCoy, Ernie Parks and Rosemary Richards. (Courtesy Henry Parks)

The schools were simple one-room structures, with perhaps an entryway or mudroom tacked on — a place where the children could hang their coats and leave muddy overshoes. There was normally a pail of drinking water with a water dipper hanging from it that was kept in the attached room. Perhaps a few supplies were also stored here, and sometimes there might be stacks of split wood with which to keep the old pot-bellied stoves going.

Then, of course, there was the inevitable outhouse out back. If you really had a modern school, there might be two outhouses — a His and Hers. The outhouses were usually supplied with a Montgomery Ward catalog for the sake of personal hygiene.

The Pargin School, which was a few miles east of Bayfield, on the Pargin homestead at Beaver Creek, and the Lowell School, which was on the east side of the Pine River by the present Pick Bar Ranch, were two of the first schools built to educate the earliest arrivals. A few years later, the Benn Springs, Moss, and Lissner Schools, to the west of the Pine River, as well as others to the South of Bayfield, had been established as more settlers arrived.

The Columbus School was at the intersection of County Roads 501 and 502, at the point where the road splits. It is called the Texas Creek intersection. The bridge going over the nearby Pine River is referred to as the Columbus Bridge. Children from Vallecito, some from Texas Creek and Florida Road, as well as some that lived down the road to the south, all went to the Columbus School.

Many times, families would donate land in order to have a school built close enough that their children could attend. Families such as the Pargins, Dunsworths, and Lissners were just a few that donated land for schools.

Changes were made in the school year to make it conducive for more children to attend. Sometimes school was held in the spring months to supposedly avoid the coldest part of the winter, but there was never a time when nature couldn't wreak havoc with the best laid plans. Of course the farmers and ranchers didn't want their kids in school during the short summers when there was all kinds of work to be done and no money to hire outside help. A few schools did try summer sessions, however.

The children walked, skied, or rode horses to school, for the most part, in the earliest times. Lots of families used unique ways of travel. Lloyd Knickerbocker, who lived up Bear Creek, talked of a dog that pulled him to the Moss School on a sled and a conveyance on a line that took him across the river.

If you rode a horse to school, you needed access to a barn by the school to keep him in during the long, cold, and perhaps snowy days. Eventually some of these one-room schools built a teacherage for the teacher to live in because there wasn't housing nearby.

Horseback riding was one of the early Vallecito children's favorite pasttimes as well as their main mode of tranportation. Pictured are: Bob Newman, Freda Beuton, Tommy Beuten and Jerry Newman perched on Rex, Freda's horse. Cool Water Ranch in background. (Courtesy Freda Beuten Brown)

In 1919 Charlie Dunsworth bought property next to the original Columbus School so that his stepsons, Dave and Sam Warlick, could live close to the school in the winter. Their ranch at Vallecito was too far away, and the road was impassable most of the winter. The rest of the family lived in the lower country where their sheep had winter pasture. Then in the spring the family would be reunited when it was time to bring the sheep up on the summer high-country pasture.

The boys weren't really old enough to be left alone, but there was really no choice. The boys certainly learned a lot about the fine art of survival at a young age. Nowadays, social services would snatch the kids up in a second if it got wind of two grade school boys batching it alone all winter. Kids learned to be tough and self-sufficient in those times.

Charles and Edith Dunsworth with cousin Marilyn McCracken on the steps of the Dunsworth ranch house. Circa 1922. (Dunsworth Collection)

In 1924 the Dunsworths traded the Columbus property to the Knights. The old school sat on the west side of the road, and since there wasn't enough level space for a barn and teacherage to be added, they decided to move the school across to the east side of the road to the Dunsworth's property. The county wouldn't allow the move since the school was just sitting on a rock foundation, so they condemned it.

Another school was therefore built at the sharp corner on the east side of the road, and eventually a barn and a teacherage were added nearby. The old school was remodeled into a home and still stands there today.

After the children went through the eight grades at Columbus, they had to finish their high school education in Bayfield. Dave Warlick, Sr. talked about some of his experiences during his high school stint in the early 1920s:

> *The Old Man [Mr. Dunsworth] bought a house in*
> *Bayfield that my brother, Sam, and I batched in while we went*

to high school there. We had a healthy competition going on between the baseball teams in Allison, Ignacio, and Bayfield. There were quite a few fights after the ball games, but this one time, Peck and Tad Morrison were really going at it. Peck had Tad down and was really pounding him when Tad's father, Bob Morrison, decided it was getting too vicious. He picked up a rock to hit Peck with to get him to stop. Probably because both boys were moving around so violently, he missed Peck and hit his own boy right in the mouth, breaking some of his teeth. I'm sure he didn't mean to hit that hard, but things were getting too rough and needed to be stopped some way.

Harold and Chet McCoy told some of their Columbus School memories:

> *Most of the kids either had to walk or ride horses to school. It took three horses to carry us McCoy kids. You had to get up at five in the morning to feed the horses since that was a must. You didn't take a hungry horse to school. Dad was strict about that. The barn at school had stalls in it to keep the horses separated, so they didn't fight.*
>
> *I shouldn't tell this, but once Glen Glover got into the X-lax and ate the whole box, thinking that it was candy. They took him to school that morning, and the kids were riding in the back of the truck, and Glen couldn't get them to stop. What a mess! They had to turn around and take him back home.*
>
> *I remember when I was in the first part of the eighth grade. Lloyd Glover and Cecil Parks were going to blow the teacher up. Where they ever got a whole stash of dynamite, I don't know. They crawled in that hole down there under the school with the dynamite, and they were going to do it, too. Old Man Glover and Old Man Parks got wind of it and beat the hell out of them before they could do it. I guess someone got word to them. They would probably have killed all the kids, too.*
>
> *When we went to the Christmas program at school, Dad would hook up the sled in all the snow. We would heat big rocks in the oven and put them in a sack to put down by our feet to help keep us warm. Boy, we'd go down there and sing our hearts out, and we'd get oranges and candy. There was usually a program, too.*
>
> *The thing I always enjoyed the most was Thanksgiving and the 4th of July. They always had a community dinner and*

get together at Columbus. One year they had it over in the cot-
tonwoods. They had a rope and barrel and everybody rode the
"horse". Mrs. Richards made the best homemade ice cream,
and Mrs. Purcell made apricot pie that would just knock your
head off. Everyone went and had a good time. There were no
bad words and no fights.

After the construction on the dam was started, and the improvements on the roads were made, some of the children would be driven to school. Doris and Johnny Caviggia had a Chevrolet coupe with a rumble seat that they would haul kids to school in. They used to give rides to Freda and Tommy Beuten, Jerry Newman, the Turner girls, and a Renfro kid. They had eight kids packed into the coupe most of the time. Freda and Jerry Newman didn't get along, so Doris had to put Jerry in the rumble seat with a blanket wrapped around him, and she put Freda in the front.

Freda Brown said that when she moved to Vallecito and started school in 1945, there were only about eight kids going to school at Columbus School. But by the time she left to go to the Bayfield School for the upper grades, there had been a big jump in attendance. Some of the increase was attributed to the families of the workers at two sawmills that were in production nearby.

Studies at the Lowell School ended very abruptly. One year the school was having its annual Christmas party. They had an especially nice Christmas tree with lots of candles on it, and there were lots of presents beneath it. Everyone was exuberant with the beauty and the excitement of the season. But when they lit the first candle, the whole tree kind of exploded and set everything on fire. Nothing was saved. People were lucky to have escaped with their lives. That was the end of the Lowell School. The Lowell students were included in the Columbus School population after that.

The 1948-49 school year was the last year that school was held at Columbus School. Most of the small schools were incorporated into the Bayfield School System at that time. The small schools concentrated on the basics. Reading, writing, and arithmetic were their focus with a little bit of history and science thrown in.

The basics were fine for the eight grades that were taught in the small schools, but by uniting all these children into one school, they could offer a variety of other classes. The teachers could also teach larger groups of children at the same grade level at one time, since there were enough children to place them in separate grades. While this method got away from the intimacy of the small schools, it was a much more efficient system. Bus service to the outlying communities was also started, which was a great advantage for many people.

In January of 1954 the Moss School burned to the ground, leaving nothing but the chimney standing. A crew of men, who were plowing snow, discovered the still smoldering ruins the following morning. The school, a stucco, and adobe structure had been in use since 1908. Fortunately this happened after the school unification, so no classes were affected.

When school wasn't in session, the children were kept fairly busy helping their parents with work around home. When they reached their teens, some of the children worked at various dude ranches and resorts to earn spending money. But there was always time for play. Most kids had horses to take them all over the mountains. The ones that liked to fish had easy access to streams that were full of fish.

The rodeos that the Sullivans put on were pure delight to the local children. Many had not been previously exposed to the delight of the bottled Nehi that was found cooling in the Sullivan's horse water tank at these events. There were baseball games to play, and swimming in the nearby Pine and Vallecito Rivers was always an option, if one could stand the spine chilling pain of the icy water. There were tables laden with food to eat while watching all the rodeo events. The rodeos were wonderfully entertaining to the children.

The Fourth of July was also a major occasion. Whole families traveled to Bayfield for these events. For weeks in advance the *Bayfield Blade* advertised the events that would take place: "Ball Games, Hose Runs, Two Teams Pulling Contest, Team vs. 12 Men, Nail Driving and Sawing Contests — Ladies, Horses, Races, Foot Race, 'Crow Race', Moving Picture Shows and Dance. Prizes."

The children would wander the streets, gazing in open-mouthed awe at the sight of the Ute Indians dressed in their finest apparel with an assortment of silver and turquoise jewelry literally dripping from them. The Utes also loved this occasion. They came in wagons and stayed around for several days to make the most of it.

In 1994 a Columbus School Reunion was held on a picnic ground on the Pine River. There was quite a large crowd, and everyone seemed to be overjoyed to get to see each other again and to relive their old school days and the other events that took place in their childhood. The consensus was that anyone who had ever attended a one-room school was happy to have had the experience. It was almost like being in another close family.

In those days children had more freedom. Life for them was so much less complicated than it is now. Children knew their limits, and most of them knew they would receive a good spanking, or whipping, if they did anything drastically wrong, but they were allowed to roam pretty much at will and explore the countryside. It was a time period where parents didn't constantly have to worry about them as they do now since the world and its people have changed so much. Those were happy days, ones the Vallecito children of that era will never forget.

CHAPTER 9

Crime and Punishment

While almost all settlers came west to improve the lives of their children and themselves, they found they couldn't escape from crime and criminals no matter how far they traveled. Crime has always crept into the lives of otherwise civilized people. The new immigrants had been exposed to crime in the old country, and discovered it followed them into their new land. There were numerous killings as the wagon trains wove their way across the prairies and farmland. Usually the disputes were over women, power, or money. Sometimes liquor added to the problem.

The settlers in the Pine River Valley didn't escape evil completely when they settled here, but it was a fairly infrequent happening. Even as the early settlers were trying to build schools to educate their youngsters, a problem emerged — crimes over water. As people started farming and digging irrigation ditches to bring water from nearby rivers or streams to their thirsty crops, disputes arose over someone not doing his share of ditch maintenance or taking more than his fair share of water.

Nick Wommer was killed over a water dispute in the earlier years, and then on July 7, 1916 the news of a second terrible tragedy quickly spread. Henry Ludwig murdered Abner Lowell and his son, Hugh. A younger son, Frank, was wounded. Then Ludwig ended his own life eight hours after committing the crimes.

The shooting took place just east of the Lowell residence on the county road south of Columbus School. The dead son and mortally wounded father had been taken to the Lowell house, and a few neighbors had arrived to try to help. Hugh, the oldest son, had been shot through the head and died instantly. Mr. Lowell was shot through the right chest and lungs, with the bullet coming out under the right arm, and he was also shot through the hips. Mr. Lowell died about two hours after being wounded. The younger son, Frank, had been shot through the fleshy part of the right hip.

One version of the horrible affair was told by Mr. Lowell before he died. He said that Frank was taking some horses to the pasture and encountered Mr. Ludwig on the irrigation ditch, which was jointly owned by Lowells, Wommers and Ludwigs. Mr. Ludwig got into a quarrel with the boy about water. Mr. Lowell was in his house at the time, but he heard the quarrel and grabbing his shotgun, went to see what the problem was.

When Mr. Lowell arrived on the scene, he didn't see Mr. Ludwig, because he was hiding in the brush. Ludwig opened fire from his hiding place and shot Lowell through the hips, causing him to fall to the ground, and then shot him again as he lay on the ground. The second bullet went clear through his chest.

Hugh, who had accompanied his father, ran to him, asking Ludwig not to shoot him, but a bullet went crashing through his brain. The next shot was fired at Frank, causing his hip injury. After this happened, Mr. Lowell, who was in desperate pain, shot twice into the brush, trying desperately to save his boy and himself, but apparently causing no harm to Ludwig. Lowell stated that he took the gun with him because he hadn't recovered fully from a badly broken leg and was afraid he might have to defend himself.

Those who heard the shots said they had heard Ludwig's gun fire six shots, so Ludwig had probably run out of shells or Frank could have been dead by this time. When Frank first met Mr. Ludwig, he was not carrying a gun, but was holding a shovel. The gun must have been hidden in the brush where Ludwig retreated when he saw Lowell coming. He waited until Lowell was quite near to start firing. Fearing trouble, Mrs. Lowell had started toward the scene and had gotten half way there when the shooting began.

Ludwig had failed to help in cleaning and repairing the ditch that year, so according to the co-owner agreement, he was not entitled to any water. Nevertheless he had come that morning and closed Lowell's outlet, and turned the water down his own ditch to water his crops. Evidently he meant to guard the ditch with the gun.

In the aftermath Mr. Ludwig barricaded himself in his home and no one attempted to go in after him, but they chose to wait for the Sheriff and his associates to arrive. Sheriff Fassbinder gathered a posse, surrounded the Ludwig home at a distance, and waited for someone to reason with the hunted man. Mrs. Ludwig called out and said her husband would not be taken alive.

Mrs. Ludwig came out and after a time, she and District Attorney Lane started toward the house to try to talk to the barricaded man. While they were still a hundred yards distant, they heard a muffled sound. When Mrs. Ludwig went to investigate, she found the room filled with powder smoke. The rifle that had done such terrible damage was lying on the floor, with her husband's body hanging over a chair next to it, dead. A loaded revolver lay on the nearby table, and a loaded shotgun lay across the stove. This closed out the second act of the day's tragedies.

The heartbroken Mrs. Lowell was left to raise a younger son and daughter, besides her wounded son. Inquests were held regarding all the bodies, and verdicts were returned in accordance with the foregoing facts.

There would be no defendant to try for the crime. Ed Wommer told another side of this story:

> *Helen Burkett said that on the day of the shooting, which was July 4th, her family had just come home from a picnic up the Florida River when Henry Wommer came and told them about a big shoot-out. They were trying to round up people to surround Ludwig's house where he had barricaded himself after the shootings.*
>
> *Lowell saw Ludwig hiding behind a tree and shot at him with his small caliber gun, which probably didn't have the capability of doing any damage from that distance. Then Ludwig shot back with his more powerful rifle. The Lowell graves at the cemetery have the year of 1916 on them, but they don't have the July 4th date on them.*

In the years before national Prohibition, different states, counties or cities enforced their own laws to stop the flow of liquor into their communities. In 1914 the Ignacio and Pagosa Springs areas were dry, while the Bayfield area wasn't encumbered with such a law. In that same year Mrs. Andres Martinez was given a one hundred and sixty day sentence for selling whiskey at Ignacio. She was soon released from the jail in Pueblo on a technicality, so she never had to serve her sentence.

The Prohibition scene was being repeated all around the county and many people became involved in illicit activity as a way to make enough money to live on. Though liquor making was indeed an illegal operation, prohibition was considered by many to be a bad law. It was just one way for citizens to eke out a living in the challenging times and at the same time meet their neighbors' celebratory needs!

The courts in Pagosa couldn't seem to get convictions when they tried to prosecute bootleggers. Obviously, the local citizens didn't agree with the law in this matter. Many people mentioned receiving packages of "dry goods" from sympathetic friends in other locales, so the post office unwittingly played a small role in the liquor delivery business.

Vallecito had its own bootleggers in those times. Two enterprising young men, George Warlick and Arthur Dunsworth, had a still located high up on the hill to the west of the present Shoreline Inn. It was located in a small hidden canyon that had a tiny stream of water running through it. It was a small operation, but it provided them with some spending money, which was always in short supply in those days.

Dave Warlick, Sr., who was just a youngster at this time, and a young friend of his came up with the idea of "borrowing" a couple of jars of this brew to sell, so they would have a little money to spend at the big Fourth of July celebration that was approaching. The Utes would be in town, and since the other boy knew how to speak the Ute language, they could arrange a transaction with the Indians. The Utes were always happy to find a source of whiskey. Everything went as planned on the day of the celebration, so the boys had some money to spend, and the Utes had some forbidden firewater. Everybody was happy.

One woman had charges brought against her when one of her best customers died after drinking a batch of her brew. The poisonings often happened when iron piping was used to make the liquor. Eventually it was found that only copper and glass products were safe to use in the distilling process.

From January 1920 until December of 1933 prohibition was enforced throughout the whole country. There were investigations and a few prosecutions in the county, but the liquor business didn't seem to slow down. The pleasure the brew gave and the money it brought in seemed to outweigh the risk factors involved.

The W.A. Bay family arrived in the Bayfield area in 1890, and soon they were such a respected family that the town was named after them. When their son was shot and killed by a young lady some years later, the whole community was up in arms.

Emerald Patrick gave this version of the event: "I remember when his girlfriend shot the Bay boy. The story went that the girl worked for old man Bay, and the Bay boy got her in the family way. Her father went to talk to the boy one night, but the boy beat the girl's father up soundly. The next day, the girl took her father's gun and went over and shot the Bay boy."

Dave Warlick, Sr., happened to be in Bayfield and saw the deputies load the girl in a wagon to take her to the jail in Durango.

Emerald Patrick remembered another killing:

> *When we lived in Durango, Dave Day had one newspaper,* The Democrat, *and a fellow by the name of Woods had the other one,* The Herald. *The two men had been feuding for years. One day when Woods came out of Tittle's Pool Hall, Day shot him just as he was coming out. I don't think the law did anything to him. There was that one pool hall, and the rest were saloons from the old First National Bank building, on the west side of the street, to the next corner, which was 10th street. Decent women wouldn't walk on that side of the street. Prostitution was in full swing in those days.*

The following covers both the story and the story behind the story of another killing as several residents remember it.

Carl Brown gave some background:

> *Lee Rector worked logging for my dad and me. He had a shrunken leg and a limp as the result of polio when he was a kid. He was a vicious fighter and after he beat Pat Simpson several times, Pat said, "No more!" Pat bought a gun and wore it after that.*

Dave Warlick, Jr., added the next part:

> *When I was a kid living on the ranch over on Yellow Jacket Creek, I went to town to see a basketball game in Bayfield with Teddy Butler and his father, who was the Forest Ranger over there. The Fahrion boys were playing in the game between Bayfield and Ignacio that night, and it was the first basketball game I had ever seen. It was held upstairs over what is now the automobile repair shop.*
>
> *When the game was over, we went downstairs, and there was a fight going on across the street, about where the restaurant is now. I remember seeing a big guy, at least to me at twelve years old he seemed pretty big. And there was no fight to it. Lee was just mauling Pat. He was just picking him up and slamming him against a car, and Pat wasn't fighting back. Lee would just pick him up, again and again, and slam Pat against that car, then kick him a couple of times, and then pick him up again and slam him again. It just went on and on. I thought, "Why doesn't anyone stop this?" The next thing I heard was that Pat had gone into a saloon in Durango the next day and shot Lee.*

Earl Sullivan told the rest of the story:

> *I was only a half block away when the shooting took place and we heard the shot. Pat and Lee had ended up in the bar and started arguing. Pat had a shoulder holster on and knew he couldn't whip Lee, so when Lee Rector crowded him, Pat Simpson blew him away. Lee was handy with his dukes and had worked Pat over good the night before. The shooting was over Helen Burkett from the Florida Road and also over a horse race. Pat Simpson had some pretty good horses. In fact, he trained some All-American horses later on. Lee had a pretty good racehorse,*

*too, and between horse races and this lady friend, they ended up
in the Silver Dollar Bar on that fateful day.*

Pat Simpson was locked up, but he quickly got out on bail and
never did have to do time for the shooting. They ruled it was self-defense.
The killing happened in the basement bar of the First National Bank, now
the Wells Real Estate office.

Glen Glover remembered a killing that happened during the
mining days at Tuckerville:

> *One time there was a miner from up at Tuckerville that
> sneaked down here and killed someone here in the valley, and
> then went right back up there. When the law went up to question
> him, his friends gave him an alibi, so he got away with it.*
>
> *People used to say, "If you want to kill anybody, take
> them to Durango and kill them, and Durango will just turn
> you loose."*

CHAPTER 10

The Miners

T he promise of gold is what lured so many eager miners to the mountainous country around Vallecito, but crime usually seemed to go hand and hand with the search for gold. There were many killings and deceptions that were involved in the search for and the possession of this precious commodity.

Long before the settlers in this country caught "gold fever," the Spanish and the French were sent over by their leaders in Europe to search for the mineral treasures that the new country might hold. The Spaniards roamed much of the West in their search for treasure. They are known to have come very near to and perhaps into Vallecito itself, as well as far beyond. The French are not known to have come any further west than the Continental Divide above Pagosa Springs and Vallecito in their search for food for their hungry miners on Treasure Mountain, near Pagosa Springs.

Some of Vallecito's earliest settlers were drawn to the general area because of the gold and silver mines around Silverton and the La Plata Canyon, where Mayday and Parrott City were located. Some of these men became disillusioned after struggling in their search to find gold year after year. They decided to settle for other occupations, such as farming or ranching, or perhaps working for or starting a business venture.

Around 1913 the Cave Basin area above Vallecito had its turn as a mining "hot spot." Cave Basin is located on Middle Mountain, which lies between the Vallecito and the Pine Rivers. It reaches an elevation of about ten thousand feet.

A Ute Indian by the name of Jim Weaselskin found a source of gold somewhere up the Vallecito River and took some of it down to the Ute Agency at Ignacio to show people. Jim also gave some of his nuggets in return for favors near Vallecito. Word about Jim's gold circulated for years and whetted a few people's interest, but the first actual discovery of precious minerals made by white men was at Cave Basin in August of 1913.

This exciting vein of ore was found at only twenty feet in depth. The vein was around five feet wide and carried a pay streak of good copper ore and galena [lead ore] that was eighteen inches to two feet wide. As hard as the miners tried to keep this exciting find under cover, the secret was soon out. Runlett, Webber, Patton and Dr. White were some of the first miners to set up claims, but hordes of eager men soon followed.

The upper portion of La Plata County had been prospected on the Pine, Vallecito, and Florida Rivers for placer gold some forty years earlier.

Silver and copper were not sought at that time, and the earlier miners missed the gold in quartz. With the discovery at Cave Basin the area would be gone over with more intensive scrutiny.

The Bayfield Blade screamed the news of the excitement. In April of 1914 a party of six, who expected to make a couple of million dollars each, left Bayfield in Grant Gifford's carryall for the Cave Basin camp. They had four horses, a suitcase full of grape smash, a few tools and tents. Billy Gill, Charley Fassbinder, George Updike, Henry Pulvermiller, surveyor George Skoog, and Frank Mars were in the party.

They left at nine o'clock one morning and arrived at the Root Ranch, which was just above the dam, about five o'clock that afternoon. They found the roads were somewhat muddy from Bayfield to Vallecito, making for a slow trip. The group left the Root Ranch for Cave Basin the next morning with saddle horses and pack animals. They got within three miles of the basin with the horses, and from there were forced to use snowshoes.

Even in May 1914 the mine operators in Cave Basin had given up on getting a pack train into the basin until the latter part of June, because heavy, new snow had fallen behind Windy Point. It was reported that foot travelers had to make their trips down from Cave Basin early in the day, while the snow was still crusted. There was no trail open for livestock at that time.

In June 1914, the first wagon load of merchandise for Cave Basin went to the Porter place (Granite Peaks Ranch). It was so top heavy it

Sammy Dowell, right, well known Vallecito miner, and John Graves packed and ready to head out for another summer of mining in Cave Basin. Circa 1913. (Courtesy Durango Herald and Sally Deckers)

tipped over in Kirkpatrick Canyon but luckily lodged against a log which kept it from rolling down into the depths of the canyon.

It was also during this same time that John Root and Mr. Salabar started the Ignacio Liveries and Transfer Company and George Taylor created the Ignacio and Bayfield Stage Line for the purpose of transporting people to and from the mining areas. As the news of the mineral strikes spread, people would travel by train to Ignacio, and from there they would use the local livery services to transport them on to the mining area. Sometimes the liveries couldn't make it all the way, so the miners had to hike the rest of the way into the camp.

The heavily mineralized region covers the headwaters of the Pine River and its tributaries. Since the rich ore shipments were made in the fall of 1913 before the deep snows fell, a general scramble among the local people to get in on the ground floor had started.

The Cave Basin District was thought at this time to be headed for the biggest mining boom since Cripple Creek. Excitement was in the air! Everyone around was dreaming of grabbing on to this golden opportunity. Gold fever was hitting Bayfield like a ton of bricks! The Board of Trade organization in Bayfield found they had to do without the wealthiest and most influential citizens in town. They, like so many others, had left for the mining camps to gain even more wealth. There were hardly any men in town left to take care of the businesses. The women and children were left to do the work that needed done.

Bayfield Mercantile sent a two-ton load of goods up to their store they had established in Cave Basin. Even the mail carrier (mail was being delivered every Wednesday and Saturday) had to be replaced when George Taylor, the veteran mail carrier and freighter, hiked to Cave Basin to seek his fortune.

The Engineer and Mining Journal recorded the following Cave Basin mines: The Holbrook, Mary Murphy, Silver Reef, Mt. Runlett, Silver Moss, Ignacio, Three Queens, Bob White, Great Western, Duke, Bob Tail, Calumet, Basin, Grand View, Iron Mask, Jessie, Tucker, and the Tuckerville. Mining expert John Sarpe of Cripple Creek looked at Cave Basin in June 1914 and was especially impressed with Sammy Dowell's mine, the Holbrook, as well as the Mary Murphy Mine

According to a federal law passed in 1872, a miner had to do one hundred dollars worth of improvements or work on each mining claim they filed on. They had to come into town to the courthouse to file the necessary information each year, usually at the start of winter, when they called it quits for the year. Of course, some stayed in the mines throughout the winter.

Copper mine near Tuckerville on Middle Mountain above Vallecito Lake. This mine was active in the early 1920s. 1913 was the start of the busiest period of mining activity at Vallecito. It ended rather abruptly in 1928, except for a few hopeful souls that hung on a while longer. This mine was probably the only one with ore cars and tracks. (Courtesy Lorene Wheat)

Another option was that the miners could sell their recorded claim to a mining company for a dollar, plus receive up to seven thousand shares of capital stock in the mining company. In turn the mining company would do the hundred dollars worth of improvements on each claim they bought.

If miners could show they had found valuable minerals and had spent at least five hundred dollars on the claim, they could acquire title to the mine and land (up to twenty acres) by paying the government two dollars and fifty cents to five dollars per acre. The government had sold over 3.2 million acres since the law's enactment. Once the title was granted, the miner owned the land outright and there was no requirement that a mine had to be worked.

Although it never did cause the stir that Tuckerville and Cave Basin had, Sammy Dowell mined west of the Vallecito River for years before he and Clyde Van Dusen formed a mining company in September 1919. The company was called The Vallecito Tunneling, Mining & Milling Company and was incorporated under the laws of Wyoming. The president was R.S. Clements, and the secretary was Clyde Van Dusen.

Sammy Dowell had a partnership with the company. Sammy probably never did receive much money from the venture, however he did exchange many of the shares in the company for food with local women such as Addie Dunsworth and Sally Decker. Some of the shares were also exchanged for supplies, so his work was not all in vain.

The Mount Runlet Metals Company, whose home office was in Cortez, Colorado, set up their mining project at Cave Basin on September 3, 1927. Clyde Van Dusen was manager of the company. They ran an impressive ad in the *Durango Herald* to entice investors to purchase shares in their holdings:

> *$10.00 buys a 300 share block of stock and gives you a free six month option on a 700 share block at $15.00, which if taken up, will make you a full 1,000 shares at 2 1/2 cents a share. All shares carry a 100% cash guarantee.*

How could any investor pass up such a deal? There were claims in all directions from Tuckerville. Ore was carried down to the dirt road by burro trains, which were contracted at one dollar per burro load. Then the ore was loaded onto wagons, and later trucks, for the twenty-eight mile trip to the smelter in Durango.

The Scott's sheep range was up in the Cave Basin area where the mines were located. Sandy Scott said that when he was still a kid, he used to pack out ore on burros for some of the miners. They paid him a dollar a burro load, which was pretty good wages at the time.

Sammy Dowel traded this mining stock certificate to Addie Dunsworth for a dozen eggs.

Sandy said,

> There were three old Dutchmen that came in there and
> stayed two or three winters and high-graded the ore with an
> anvil and a hammer. They would break it up and pick out the
> good pieces. They would have several ore sacks full. I would go
> in and pack it out with burros, and they would send that to
> Leadville and have it processed. Then they would have a grub-
> stake to go back there the next winter and stay all winter again.
> They just never did come out in the winter.
>
> They weren't in Tuckerville, they were over in the other
> mine. It was the one way up on top in the cliff and the Mary
> Murphy Mine. There were two cabins there on top, and then you
> went on down the side of this steep cliff on a trail. You would go
> down, and there was one hole, then go down further to the next
> one, and then go on down to the third one. That's where the mine
> was. The Forest Service came up to talk to us about the
> Dutchmen, but the road got so muddy from the Vallecito side that
> they never came back up again. This was in 1924.

The Colorado No. 1 claim had a fifty-four foot tunnel with a
twenty-six inch silver vein that produced thirty-two ounces of silver per
ton. It also had a small percentage of copper and lead and a trace of gold.

The Excelsior Mine, which was located one and one-fourth miles
north from the Colorado, is on the same vein. Ore from the Excelsior has
been assayed from one hundred fifty to two hundred ounces of silver per
ton. John Moss, Charley Ylingling, Joe Grobecker, and Oscar Sims each had
one-quarter interest in the mine. In the same area, the A.R. Pierce claims
showed copper as high as thirteen and one-half percent.

There was a big meeting at the Strater Hotel for all the mine
owners in the Cave Basin and Tuckerville areas. A large mining company
wanted to buy the whole area for seven million dollars and then pro-rate
this to the miners, but fifty-seven percent of them rejected the deal, so it
all fell apart. Not long after that, everyone suddenly cleared out of that area
because there was no longer enough production to make it worthwhile.

An August 1914 article in *The Bayfield Blade* said, "The war has
knocked the bottom out of the metals market, or else shipments of ore
would be in full swing. Ore is there in great quantities when the market
goes up."

The Mineral Resources of the San Juan Primitive Area recorded that
the Holbrook, Mary Murphy, and the Silver Reef Mines brought fifty-four
tons of ore to the smelter from 1913 to 1928. Only twelve ounces of gold,

two hundred thirty seven ounces of silver, and twenty-nine hundred pounds of lead were removed. Their total worth was $3,200. It wasn't much to show for all the backbreaking hours of toil and all of the hardships the men and their families had to endure.

In 1929 L. M. Addington arrived on the scene and took over most of the claims in the Tuckerville area. He started the Hinsdale Mining, Smelting and Milling Company and promoted it extensively.

Sandy Scott remembered him well:

> *A man named Addington came in here and promoted those mines and sold stock back East and then got away with all the money and took off. He was a real crook. He had Frank Ludwig and Dad build the road that starts from the old bridge and goes on up through there to Tuckerville for him. And of course they built it with horses, since that was the only way they had to do it then.*
>
> *When they put that road in to Tuckerville, it had one little switchback that Addington's cars couldn't get around. I used to give him a little pull with horses around this switchback so he could make it on up. He had a Packard and a Model A Ford. I remember he always reached behind the seat and grabbed a pint of whiskey. Then he'd pull out the cork and take a big swig, cork it back up, and put it back before he drove on up.*
>
> *He owed Frank Ludwig and my dad $750 apiece for the roadwork. They attached his Packard for this work since he owed them the money, but he came to Frank and Dad and talked them out of it. That's the last they ever saw of Addington. And that was the end of the big mining boom at Vallecito.*

The main mining area at Cave Basin was called Tuckerville. It had a cook's building with a dining room and a storeroom in the back. There were some cabins built there that were still in use in the 1950s as hunting cabins. Many of the miners lived in tents. One can still see numerous old holes sprinkled all around the Tuckerville site.

Another mining site is a little ways up the mountain from Tuckerville and a mile or so to the right. It is in the flat, open area that still shows the blue and green copper-laden rocks that were uncovered during the mining days.

Cave Basin is on the Vallecito River side or the "back side" of Middle Mountain. It can be reached by turning left on a trail before you reach Runlett Park and Tuckerville. It circles down and around the back-side of the mountain and is at a slightly lower elevation. It is also pockmarked with mining sites and the remnants of a few old cabins are still visible. Unlike Tuckerville and the Mary Murphy Mine, which can be reached by vehicles, Cave Basin can be accessed only by foot or horseback.

The Mary Murphy Mine, which is on the cliff overlooking Cave Basin, can be reached by four-wheel drive vehicle by going through Tuckerville and on up the mountain approximately one-half mile before turning toward the left. From there one may continue climbing on up to the rim. The remnants of a cabin still stand near the trail that heads down the side of the cliff to the Mary Murphy Mine. The first tunnel is difficult to reach, but the second and third ones that are below it are easily accessible, if one doesn't let the fear of falling into the canyon far below hamper him.

George Parks and his son, Irvin, worked the old mine on Parks Hill for years. It gave them a dream of riches, but actually, it gave them more hard work than anything else. The mine was reached by going up the old trail through Dunsworth Park to the higher mountain above, which was known as "Parks' Hill" to old-timers, but is now known as West Mountain. There are still remnants of the old mine and cabin that bear witness to the Parks family's mining efforts.

Mutt Decker told of the mine that Elmer, Claude and Jim Decker had up by Roell Creek called the "Reggie King Mine." After you left the

Remnants of Tuckerville mining camp on Middle Mountain. Some of these cabins were still used as hunting cabins in the 1950s by Sandy Scott, Martin Safley and others. Circa 1954. (Courtesy Martin Safley)

Vallecito River Trail and turned east, it took about one and one-half hours to reach the mine. It was a switchback trail that did a lot of climbing. They packed the gold and silver out on burros and took it to Durango to be shipped. The vein ran out eventually.

Mutt remembered that once in November, when he was a junior or senior in high school, his dad wanted him to move all the stuff out of the mine before winter closed in. He started up there at sunup, taking four mules along to pack the camp equipment out on. It was snowing and the trail was slick by the time he got to the Vallecito Trailhead, so he had to be especially careful.

When he started up Roell Creek, the snow started coming down harder all the time, and he hated the job more and more as the snow got deeper and deeper. He had an eerie feeling, knowing that he was the only one up on that mountain. No one would know if he got hurt and he couldn't make it back down until it was possibly too late.

Mutt made it to the mine, got everything loaded on the mules, and started back down the trail with the mules slipping and sliding all the way down the switchbacks. He finally made it down off the mountain before dark and was very relieved to be back to civilization again.

The remnants of still another old mine site can be found by taking the Vallecito River Trail past the second bridge and going up Second Creek on a difficult trail. There are several old cabins and an old workshop with a wheelbarrow with the price tag still on it. The buildings are scattered over a rather large area on both sides of the creek. There are also remnants of an old stamp mill and a steam engine by the old mine shaft. Someone put a lot of effort into building the trail and the bridge coming into the mine. One source says this was the Decker Mine, but since Mutt Decker says the Decker Mine was on up Roell Creek, it's anyone's guess who the owner was.

Emerson Patrick talked of the stamp mill up the Vallecito River by Sheep Lake and Soda Lake, just above the falls. It was run by water, and it would stamp the ore (break it up) so they could pack it out on burros. He didn't give the name of the owner.

There were also mines around Log Town above the Florida River. Instead of reaching them from the Vallecito side of the mountain, the miners went up the west side on the regular trail from Transfer Park above present-day Lemon Lake. They stayed there in the mines all winter, because it was so difficult to get in or out at that time.

The Waldner family, who lived above the present-day Lemon Lake in the late 1800s and early 1900s, spoke of a band of Indians that did some mining in the area. These Indians would come to the Waldner place and trade gold for supplies. After John and Marion Kelley bought the Waldner property in 1930, they lived in the old log house for nine years while they were building a new log home. They pulled out a piece of chinking on an inside wall and found it to be a piece of a German newspaper dated before 1900.

It seems that few people really benefited from the hardships the miners and their families went through in their search for treasure, but it did however give them excitement and high hopes for a time. The gold that the Spanish miners found nearby is documented. Who knows, some lucky person may find the famed "Mine of The Window and "Weaselskin's Gold," both located far above Vallecito.

CHAPTER 11

Vallecito Dam

T he mining years had come and gone at Vallecito, and the population was holding fairly steady, when suddenly there was news of a major development that would change this quiet valley forever. A dam was going to be built, and a reservoir would displace some of the ranchland in the bottom of the valley! The news sent shock waves into the hearts of the people involved. If this happened, life at Vallecito would never be the same.

There was so much water coming downstream from melted snow in the high country, that both the Vallecito and Pine Rivers were filled to overflowing at times. So water was not usually a problem in the spring and early summer. However in late summer or during dry years, the farmers would see their crops burning up in the sun when there was no irrigation water left. There was also a great deal of land that could be planted and put to beneficial use, if water could reach it.

The influx of new white settlers who farmed and ranched and needed water for irrigating their crops was becoming a critical issue. When the U.S. government moved the Southern Ute Indians to a reservation on the lower Pine River Valley, the Indians were encouraged to take up farming, so they too needed the water. The Utes thought correctly that they should have first rights to the river's flow. Colorado's riparian water rights system gave them first rights, since they had been using water from the river long before the white man arrived. The 1868 Treaty that the government made with the Utes was the basis for their earliest water priority rights.

According to Colorado water law, which was established first in eastern Colorado, the first person to put the water to beneficial use is the first in line in the chain of water users. It was first come, first served. If there was only enough water for the first ten in a group of twenty men who filed for water rights, then so be it.

Eventually, there were dry years when the Utes needed what little water that was available, and many ranchers were left high and dry. The ranchers had already put in irrigation ditches, but if they didn't have water flowing through the ditches, they were useless. One year, Buckskin Charlie had to bring his tribe clear up to the Columbus Bridge area before they found water enough to carry back to the reservation. Something had to be done!

In October 1911 a flood washed out part of the town of Bayfield. After the June and September floods in 1927 did terrible damage, including washing out several bridges, it was generally agreed that it was time to do something about the situation. The ranchers, farmers, and Utes decided to work together on a solution to the water shortage. A dam would solve the water shortage problem and also help with flood control on both the upper and lower Pine River Valley.

After years of studies and meetings, a delegation from the Pine River Valley worked together, through a chain of command, to reach the top officials of the government, and a plan was successfully negotiated. The Pine River Project was drawn up and signed by President Franklin D. Roosevelt on June 17, 1937. This happened at the tail end of the Great Depression, so the President was still trying to provide jobs for the people and was quite receptive of the project. The original name of what we now call the "Vallecito Dam" was the "Pine River Dam;" however, even during construction, both names were in use.

The Bureau of Reclamation was put in charge of planning and building the project. One of the first jobs was to secure title for the land that would be involved from the present owners, and there were a number of them. Most of the landowners were not at all pleased to have their land taken, but they went along with it and accepted the government's offer of payment. Charlie Dunsworth was the holdout, but the government even-tually took part of his land by right of condemnation.

The Sullivans, Deckers, and Dunsworths owned most of the land needed. The other owners were the Pearsons, Wilmers, Oberts, and Curries. Most of these people would lose their homes, or would have to move them, if that was possible.

After the land acquistion phase was accomplished, the Bureau awarded the contract for logging the timber from the dam and lake site to Western Lumber Company. The timber to be removed was estimated at five million feet, log scale, merchantable timber, and the removal was done in one thousand days. How sad it was to see those beautiful old pines and firs fall to the ax.

Planning stage of Pine River Dam in 1936 looking south towards the Hugh Curry ranch. This ranch had to be moved to higher ground up Jack Creek. (Courtesy Fort Lewis Southwest Studies Center)

The Martin Wunderlich Company, which recently finished the construction of Wolf Creek Pass, was awarded the dam construction contract, which was estimated to take three years to complete. The company arrived on the site in May 1938 and started setting up an office, school, and cabins where the Vallecito Resort is now.

The Bureau of Reclamations began setting up its office and cabins on the other side (west side) of the road. Some of these cabins had been used for a Civilian Conservation Core (CCC) camp at the north end of the valley and were moved to the area to be used for a new set of government employees.

The Wunderlich Company soon established an employment office to aid local labor, and a special patrol was established on the road to the site to turn back the increasing number of outside men. Special Deputy Sheriff Norman Young's duty was to explain to the outsiders that local men were to be given the available jobs.

Three bulldozer-equipped diesel Caterpillar tractors were the first of the dam-building equipment that would be needed. The Caterpillars were to be shipped by rail to Ignacio, and then trucked up to the dam site. There was a problem, however. The road from Bayfield to Vallecito was a narrow dirt road that would never stand up to the weight of the heavy equipment. So contracts were given to build the roads that were needed. A huge old pine tree, which the road had simply been built around, had to be removed from the

View from southeast end of dam during dam construction. Some of Dunsworth ranch building and Sawmill Point in upper background. (Courtesy Fort Lewis Southwest Studies Center)

middle of the road, and a curve straightened out by Black Dog Corner to make way for the big machines.

Wunderlichs employed around seventy-five men by the end of May. Most of them were removing extraneous material and undesirable topsoil from the dam site or building the mess hall and office.

As more and more men were hired the need for employee housing became so great that more cabins were hurriedly thrown together to accommodate them. Soon the meadow around Red Creek took on the appearance of a small village. Tom Marshall, taking advantage of this situation, quickly put together a grocery store and a liquor store. Bill Miller and Bill Orchard ran a dance hall and a gambling hall. There were also rumors of a house of ill repute.

Housing was so scarce that people started boarding with nearby residents, and some even set up tents to live in. Every able-bodied man who had the desire to work had a job. If he didn't work directly in the construction project, he could supply meat or produce to the contractor's camps. Reed and Lucy Hammond capitalized on the situation by opening up a little restaurant close to the workers' cabins.

Their son, David Hammond, remembered that, for a time, there were two schools below the dam. One was for grades one through four, and the other was for grades five through eight. The contractor's school was there first, and a government camp school was built soon thereafter. The two schools eventually combined.

The Cole brothers started the Vallecito Transportation Line that carried workers from Ignacio and Bayfield to the dam site. They also had a bus that started in Durango and came to Vallecito via Florida Road. Return trips were made at the end of shifts.

Soon freight trucks started hauling 345,000 pounds of steel from the railroad at Ignacio to Vallecito. With all the comings and goings of people and vehicles, Vallecito was becoming a lively place.

Dee McCoy worked for the Bureau of Indian Affairs when they did some preliminary surveying in the dam area to decide exactly where the dam would be located. When the Bureau took over the project, he worked for them until he had trouble with a supervisor and suddenly quit. As he was walking off the job site, a boss from the Wunderlich Company stopped him and hired him on the spot. Good, experienced workers were in demand.

One of his first jobs up there was to pull a surveyor's car out of the muddy road where it was stuck. The old roads could be impassable. But as the roads were improved from the south, and then to the north along the west side of the lake, they soon were quite passable.

It took 3,738,000 cubic yards of crushed stone and earth to finish the dam structure. Much of the rock and gravel was taken from the very northwest end of the valley, close to the Vallecito Campground. The rock and gravel were taken to the construction site in huge dump trucks along the road on the west side of the valley. The resulting dam stretches over 4,000 feet across and is 162 feet high. Its width at the top is 35 feet, and the base width is 900 feet at its thickest point. The reservoir's capacity is 129,700 acre-feet, and its surface covers 2,720 acres.

In 1940 Annabelle Williams, a seventh grader from the Indian School in Ignacio, gave a good description of the work under progress during her visit to the dam. Annabelle wrote:

> We looked down the long ditch they called a conduit and watched the men working to spread concrete on the base of this part of the dam. The big spade would dig up the dirt and dump the dirt into one of the waiting dump trucks. The dump trucks hauled the dirt away and spread it out about six or eight inches deep. There was the roller with iron spikes about eight inches long they used on it. Then a tractor pushed this roller along the base of the dam. This was to harden the surface so the water wouldn't wash the dirt away.

View from the south of dam during construction. Bureau of Reclamation office and Government Camp at lower right. Wunderlich construction camp across the road above it in picture. (Courtesy Pine River Irrigation District)

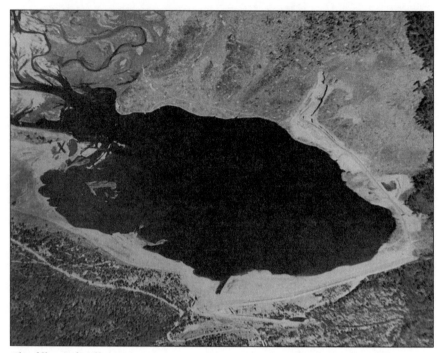

The filling of Vallecito Reservoir in 1939-1940. The cabins on Sawmill Point can still be seen (X). These cabins would still have to be moved. (Courtesy Dunsworth Collection)

As the water level in the new reservoir started rising, some of the old irrigation ditches that had been so painstakingly put in by Vallecito ranchers were inundated. The Patrick Ditch, which was put in around 1885, was one ditch that survived a watery grave, and it continues to wind its way from Grimes Creek to supply the surrounding area with water.

Although a few of the ditches were lost, the dam enabled many more ditches to be built, therefore benefiting many more people. The ranchers below the dam would have the water they needed to irrigate their crops in the dry years.

When the Vallecito Dam was finally completed in 1941, seven thousand people came to the dedication ceremony. The road leading to Vallecito was a big cloud of dust all day long. People from miles around came to see the amazing new lake and dam and were awe-struck by the beauty of the place.

Carl Goshorn landed the job of security guard, and he lived in the first government cabin. His job was to guard the road that went across the dam. He had one very strict rule that he made himself. For some reason, he would not allow Texans to cross the dam to fish on the other side. There were several disputes over the rule. When World War II started in 1941, no one was allowed to cross the dam due to security concerns — Texans or anyone else.

Johnny Caviggia was another local who worked on the project. His first job was pulling stumps out of the lake. He drove the government's speed boat, and he would hook onto the stumps and then pull them out. Then he would set the stumps on fire at the head of the lake. The experts thought the stumps would disintegrate within three years, but that didn't happen. The stumps seemed to petrify instead. When the lake is down those old stumps are still quite visible. They are proving to be useful as hiding spots for pike and other fish.

Johnny also had the job of painting part of the dam, by the spillway, all the way to the top. He talked about the good and the bad:

> I had to sweep it and put linseed oil on the top where the spillway goes over, and on down about a foot, all the way to the spillway. I made a scaffold to take me over so I could hang there on it to paint.
>
> One day I got real thirsty, so I was going down to get a drink of water. I let the scaffold down and got it too low, and the force of the water threw the scaffold and me up in the air, and I went over the spillway and landed in the pond below. I had to swim my way out of the pond. It was lucky for me that I could swim.
>
> The easiest job I ever had was testing the automatic gates at the dam with weights. Two weeks we were pumping water. We had a little old pump and would pump the water into the gates. All I had to do was smoke cigarettes and fish until the water got up to the gate level. It was the easiest two weeks of my life. I also painted all of those steps, from the bottom to the top of the inside of the dam. When I would come out for lunch, I couldn't hear anything after that pressure under there. Those big motors would drive me up the wall. It would take me a day to hear again.
>
> I was working there the night that the gates on the dam tripped. We had chained the gates so they wouldn't open so we could hold all the water we could for the irrigators and boaters. But we suddenly found there was too much water, and it was in danger of spilling over the top or breaking the chains.
>
> Steve Newman went down to phone a warning to the people below and tell them that the lake was too full, and he was going to have to release the gates and let some water out. But the weight of that water had so much force that it broke the

chains before he got back, and the water came over the spillway causing a flood below. I stayed up all night watching what was happening for Steve. My watching didn't help those people who got flooded though.

There is a fine line on how much water to keep stored in the lake. If you leave it at a high enough level to keep the boaters satisfied in the summer, the ranchers and farmers might not get enough to use on their crops. Because the lake is primarily for irrigation, the ranchers have the next right to the water after the Utes. If you end up in the fall with too much water in the lake and there is a heavy snowfall in the mountains above, there is a danger of the lake getting so full that a calamity might happen again. The lake superintendent has a difficult, high stakes job.

The Vallecito Dam has been a blessing for all concerned, as it collects water year after year. Today there isn't the extreme drop in water downstream on the Pine River in the late summer and fall, nor are there devastating floods.

Most of the visitors to Vallecito who go boating or fishing on Vallecito Lake don't realize the effort involved in the years of planning and the struggle to actually bring this project to fruition. They don't understand that the lake is here only because the old-time farmers and ranchers and the Ute people had the foresight and exerted tremendous effort to get it accomplished.

On January 10, 1983, these farmers and ranchers paid the government the final payment on the debt they had incurred in the construction of the Vallecito Dam.

Looking down on Vallecito Lake from Middle Mountain Road after the lake was filled. (Warlick Collection)

Disaster Strikes

T he summer of the year 2002 proved to be a season of historic drought and fire destruction throughout the West. As the drought worsened, fires rampaged in many locations, especially in the state of Colorado. Fire companies were overwhelmed with fire after fire in the tinder dry forests. The small mountain community of Vallecito Lake, located in the southwest corner of the state near the town of Durango, was certainly one of the hardest hit. The evacuation of Vallecito was perhaps the least timely, and the behavior of the fire in the mountains that surround Vallecito Lake was perhaps more extreme and caused more devastation than anywhere else in the state.

The thirty-nine day Missionary Ridge fire burned with a horrible ferocity that the firemen who worked to control said they had never before witnessed. Many stately stands of spruce, fir and pine trees were reduced to blackened hulks, lurking over the ruins of burned homes, downed power lines and poles, and the half-empty lake bed below. Over $40.8 million dollars was spent fighting the seventy thousand acre fire, and millions more are being spent on rehabilitation efforts in its aftermath.

Life will never be the same for the people of Vallecito as they now live under the perilous shadows of repeated floods and mudslides, which will wash the burned trees, ash and loosened rock down the steep, barren mountainsides. The aftermath will cause still more devastation to the remaining homes, businesses and roads below. Many harrowing nights and days were spent during the rainstorms that followed the fires, and many more likely lie ahead.

June 9, 2002 was a gloriously beautiful summer Sunday. The summer was starting out to be an unusually warm one, but the weather was great for the outdoor-loving people of Durango and its surrounding communities. Many people live at Vallecito for the area's lifestyle and its crisp mountain air. Exceptional hiking, biking, skiing, boating, fishing and camping are among the many activities that the Four Corners area is noted for. Not a soul had an inkling that this day was the start of a disaster such as this part of the country had ever before experienced.

Although great for outdoor activities, the warm weather wasn't good for the surrounding forests. The drought was the most severe in the 107 years of record keeping in Colorado. The winter of 2001-2002 had seen even less snow than the three previous low-snowfall winters. Rain had been in short supply for several years, leaving the scorched land in critical condition. As the water table dropped, wells were starting to go dry.

The pine trees seemed to be taking the worst beating. During the past two years they had shed an unusually large number of needles trying to survive. They were at an extreme point of distress, and everyone was praying for a rainy summer to help make up for the lack of snow and its accompanying snowmelt.

In the year 2002 the run-off from snowmelt was almost nonexistent at Vallecito. There was precious little snow in the high mountains surrounding the valley to funnel down the small streams into the lake. Much of it just soaked directly into the ground. This meant that the reservoir known as Vallecito Lake would not be replenished by the spring run-off as it normally was, and the lake would reach a record low.

The water in the lake never attained the depth needed to float the commercial marinas, so they didn't open for the season to the usual horde of eager fishermen and boaters who normally milled around them in the summertime. The concrete boat-launching ramp soon sat far above the water, which left it unusable. Without the availability of the boating concessions, business owners were starting to worry about losing much of their summer business as much of the reason that visitors came to Vallecito to vacation or to spend the summer months was because they liked to fish or boat.

There were meetings between County Emergency Preparedness Manager Butch Knowlton, Sheriff Duke Schirard and the La Plata County fire chiefs to discuss the extreme fire danger that the warm weather and the dried-out forests were causing and to work out a disaster plan. Fire bans were put in place that disallowed any open burning, and citizens were implored to create a defensible open space around their homes. The men knew this parched, tinder-dry country was ripe for disaster as any tiny bit of carelessness could start a major, far-reaching fire.

The people at Vallecito were starting to worry about getting out of the area if a major fire started in their valley. With only one way in and out of the lake community, they would have no way of escaping if County Road 501 was to become blocked by fire.

A community meeting was held at the Vallecito Chamber of Commerce building at which county representatives explained to the residents that they had a safe zone readily available to them if such a problem arose. Since the lake was extremely low, there was a large expanse of empty land at its upper end where there were no trees or vegetation to burn. The people were told this would be an excellent, easily reached safe place for people to bring their prized possessions and to come and stay until the danger had passed or they could be rescued.

Therefore on this sunny Sunday people in the community went about their normal activities. It was the start of the summer tourist season, and the lodges and restaurants felt it was the beginning of what, they hoped, would be a profitable season. People were hiking, horseback riding, or engaging in work around their homes that day. Virginia's, The Buffalo Gap, Shoreline Inn, and Marilyn's restaurants were all starting to get larger groups of customers. It was needed as most of the restaurant and lodge owners' income was derived from the summer's tourist population and the summertime residents.

The peaceful day was suddenly interrupted at 2:30 P.M. when Durango dispatched a fire crew to a small fire that had started in a ditch near the first switchback on Missionary Ridge Road, about twelve miles northeast of Durango. Investigators later reported that it was apparently started from a spark of undetermined origin. The temperature at the time was 87 degrees, and with the scant 1.31 inches of rain that had fallen that year, it didn't take much to cause a spark. Perhaps a cigarette ash or vehicle muffler was the culprit. Perhaps the spark came from a slack safety chain between a truck and horse trailer that a wrangler was driving up to a base camp far up the mountain. No one will ever really know.

A few Vallecito residents happened to be near enough to their police/fire scanners to hear immediately that a fire had started north of Durango. Boy! They sure breathed a sigh of relief that it was all the way over the mountain — far away from Vallecito. The local people had just been holding their breath for fear that a fire would start in their area. There were so many out-of-state people visiting who didn't understand the extreme fire danger in the dry, high altitude country, that they may not have been as careful with their cigarettes, outside trash burning, or barbeque grills as the year-round residents were learning to be. Not every one was aware of the strict fire bans put in place by wary county officials.

The century-long fire suppression efforts, as well as the pressure put on politicians to curtail logging, had created densely thick forests which were ripe for a catastrophic fire. The San Juan National Forest around Durango and Vallecito had the driest air mass in the nation at the time the fire started, and it took off at an amazingly fast pace. Within four hours it had consumed almost six thousand acres as it raced from a 7,500 foot elevation, right up the mountains to an elevation of 11,000 feet — totally devastating everything in its path.

The responsibility of managing and suppressing the fire fell on the shoulders of Ron Klatt, fire management officer for the Columbine Forest Service Ranger District and Bureau of Land Management Field Office, which was responsible for the area that included Durango and Bayfield. Klatt soon realized that the furiously burning fire was not going to be quickly stopped. The rugged, steep mountains and deep valleys would be extremely difficult for fire fighting. Some of the area was in the wickedly dangerous terrain of the Weminuche Wilderness.

During the first few days, the fire would make swift uphill runs on the ridges, and then stop, sometimes throwing embers for a half-mile ahead. These new fires would make runs of their own, spreading the blaze farther and farther at an ever-quickening pace.

Forest Service tanker planes started dropping slurry on the advancing fire to try to stop its progress into the wilderness area. Smaller spotter planes and helicopters were in use by officials who were looking over the fire scene to try to plan their fire-attacking strategy.

For the first couple of days, a local Type III Forest Service team and members of local fire departments battled the spreading blaze. On the third day the fire had grown to 9,500 acres and was large enough for a higher-level Forest Service Type III team to be called into service. They would bring added reinforcements to help with this monstrous fire, which had already spread eastward up Missionary Ridge and then made runs both north and south, lapping up vast stretches of forests in its ever-broadening path.

Fire doesn't usually burn aspen groves because of their normally high moisture content, but due to both the drought-ravaged condition of the aspen and the heat generated by the rampaging fire as it consumed the dense forests with its dry underbrush, the aspens didn't begin to stop or even slow the fire. It simply devoured them along with the spruce and pine.

The people at Vallecito weren't comfortable with the direction the fire was heading, but with the Florida River and Lemon Reservoir in its path, they figured that it would be stopped even if it reached that far. Many felt that surely it would never get over on their side of the mountain. Still there was unease. People were getting tense.

Carl and Freda Brown on Cool Water Ranch were quietly packing up some of their most important possessions and hauling them out to a safer area. Some thought they were really jumping the gun. Surely this wasn't going to be necessary, although it did make some neighbors wonder what the Browns knew that they didn't know. A few residents started loading a few of their own important things into their own vehicles, just in case the Browns' fears proved to be justified.

By Wednesday, June 12th, the fire had reached the hills directly above Lemon Reservoir's northwest side, gobbling up the forest as it spread with outstretching fingers, and leaving ghostly, black hulks of trees on the smoking, ash-covered slopes in its wake. Now and then there were patches of green trees, left untouched, but next to them were huge swatches of burned areas covering much of the mountainsides.

By the next day, a smoke plume that rose thousands of feet high could be seen over Durango. It was visible for many miles. Smoke was getting thick as far away as the New Mexico state line, especially in the early morning hours. There were frequent gusty winds that pushed the fires along at incredible speeds at times. Several new fires were started as the clouds of fiery embers fell into Young's, Shearer and Red Creek canyons. Some smoke was drifting into Vallecito by this time, and the locals were realizing that the fire was getting closer and closer.

Someone noticed that a horse trailer and other vehicles had been left at the Burnt Timber Trailhead above Transfer Park at the north end of Lemon Reservoir. Locals knew what this signified. Fire officials were informed that there were still hikers and horses on the trails above Lemon Reservoir. Planes were sent over to try to spot the unsuspecting souls, and helicopters were put in service to make some daring rescues.

Many of these hikers and trail-riders hadn't known about the start of the fire, and others had no idea it was heading their way. The whole atmosphere became more alarming as each day passed and the many-headed monster spread its tongues of flame in varying directions.

As the winds blew the fire toward the southeast, causing it to burn down towards the Lemon Reservoir's west side bottomland, the firefighters waged a desperate battle to save the historic ranch buildings that were built by the Waldner Family around the year 1900. The ranch, owned by John and Marion Kelley for the last thirty-five years, is the ranch where the old Ute Indian, Weaselskin, used to stop and trade gold nuggets for a hearty meal as he made his way across the valley.

The ranch has been in the Kelley family since 1930 when John's grandfather purchased it. The Kelleys chose to stay and risk their lives to care for their livestock and protect the log home they had worked nine long years to build. They soon had plenty of help as friends with water trucks and pumps, Upper Pine firefighters, and volunteer firefighters from New Mexico streamed over the narrow, wooden bridge to gain access to their remote ranch.

The two subdivisions on the east side of Lemon Reservoir would be in danger soon if the fire came across the Kelly ranch or over the upper end of the valley. So far the fire had burned in the higher country where it hadn't endangered very much private property, but the whole situation was changing to a more critical stage. The fire was spreading to the lower country, nearer and nearer to housing developments.

On the fifth day Ron Klatt and other county officials met with the fire-behavior analyst at the La Plata Fairgrounds, where a camp had been set up to house the fire crews arriving from out of the area. The analyst predicted that, based on his models and the way the fire had acted until now, it would be at least four or five days before the fire could reach the subdivisions near Lemon Reservoir and Florida Road.

This information was passed on to the people from Aspen Trails, Los Ranchitos, and other subdivisions north of Florida Road at a meeting. No sooner had the meeting ended than County Commissioner Fred Klatt, Sheriff Duke Schirard and Emergency Manager Butch Knowlton knew they would have to eat those words. They were hurriedly informed that the fire was behaving in a very unusual manner and was advancing along with a southeasterly wind at an alarming rate. The subdivisions were indeed in danger because of the monstrously growing wall of flame. It was decided that three of the nearest subdivisions needed to be evacuated immediately.

As one of these subdivision residents said later, "One minute they said we had four or five days; an hour later they were beating on our doors telling us to get out as fast as we could. We couldn't even take time to find our pets before we had to leave." Fortunately the wind quieted and the fire calmed as night fell. At this time the local firefighters, who are more attuned to saving structures, worked endless hours to keep the fire from reaching the homes.

The federal firefighters were geared more towards fighting forest and land fires than they were to structure fires. They had strict rules governing how many hours they could work before taking a rest period. Local firefighters had none of these guidelines to follow, and sometimes it was their neighbors' home or even their very own home that needed protecting. They worked frantically for seemingly endless hours, so these people would have a home to come back to. A few homes were lost, but they succeeded far beyond their own or anyone else's expectations.

A few ranchers and other individuals with heavy equipment donated their time to carve fire lines around the houses to keep the fire from spreading closer. Tiffany rancher, Steve Pargin, drove his huge 10,000-gallon water truck, normally used to supply water to his herd of cattle, to the fire scene to add to the firemen's limited water supply. Everyone and anyone who was able contributed to the effort to stop the spreading monster that was coming nearer and nearer to the populated areas of Lemon Lake and Florida Road. If the fire moved through the subdivisions to the east, there was a very good chance it would come over the hill to the Vallecito side of the mountain.

By Friday the fire had enlarged so much and was threatening so many homes that the National Guard was called in to assist in the attempt to stop this raging giant. They also manned the road blocks that kept unneeded people out of the critical areas. There were now nine hundred people fighting the fire as it engulfed more and more land. Insurance companies no longer wrote policies on property anywhere near the fire zone.

The Red Cross opened a shelter for the evacuees in the Bayfield High School so displaced people would have a place to go. They would need food and other necessities that they didn't have time to gather up before leaving. Motel rooms were scarce in Durango during the tourist season, so cots were provided until these folks could make other arrangements.

On Saturday, the southeast winds drove the fire into such a frenzy that a two-hundred foot wall of flames towered so high that it could be seen from as far away as Bayfield. The Tween Lakes and Enchanted Forest subdivisions, near the intersection of Florida Road and Highway 501 leading to Vallecito, were evacuated.

West Mountain, which lies between Lemon and Vallecito reservoirs, kept Vallecito residents from seeing the advancing flames, but they could see the billowing smoke to the west at times. Anxiety ran even higher. Radio reports were sketchy on the weekend, but residents with scanners knew that the danger of the fire reaching Vallecito seemed imminent and some people started to load valued records and possessions into their vehicles.

Around 6 P.M. scanners broadcast the excited voices of local firemen, warning each other that the fire had topped the high ridge to the west of Cool Water Ranch and was starting to head down the hill towards the east, spreading outward as it came. People with scanners started to call friends who had asked to be warned if the situation got too alarming. Many of the summer residents were older and didn't want to be trapped in the valley away from medical help. They all knew about the safe zone, but many didn't want to be trapped there with only the food or water they took with them and with no toilet facilities for who knew how long.

As the news of the fire's progress got more alarming, some residents hurriedly finished loading their vehicles with whatever they thought they might need and started down the road leading out of the valley. This author insisted that her husband take down the bear rug that hung on the wall and load it into her car before she would leave. I had killed that bear a few years ago and doubted that I could ever replace it. I had already placed the manuscript, tapes and pictures for this book in my car several days earlier as a precautionary measure, and I now also loaded my computer. Different people had different things that were important to them.

Many people didn't get word about the seriousness of the situation right away. The officials at a meeting at Vallecito had told them just two days ago that the fire couldn't get here for four or five days and hopefully it would be stopped far short of Vallecito. So on Saturday evening, Virginias Restaurant and the Buffalo Gap were still serving dinner to locals and tourists alike. By the time the Sheriff's Department decided that Vallecito needed to be evacuated, the restaurant owners and employees weren't given time to put away food or do anything else. They had to get in their vehicles and leave!

Some people, including health-impaired Don and Jean Lochtrog, were desperately trying to get out of the valley but found themselves herded to the "safe zone," where they had to spend an uncomfortable night in their automobiles as the chilly mountain air settled in. A number of people had already brought vehicles, boats and campers out to the safe zone for safekeeping. Don and Jan McCain brought their antique car collection, so it would be safe.

As people made their way down Vallecito's only road out, they saw the fierce fires up Jack Creek and Red Creek canyons and the flames that were lapping their way over the ridge across from Carl and Freda Brown's home on Cool Water Ranch. As the fire progressed along the ridge, it was throwing fireballs that could reach out a half-mile. The fire ran like molten lateral rivers across the thickly wooded mountainside, spreading the ever-growing fire onto new territory and always closer to the Browns' ranch buildings.

It was a monster that no living person in the locale had ever witnessed before, and they hoped to heaven they would never be a witness to such a sight again — especially not so close to where they lived.

Florida Road was now closed due to fires still burning over there, so the train of vehicles had no choice but to head on down to Bayfield where they were informed that they needed to stop and check in at the Red

Beauty along with destruction. Photo taken near Warlick's boat dock on the southwest end of Vallecito Lake. (Courtesy of the Denver Post, *Shawn Stanley photographer)*

Cross Shelter at the Bayfield High School. It would allow their friends or relatives to locate them and find out if they had made it out safely.

Quite a number of Vallecito's summer residents had motor homes or travel trailers, which they brought out with them, so one section of the parking lot was soon filled almost to capacity with such vehicles. These people were the lucky ones, since they had their own beds and facilities with them.

Snacks, drinks, and necessities were provided; and rest rooms, showers, and cots were available. By morning, meals were being served, and Alltel had set up complimentary phone lines for the evacuees' use.

Many people tried to sleep on cots under the bright lights of the school auditorium amidst the unsettling noises of people stirring all around them. Some of the folks soon chose to try to catch a little sleep in their cramped but somewhat quieter vehicles. Cars streamed into the parking lot until it had almost reached capacity, and still they came. The Bayfield high school had probably never hosted a larger crowd than it saw in the coming two weeks as the Red Cross registered 2,183 people at the location.

Some people had friends or relatives nearby who could put them up. Motel rooms in Durango were at a premium, since the summer tourists that swarmed to the area every year usually filled them. A few people found they could get reasonably priced rooms at Sky Ute Lodge in nearby Ignacio and gratefully made their way to the solitude of a quiet place to get some sleep. Some of the people were from Vallecito's elderly community and were not in the best of health. They were perhaps the ones that suffered the most.

The day following the mass Vallecito exodus was a Sunday. The Red Cross and local volunteers were serving meals, snacks, and drinks to the horde of bewildered evacuees who milled around like sheep as they began to realize that this disaster had really happened, and they tried to figure out what to do next. Some were in an almost dazed condition.

Some had forgotten their urgently needed medicines, and others wanted desperately to go back to get a tent or camper and warm clothes and sleeping bags that they hadn't had time to bring out. Sheriff Schirard finally granted the people with the most urgent requests permission to go back into the closed areas for just long enough to get what they needed and then come immediately back. The fire was close to the highway, the only escape from the area, and it was anyone's guess how fast or in what direction the prevailing winds would take it.

One couple, Glenn and Linda Trewet, had to leave without their treasured camper on Saturday night. It was parked alongside a friend's storage building just below the dam. It was hurriedly retrieved Sunday morning just as the fire was trying to cross the road by Vallecito Resort, and they had to make a desperate run to out-flank the flames. Firemen were trying to keep the fire from burning the homes and the resort at the base of the dam near Jack Creek. At least the couple would have a temporary home for them and their four dogs for the next two weeks. The building the camper had been parked beside burned to the ground that very night.

Others who had made hurried trips back home brought whatever tents and gear they could rustle up to share with needy friends or strangers, who would soon become new friends. Helping each other so all could survive this ordeal was the unspoken agreement amongst the people.

Later that day a small tent city appeared on the school's soccer field — a place where many Vallecito residents camped for the following two weeks. The school was kept open for rest room use and showers, and the Red Cross was always supplying food, water, or most any small item anyone might need. Many people with campers or tents moved to Bayfield's RV Park in the next few days. It soon became jammed with the unexpected guests, but the owners wouldn't turn anyone away in this hour of need.

A most beautiful thing happened during this dark time when people didn't know if they still had a home to go back to or not. People were helping other people in any manner they could. The traumatized evacuees shared what few items they had managed to grab as they made their escape with anyone around who needed them. Tylenol, aspirin, and hairbrushes were bandied about along with tents, blankets, and clothing. The clothing didn't all fit perfectly, but it served its purpose. Tears were shared. Old feuds and grudges were forgotten and hugs and kind words took their place as the people all worked together to survive the disaster.

A few single women, who had never slept in a tent before, gladly accepted the loan of a tent from some kind friend or stranger. They simply needed a little space of their own to sleep in, and a place to keep what scanty possessions they still owned.

Jan Alexander, the former owner of the Buffalo Gap Restaurant, gladly accepted the loan of a camper from the friend of a former customer and joined the Vallecito gathering at the campground. Bayfield friends and the Vallecito folks who were lucky enough to have a relative nearby, kindly brought meals to help their homeless friends keep their spirits up.

The Bayfield residents weren't under the black cloud of uncertainty, but many of them turned out to help the Red Cross serve meals or help in any way they could. Many kept other people's evacuated pets in their own homes, and offers were extended for various types of help.

The evacuees were overwhelmed by the offer of generosity. Some were offered a number of places to stay, but as they watched the billowing clouds of smoke and flames to the north, they were under tremendous pressure to get back and see if they still had a home or a business to go back to.

Sheriff Schirard, Butch Knowlton, and various Forest Service Officials would meet with the evacuees every morning at the High School to inform them of the fire's progress. A new map was presented every day to show the path the fire was now taking and to explain what they expected to happen next. It was a waiting game as the fire roared on and on.

By Sunday night the fire had enveloped much of the mountain on the west side of Cool Water Ranch and made its way into the lower reaches of Red Creek and Jack Creek where they crossed Highway 501. The Pine River Irrigation buildings and nearby homes, as well as the Vallecito Resort RV Park near Vallecito Dam, were perilously close to being incinerated. The many firemen who swarmed in from nearby communities fought a tremendously hard battle that saved these structures, but one home and another building on the opposite side of the highway were lost that night.

As the flames crossed Jack Creek, the winds drove them at a furious pace through the heavy timber, and then they went up and over the steep slope to the north into Dunsworth Park and Lake Vista Estates. The flames reached from two to five hundred feet in height and consumed eleven homes in that area with such an intensity that scorched foundations, a few chimneys, charred remnants that once had been vehicles, and an almost unrecognizable horse trailer was all that remained. The towering, steep hills surrounding Dunsworth Park were now covered with nothing but smoking blackened sticks and ash.

Amazingly six homes and a well house still remained standing, even though a few of the homes were located beside structures that were now charred ruins. The well house that remained, housed the well that served the subdivision, so the water supply was spared and could be ready for use again after new wiring and electric service was restored.

By Monday, June 17th, the fire had burned 30,800 acres and was still growing at an amazing speed. Dave Warlick was able to make his clandestine way to the Dunsworth Park and Lake Vista Estates area and see that the fire had already swept through with a ruthless vengeance and taking a tremendous toll. The few firefighters who still remained at this nightmarish, smoke-filled scene looked like ghostly apparitions as they tried to put out the numerous smoldering fires where once homes had stood amidst a magnificent stand of old growth timber.

The cabin that Dave had grown up in was now a smoldering pile of rubble. Only the tall chimney remained intact. His other, smaller cabin, with its once thick stand of trees, was also burned to the ground. A long length of fire hose had been left lying along the road. His experience as a fireman, coupled with the obvious intensity of the fire, told him that the firefighters working on the fire had almost stayed too long and finally had to just "cut and run" as the wall of flames came down on them. It was almost a miracle that the firemen could have saved any of the homes without losing personnel.

As Dave drove on north on Highway 501, he found that his residence, which was nestled along the cabins and businesses stretching along the south end of the lake, was still standing, and he breathed a grateful sigh of relief. Now he faced the task of going back down the mountain to tell his anxiously waiting neighbors which homes were lost and what still remained.

The relentless flames next jumped across the road near Camp Kanakuk, with its multitude of structures, which stood on the old Glover Ranch. It took a major effort involving slurry bombers and firefighters to save the camp. However the firefighters couldn't keep the fire from jumping the nearby Pine River to the east. The fire was too large and too hot to let a river stop its progress.

The flames burned along the lower side of the dam, swooped through the forested land below, then plunged across the Pine River at this location. It burned both to the south and to the north as the prevailing winds changed. The fire swept up the slope near the Forest Service campgrounds on the east side of Vallecito Lake and then raced up the steep mountainside burning two more homes. Then it turned south and headed towards the densely populated Forest Lakes Subdivision. The residents

Fire charred remnants of the home that Dave Warlick, Sr. built in 1937 near Dunsworth Park and Lake Vista Estates. Eleven homes burned in this area during the fire. Only six remain. (Photo by D. Warlick)

were soon evacuated and joined the other refugees; however the Forest Lakes homeowners were allowed to return home much sooner than Vallecito residents since their homes were soon out of imminent danger.

At the same time, the fire was lapping its way through the heavy timber on the west side of Vallecito Lake. Flames reached hundreds of feet above the treetops. Normally, a fire slows down as it heads downhill, but this one didn't. Sheets of flame broke off in a rolling vortex as it came racing down the mountain as a tree-scorching crown fire and roared into the north end business district where the Chamber of Commerce Building, Buffalo Gap Restaurant, and other buildings were located.

At this point a remarkable thing happened. It just so happened that Detective Dan Bender, Sheriff Duke Schirard, and Emergency Manager Butch Knowlton were nearby and witnessed an unimaginable spectacle. No one would have ever believed their story if Lieutenant Dan Bender hadn't caught it on his video camera.

As the fire came raging down upon the buildings, a series of fiery tornadoes developed and swirled across the ground onto the empty lakebed, which had been declared a "safe zone." The swirling dervish, called a vortex, scooped up the dry sand and whirled it high in the air along with the fire, causing a fantastic entity that rolled across the barren lakebed and the surrounding area. One after another, the tornados formed, mixing fire with swirling, flaming sand and taking it hundreds of feet into

Vortex forming on west side of dry lake "safe zone." Note vehicles parked in foreground for safety and Rocky Mountain Store and Buffalo Gap Restaurant. (Courtesy Heather Kinailik)

the air as it skipped here and there along its merry path. The tornados pulled up giant full-grown pine trees by their roots and snapped others like twigs. It was a truly awesome spectacle!

Not a soul who witnessed the amazing event expected either the Chamber building or the Buffalo Gap to be standing when it finally ended after some twenty minutes. But when it came to a stop, the Chamber building had some roof damage, but the nearby businesses all remained intact. However, the so-called "safe zone" looked like a war zone with scattered cars, trucks, campers, and boats that were burned or blown away in a scene of wild disarray. Thankfully it happened while the spot was uninhabited — or almost so.

Seventy-nine year old Shelby Parmenter had stubbornly refused to leave his home on Ho Hum Drive near the north end business district. Deputies couldn't force anyone to leave, but they did their best to encourage them to go. Shelby felt he could save his home if he stayed by keeping it and the surrounding trees wet. If the fire got too close he could retreat to his basement. Later that day, firefighters came by and told him that there would be no oxygen for a period of fifteen to thirty minutes while the fire passed over his house. They finally convinced him to at least go to the "safe zone" in the dry lakebed.

Shelby drove down and parked beside a twenty-foot pontoon boat, thinking it would afford him some shelter, but soon realized that wasn't going to be enough protection. Giant embers started falling and swirled all around him. Boats and other flying objects went sailing over his head, and

Vortex aftermath and remains of Northend Marina. (Courtesy Heather Kinailik)

debris broke all the windows out on one side of his car. The inferno sweeping the west side of the lake, and the fire-spawned tornadoes that came roaring through the lakebed combined to make a deafening noise. The smoke-filled air was so thick he could hardly breath.

"It sounded like ten freight trains going through, and you were standing right there," Shelby said. "When I looked around once, flames were all around. It looked like a picture of hell."

After the whole episode was over and he looked at the devastation around him, Shelby had to wonder how he had remained alive in all this destruction. Burned out vehicles and parts of boats or trailers were scattered all around him or in some cases had completely disappeared.

He slowly drove up the road toward his home, not knowing what to expect in the fire-stormed neighborhood. But there it was — his home was still standing. Three of his neighbors' homes burned to the ground, but his efforts had not been in vane. Surely someone up there had been looking after this determined man and his home.

Sheriff Schirard had this to say about the incident, "It created at least six tornadoes. It pulled a car off the ground and flipped it, and a boat just disappeared. Buffalo Gap and the Chamber of Commerce were engulfed in fire, yet it now looks like it always did."

The spectators told of birds in flight dropping dead to the ground, and how one of the tornadoes knocked down a whole swath of large trees near the old Meadowlark Ranch, breaking them off or uprooting them.

Unfortunately the upper side of the highway didn't fare much better than the "safe zone." The green was gone from the surrounding hill, and only black sticks remained standing amidst the ash and smoking embers. Several more homes had been consumed on or near Ho Hum Drive as the wall of flames came in. The raging giant had grown so huge that it was totally uncontrollable. The hope was that it could somehow be herded from the populated areas of Vallecito towards the wilderness above, where it might burn itself out in the thin air of the higher altitude.

Fire Incident Commander George Custer said that this fire was so powerful it created its own weather. Its extreme behavior induced the vortexes that literally sucked all the oxygen out of the fire. They are incredibly dangerous because there is no way to control them.

By June 19th President Bush declared the State of Colorado, with its numerous fires, a major disaster area, meaning that the Forest Service could send in the top firefighting teams in the country. Fires were still spreading on the Animas River side of the fire, and firefighters from all over the country were swarming into the Durango Fairgrounds where a shelter had been opened for the people who had been evacuated from the western side of the fire. A tent city was set up to house the ever-growing number of firefighters.

Helicopters were very much in evidence as they scouted out the directions of the fires and sucked up slurry or scooped up water to drop on the edges of the crawling blazes in the hopes of slowing them down. Air tankers were constantly flying between their base at the airport and the fire scene with their precious loads of slurry. At one point they ran out of fire retardant and had to lose valuable firefighting time until it could be replenished.

When the fire that was sweeping north along the east side of Vallecito Lake reached the Pine River, it roared up the canyon to the east where the Wilderness Trails, Teelawuket, Granite Peaks, and Penn ranches were located. Wilderness Trails was still operating as a guest ranch, and guests and horses were quickly evacuated down the narrow Pine River Canyon.

Because of the narrowness of the canyon, the fire surged across the Pine River to start a huge blaze on Middle Mountain to the north. As the fire crews made a little progress in one place, it took off in another direction. It was on Middle Mountain that Oregon firefighter Alan Wyatt was killed when a huge, fire-damaged aspen tree, without any warning, fell on the experienced woodsman.

While Wyatt was the only human casualty of the Missionary Ridge Fire, there were unknown numbers of animals that met their demise. The National Guardsmen and deputies who manned checkpoints and road closures witnessed the injured animals. At one checkpoint a deputy transmitted a message that a bear had come out of the burned area towards the

July 2002 air view of fire-scarred mountains surrounding Vallecito Reservoir which was at it's lowest water level since 1977. Grass was now growing in the empty lake bed. The Vallecito Dam is at the far left of picture. (Photo by D. Warlick)

men, as if he wanted them to help him. He had very badly burned feet, as well as burns on other parts of his body, so he had to be killed.

A deserted bus was discovered at the Pine River Trailhead. Someone learned that the passengers had left on foot into the Weminuche Wilderness days earlier, and they were no doubt unaware of the danger from the rapidly spreading fire. Helicopters were again sent out to rescue the hikers before the flames overtook them. Flying the choppers and attempting rescues at high altitudes could be a risky business, but soon all of the people were found and shuttled down off the mountain to safety.

During the whole time that the fire was in the Vallecito Valley and the residents were being evacuated, there were a few other brave souls who remained. EMTs Gail Rush and Billie and Gordie Retoike stayed to be available for firefighters who might be injured or become ill. Many of the firefighters coming to the high altitudes were from low altitude states, such as Oregon and Georgia, and came down with altitude sickness. Others who stayed in the tent camps experienced what was called "camp crud," an intestinal ailment. The EMTs took care of everything that came along, even the one fatality, who was injured too badly for them to save.

Travis Leonard, who has an excavating business, worked endlessly building firebreaks along Highway 501 and clearing fallen, burning trees from the road with his heavy equipment. He was trying desperately to keep the fire from crossing the highway and burning the Cool Water Ranch and Kanikuk Camp buildings and the homes and cabins beyond.

Fireman Chuck Flores, who lived near the foot of the dam, continued to stay on, trying to save his own home as well as any nearby homes that he could. He worked for endless hours without stopping for sleep, and he and other firemen managed to save many homes, including his own. He did however lose another large structure on his property, and he agonized over the fact that he couldn't save a nearby neighbor's home.

Justin McCarty, who also has an excavating business, stayed to save his home and buildings. He also risked his life to keep the roads cleared from burning trees so fire crews and officials could get through to fight the fires that were spreading to the north end of the lake. He, and others, bulldozed fire-lines to try to stop the fire from spreading into populated areas. They did anything and everything asked of them, and more, as they worked desperately to try to stop the fiery invasion. The survival of the community was now at stake.

Ironically, while Justin was helping firemen along the west side of the lake when the firestorm came through on June 17th, the Robinettes and the Animas firefighters saved one of his buildings. The Robinette family, owners of the Buffalo Gap Restaurant, refused to leave, keeping the place open to feed the hungry firemen. Every single person seemed to do whatever he or she could to help anyone that needed help. Such teamwork hadn't been seen at Vallecito for a very long time.

On Tuesday, June 25th, Sheriff Schirard and Butch Knowlton decided that during the mornings when the fire was at its' quietest, they would start letting people go to their homes and empty out their freezers and refrigerators, even if they had to just throw the spoiled food out in their yards for the bears and racoons. Deputies then loaded groups of residents into vans and dropped them off at their homes with an order to be ready to be picked up again within twenty minutes.

The fire had burned the power poles and power lines in the valley nine or ten days earlier, leaving all the appliances without power. Most of the food had spoiled and needed to be removed to keep the appliances from being ruined. Those were the lucky people. The others needed to see for themselves that their homes had been burned to the ground along with all the contents. It was a sight that brought tears to many an eye. Now some people knew they really were homeless — not for just the duration of the fire, but until they could find another home. It was a grim reality to face.

Every day the authorities gave their report. At times it was thought that the business area at the south end of the lake below Lake Vista Estates had burned, but somehow the firemen and bulldozer operators kept it intact, and the news gave some hope to the traumatized listeners.

Days grew to weeks. There were ups and downs, tensions increased, and the tears came more readily as people met and discussed the rumors and facts they had heard. One couple was told by authorities that their home in Lake Vista Estates had burned. A neighbor who had managed to visit the location the day before had told them that it was still standing. The authorities were trying very hard to avoid such mistakes and to cause needless suffering.

Mountain subdivisions are notably unorthodox, as the roads curve around, go up and down the mountainsides, and intersect with various smaller roads. The Lake Vista Estates subdivision had been burned so badly that there were practically no house numbers in place. There were so many burned structures that it was extremely difficult for someone who didn't know the area well to distinguish one ruin from another.

Butch Knowlton and Sheriff Schirard knew something had to be done to ease the worried couple and to avoid another mistake. When they found out that old timer Dave Warlick, who owned two of the burned homes, was in the crowd, they sent him, Dewey Menter (the owner of the disputed home), and Under Sheriff Robin Harrington to make an accurate determination of the ownership of burned homes. Dewey breathed a huge sigh of relief when he actually saw his home still standing. It was hard to understand how the house had survived since the neighbor's home and shed, which was only ten feet away, was totally burned.

Finally on Friday, June 28th the power was restored and the harrowing evacuation period was over for most of the Vallecito residents. They were at last allowed to go back to their homes. Trees still smoldered in many areas around the lake, but the main part of the fire was thirty-five percent contained and was being fought primarily up the higher reaches of the Pine River, above the lake and on Middle Mountain. It was also still burning along Falls Creek in the wilderness area above the north end of Vallecito.

At times thick smoke still filled the air. The sound of helicopters and planes, dropping slurry or dipping water from the lake to be released on smoldering fires, still filled the air during the daytime. To the residents it sounded like they were living in a war zone, although the helicopters were a welcome sight as they worked to put out each spot where the fire flared up.

The Forest Service C-130 tanker planes could drop 3,000 gallons at a time and were used on the larger fires, but the helicopters, with their smaller loads, were also very important in the firefighting effort. After the west side of the fire was fairly well contained, the residents of Vallecito saw more of the larger, ungainly Sikorsky helicopters in use as they ferried their 600-gallon loads of water to fire sites. What an air show it turned out to be!

By the Fourth of July the activity had calmed down considerably for the people who lived in the fire-scarred areas. The dry conditions stopped any display of fireworks. People were just thankful to have survived the catastrophe. Most of the newly homeless had managed to find temporary living quarters and then tried to decide what to do next.

An organization called "Helping Hands" was formed to make sure the homeless people received clothing or other items. The residents banded together as they tried to bring the community back to some semblance of what it had been before the fire.

Before the fire even occurred Sheriff Schirard and Emergency Manager, Butch Knowlton, with the help of local fire chiefs, had put together an excellent disaster plan, which the whole community benefited from during the Missionary Ridge fire. Although forty-six homes and cabins were destroyed in the seventy thousand acre fire, many more survived because of the hard work of many agencies working together.

Schirard and Knowlton have received much credit for their exceptional handling of the situation, but it is the firefighters that have been honored more than anyone. They are the true heroes. Signs were placed randomly all along the area roads thanking the firefighters for their work. Many dinners were given to honor them and to show the deep appreciation of the community.

Much of the beauty that drew people to settle at Vallecito still remains, but now ghostly, blackened canyons and slopes mingle with the green as a reminder of the power and wrath of nature that descended upon the valley in the summer of 2002.

When the once longed for rains began to fall, new problems arose. The ash-covered slopes did not absorb rain like the grass and shrubbery once had. Water ran down across the ash as swiftly as it would from an ice-covered surface, bringing downed trees, rocks, or anything else in its path to the lower areas. Gullies near the highway, which had never been known to have running water, were now raging streams of water, ash, rock, trees and mud. The debris washed against and into homes and businesses, blocking the roads in many areas of C.R. 501 from the old Glover property below Cool Water Ranch, and even on north to C.R. 500 and beyond.

When the rain finally stopped, destruction was everywhere. Red Creek, Dry Gulch, Sawmill Gulch and Jack Creek on the Cool Water Ranch all brought down torrents of water, mud, rocks and tree debris that poured across C.R. 501, moved through the fences, and spread far out into the fields beyond. Four to six feet of mangled mud and tree debris filled the now unusable road in some spots, all of which had to be cleared by heavy equipment. Then the small amounts of mud that were left on the pavement were treacherously slick.

Red Creek came out of its banks and pushed tons of trees and branches against Bob Niggli and Doris Andrew's nearby home. The Browns' fences were knocked down, their home was in danger of being washed away, and their rock and ash-strewn fields will never look the same again.

The steep, barren slopes above Dunsworth Park sent a giant wall of mud and debris across the meadow and down tiny Root Creek canyon, causing havoc along the way. It pushed its way into the McCracken home, which sits on the upper side of the highway, and took a good portion of the front yard along with it. Marilyn's restaurant and the homes and businesses near Shoreline Inn and Sawmill Point, all at the base of steep drainages, also took a major hit.

Diane and Roland Healy's Vallecito Country Store found itself almost afloat with mud and water. The mud also engulfed their home situated on the hill above the store, leaving several feet of slime inside the home. The store's ice machine was washed across the highway into Steve Dudley's Virginia's Restaurant.

The two businesses were probably the hardest hit, but as soon as the rain stopped and the road could be opened, the whole community appeared, armed with shovels and cleaning equipment, and pitched in to help their neighbors clear out the mud, rocks and debris. The fire department washed most of the mud from inside the house with their powerful water hoses. A diversion ditch was dug to re-route the path of future floods and to try to keep the businesses safe.

Wit's End's Chain Lakes partially filled with mud that came down the steep slopes to the west and crossed the highway. The Buffalo Gap Restaurant and many other places sustained similar fates during other rainstorms. It almost made one forget about the fire for a short span of time.

Travis Leonard, Justin McCarty, and others who had excavation equipment made their way to the worst hit areas and started moving massive loads of mud, rock and burned trees to clear the road. The La Plata Highway Department equipment started clearing the lower areas as they made their way up the debris-covered highway.

La Plata Electric, whose crews had done a truly remarkable job restoring power after the fire, still had equipment along the highway laying new power lines, and their men also went into action, clearing the roads and the ditches where they were working. Everyone was helping, in any way they could.

Then more rains came, and some of the same problems arose at new and different places. Valley residents constantly watched the sky and the weather reports. Some had scanners to monitor the fire and rescue reports of rainstorms and flooding problems. Some of the residents, who live on low-lying ground at the base of steep, burned off mountainsides, even moved to higher ground until the rains were over.

No, life will never be quite the same for the people of Vallecito. They will perhaps face the danger of avalanches if winter brings heavy snows. But there are signs of new beginnings as a few burned homes are being replaced with new structures. Nature is pushing up new grass and other plants to cover the burned earth, and the re-seeding efforts are now bearing fruit. The healing power of nature can be seen as the ground cover is replenished. The rains have brought more water into the gradually rising lake, and as we gaze up and down the valley, we see that much of the beauty still remains and waning spirits are revived.

The smaller trees and brush that remain have more room to grow and can multiply. Little aspens, which spread from the roots, are coming back in thick groves. Grasses that once were inhibited by the lofty pines, will now be able to spread and cover the ground where the pines once grew, perhaps making the area even more spectacular. It may look different, but Vallecito is still a beautiful place.

The people of Vallecito have always been known to be a defiant, strong-willed bunch when faced with opposition. Their sheer determination, tenacity, and generous spirits will continue to bring the community through whatever may lie ahead until the shadow of danger is lifted in Southwest Colorado's "Hidden Paradise."

SOURCES OF INFORMATION

La Plata County Courthouse — Records Department

National Archives — Denver Federal Center — Denver, Colorado

Spanish Archives Records Center — Santa Fe, New Mexico

History Museum — Santa Fe, New Mexico

Ft. Lewis College Library and Southwest Studies Center — Durango, Colorado

        Colorado Bureau of Mines Annual Mining Reports
        Engineering and Mining Reports
        Colorado Year Books
        Bureau of Reclamation Pine River Dam Reports
        1921 San Juan Basin Directory

Durango Public Library — Durango, Colorado

Newspaper and magazine articles from:

        Durango Democrat, Durango Daily Herald, The Durango Evening Herald, Bayfield Blade, Ignacio Chieftain, Farmington Times Hustler, Pine River Times, The Denver Post, The Rocky Mountain News and *Colorado Magazine.*

Various other sources including:
Colorado State Brand Inspector records
Southern Ute Tribal Center and Museum
Pargin Family History by Leon Pargin
Sheepherder's Gold by Temple Cornelius
Colorado Handbook by Steven Metzger
People of the Pine — 1979 Bayfield Eighth Grade Class
The Ute Legacy by Richard N. Ellis
People of the Shining Mountains by Charles S. Marsh
Citadel Mountain by Maynard Cornett Adams
True Stories of Early Days in the San Juan Basin by Leta Pinckert
Rocky Mountain Boom Town by Duane A. Smith
Columbia Encyclopedia
Cattle Camp Cookie by Kathy Webber

Many old-timers also shared precious memories with me. I am deeply indebted to all of these people who so generously gave their time and efforts to help in my quest to keep segments of history from forever being lost.

Euterpe Taylor
Sylvian Valdez
Edna Baker
Belle Cuthair
Annetta Frost
Jack Frost
Neal Cloud
Dave Warlick, Sr.
Gertrude Pargin Warlick
Dave Warlick, Jr.
Monte Warlick
Laura Dunsworth Sower Petri
Jessie Wommer
Ed Wommer
Emerald Flint Patrick
Donna Patrick Becker
Lee Patrick
Keith Graham
Dianne Graham
Bill Penn
Lucinda Penn
Henry Parks
Helen Lissner Burkett
Anna Tubs Wilmer
Harold Wilmer
Glen Glover
Lloyd Glover
Sandy Scott
Harold McCoy
Chet McCoy

Melba McCoy
Lavenia McCoy
Sally Decker
Vera Decker
Kennon Decker
Earl Sullivan
Norman Payson
David Hammond
Georgie Carmack Fahrion
Carl Brown
Freda Brown
Jimmie Shadden
Doris Caviggia
Johnny Caviggia
Lorene Caviggia Wheat
Dobbin Shupe
Guy Shupe
Gordon Shillingburg
Jan Roberts
Claude Crane
Maxene Safley
Martin Safley
Bob Burch
Roberta Stumberg
Dick Stumberg
Laura Percell
Lloyd Knickerbocker
John Kelley
Marion Kelley

BAYFIELD RURAL ROUTE #1-UPPER PINE RIVER, TEXAS CREEK, BEAR CREEK, WALLACE GULCH AND VALLECITO 1921

From A.K. Skinner's San Juan Basin Directory

Amon, P.H.
Barr, John B. — Alice
Brown, Nettie Mrs.
Clark, Robert P. — Mrs. Robert
Clouse, Jim — Nora
Conrad, Donald — Matty
Coon, R.W. — Mrs. R.W.
Coulson, D.E. — Mary
Currie, G.H. — Grace
Duffy, Ray — Mary
Dunsworth, George L. — Rena
Dunsworth, C.W. — Addie
Ellston, Jessie Mrs.
Epperson, Albert — Mamie
Foster, Mancy Mrs.
Foster, Fields
Frahm, Fred — Lulu
Garrick, J.B. — Mattie
Glover, A.I. — Lenta
Gray, F.L. — Lena
Greathouse, Fred
Greenlee, Frank — Edna
Groves, M.C. — Lyda
Hainds, Albert — Lillian
Hickman, Elmer E. — Bertha
Humiston, Henry — Mrs. Henry
Jaquez, E.K. — Mrs. E.K.
Johnson, Roscoe G. — Winifred
Knickerbocker, B.H. — Mae
Koon, W.A. — Naoma
Lawson, Harry — Miner
Lowell, J.P. — Mattie — saw milling
Lyons, John — Mrs.
Lyons, Dennis — Mrs.
Lyons, Luther — Catherine
McCoy, Fred — Mrs. Fred
Mikel, W.S.
Montgonery, Frank — Cora
Morris, B.F.

Nelson, Nels
Owen, W.H. — Edna
Palmer, I.L. — Mae
Richards, W.R. — Ester
Richards, John — Mrs. John
Richards, Howard
Rollman, C.R.
Rollman, Elva Miss
Salabar, Effie Mrs.
Sapp, Henry — Ida
Sapp, Geo.
Sheets, A. Mrs.
Smith, Earl — Marjorie
Sommers, Miles — Florence
Steele, Frank — Mrs. Frank
Sullivan, T.B. — saw milling
Sullivan, Geo. J. — saw milling
Sullivan, Joe — Mrs. Joe
Swain, Joe — Bernice
Trone, Haley E. — Nettie
Trone, Geo. — Mrs. Geo.
Upchurch, Jim
Vaughn, Jim
Vinton, R.O. — Needa
Warlick, Geo.
Webber, E.T. — Julia
Webber, Rex
Wilbourn, Luther — Cora
Williams, Tom
Williams, John
Williams, Manford — Clara — saw milling
Willmet, Elmer — Sercke
Wiser, Geo. — Metta
Wommer, Henry — Mrs. Henry
Wommer, Louis — Rosa
Wommer, Frank — Hattie
Wommer, Jacob—Emm

FEDERAL ARCHIVES LIST OF
EARLY UPPER PINE HOMESTEADERS

The Homestead Act of 1862 gave any U. S. citizen over the age of 21 the right to claim 160 acres of land if they lived and "proved up" on it for five years. This list of early settlers shows many names did not appear in the postal records of 1921. An H is a Homestead claim, T&S is a Timber and Stone deed (obtained for stone, timber, grazing, or just more "elbow room"), and UN means the land was unsuitable for farming and was vacated. Some claims were recorded long after the actual claim was established.

H	1884	William B. Asher
T&S	1908	Clara Barker
H	1895	Bennett Bishop
T&S	1903	Anna M. Boyle
H	1903	Mathias Boyle
T&S	1898	Owen F. Boyle
H	1886	George Browner
T&S	1903	Mattie J. Brown
T&S	1902	William Chapman
T&S	1917	Birdie A. Cordell
H	1893	Adolphus P. Crisswell
H	1891	John Dawe
T&S	1903	Evelyn Nora Eldredge
T&S	1903	Frank Eldredge
UN	——	Paris Engler
T&S	1902	Hiram S. Farley
T&S	1903	Della Farrell
T&S	1903	Johnny Farrell
H	1885	Michael Foster
H	1888	Theodore Fulton
H	1886	Adolphus Germain
H	1903	Al Glover
H	1903	Jasper Glover
H	1886	Charles C. GrahamH
H	1885	John T. Graham
H	1890	Joseph H. Graham
UN	——	Ira & Sherman Hatch
H	1888	James Highland
T&S	1903	Uriah Hollister
T&S	1902	Loyd R. Huntsman
H	189-	Wm. H. Jack
T&S	1894	Wm. Kirkpatrick

H	1889	Edmond P. Lowe
H	1889	Ephram A. Lowe
T&S	1903	Mattie Lowell
T&S	1917	Thomas H. Marshall
T&S	1902	Hurlbert D. McBride
T&S	1903	Netta McBride
T&S	1903	Mary A. McGalliard
T&S	1903	Mang O. McLin
H	1888	Charles McLoyd
T&S	1902	Anna Melville
H	1887	John A. Moore
H	1887	Mellisa Moore
H	1905	Warren Mullen
H	1882	Jewett Palmer
H	1884	Lester Palmer
H	1890	Benjamin Pargin
H	1902	Samuel Parks
H	1885	John M. Patrick
H	1888	Washington E. Patrick
H	1891	George Patton
H	1913	Pearson/Wilmer
T&S	1902	Clayton C. Perkins
T&S	1895	John A. Porter
T&S	1903	Ben W. Ritter
H	1885	William Robbins Estate
T&S	1902	Thomas B. Rockwood
H	1903	David Roe-assg. to Sanford
T&S	1903	Candace Root
H	1902	John N. Root
T&S	1917	James D. Scott
H	1901	Jeanette Scoville
T&S	1903	Daniel Shively
T&S	1901	Edna Short
H	1906	Sidney-assg. to J. Sanford
H	1901	Bertha N. Snyder
H	1908	Rose Steans
H	1889	Charlie Sublette
H	1884	Ellis C. Taylor
H	1890	Norman W. Titus
H	1900	Edmond B. Trussler
H	1901	Schuler C. Whitney
H	1889	Thomas Wilson

VALLECITO HOMESTEAD MAP

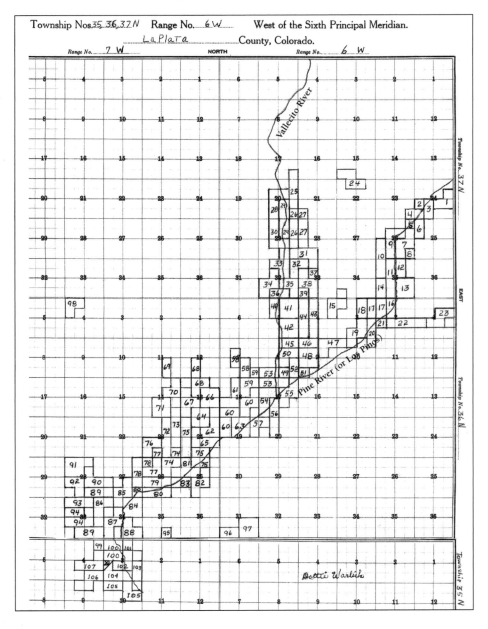

Township Nos. 35, 36, 37 N   Range No. 6 W   West of the Sixth Principal Meridian.
La PlaTa County, Colorado.

NAMES OF PIONEERS ON VALLECITO HOMESTEAD MAP

1. Charles Sublett
2. Jethro C. Sanford
3. William T. Kirkpatrick
4. John A. Porter
5. Jethro C. Sanford
6. Jethro C. Sanford
7. Joseph H. Graham
8. Luella B. Rockwood
9. Hiram S. Farlay
10. Clayton C. Perkins
11. Charles C. Graham
12. Loyd R. Huntsman
13. R. W. Ritter
14. Thomas Rockwood
15. Anna Melville
16. Uriah Hollister
17. John T. Graham
18. William Chapman
19. William T. Kirkpatrick
20. Jeanette A. Scoville
21. Jeanette A. Scoville
22. Evelyn Nora Eldredge
23. Frank Eldredge
24. Henri Beri
25. Edna A. Short
26. Garret N. Rhodes
27. Schuyler C. Whitney
28. Anna M. Boyle
29. Charles McLoyd
30. Heirs to John M. Patrick
31. Washington Patrick
32. Ephrim N. Lowe
33. Wm. Robbins
34. George Newell
35. Michael Foster
36. Edward P. Lowe
37. Daniel Shively
38. Mellisa A. Moore
39. Michael Foster
40. Edmond P. Lowe
41. Norman N. Titus
42. James S. Highland
43. Mathias Boyle
44. Edmond P. Lowe
45. James Highland
46. O.F. Boyle
47. Bennett Bishop
48. C.C. Graham
49. Ellis C. Taylor
50. Ellis C. Taylor
51. John T. Graham
52. John T. Graham
53. John Dawe
54. Edmond B. Trussler
55. William B. Asher
56. Thomas Wilson
57. Rose Steans
58. John M. Root
59. Heirs of Adolphus Germain
60. George Patton
61. Candace Root
62. William H. Jack
63. Schuyler Whitney
64. Alpheus P. Criswell
65. Josa Trussler
66. Charles A. Lewis
67. Della M. Farrell
68. Maude O. McLin
69. Green Barker
70. John Farrell
71. Tina J. Marshall
72. Thomas H. Marshall
73. Hurlburt D. McBride
74. Metta McBride
75. Bertha Snyder
76. James D. Scott
77. Clara Barker
78. Susan A. Scott
79. Chas. Gerard
80. Jewet Palmer
81. George F. Brawner
82. Mattie J. Brown

83. James Edwards
84. Jasper Glover
85. A.I. Glover
86. Birdie A. Cordell
87. Lester H. Palmer
88. Warren L. Mullen
89. Samuel Parks
90. Mary A. McGilliard
91. Marion Mayn
92. Edward B. Trussler
93. Peter Ward
94. Theodore Nulton
95. Leonard Zipperian
96. Mattie Lowell
97. Joseph P. Lowell
98. John A. Gallagher
99. S. Parks
100. James W. Verteh
101. Frank Webber
102. Charles Lignoski
103. Daniel Myers
104. Benjamin H. Bennett
105. Willaim T. Richards
106. David D. Day
107. Chas. M. Waggoner

X Columbus School

BRANDS THAT MADE HISTORY IN THE VALLECITO AREA

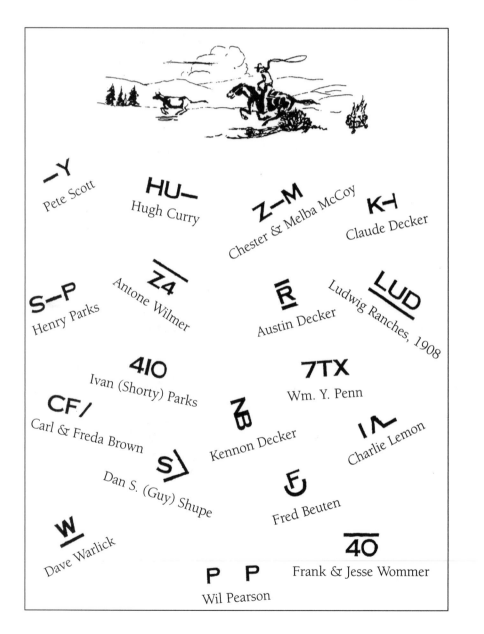

−Y
Pete Scott

HU−
Hugh Curry

Z−M
Chester & Melba McCoy

K−|
Claude Decker

S−P
Henry Parks

Z4
Antone Wilmer

R̄
Austin Decker

LUD
Ludwig Ranches, 1908

4IO
Ivan (Shorty) Parks

7TX
Wm. Y. Penn

CF/
Carl & Freda Brown

NB
Kennon Decker

I∧
Charlie Lemon

S⌐
Dan S. (Guy) Shupe

FJ
Fred Beuten

W
Dave Warlick

P P
Wil Pearson

4O
Frank & Jesse Wommer

INDEX